WHO KILLED MR DRUM?

GW00373810

WHO KILLED MR DRUM?

Sylvester Stein

**With a foreword by
Anthony Sampson**

Mayibuye History and Literature Series No. 93

MAYIBUYE
BOOKS-UWC

Published 1999 in South Africa by Mayibuye Books, University of the Western Cape, Private Bag X17, Bellville 7535, South Africa

Mayibuye books is the book publishing division of the Mayibuye Centre at the University of the Western Cape. The Mayibuye Centre is a pioneering project helping to recover areas of South African history that have been neglected in the past. It also provides space for cultural creativity and expression in a way that promotes the process of change and reconstruction in a democratic South Africa. The Mayibuye History and Literature Series is part of this project.

© Sylvester Stein
All rights reserved
All photographs by Jurgen Schadeberg.
ISBN 1-86808-451-5
Cover illustration, Malcolm Hart
Cover design, layout and typesetting by jon berndt Design
The book was set in Times New Roman with all chapter Heads in Univers 67 Bold Condensed to echo the design style of Drum Magazine. All adverts from Drum Magazine of the 1960s are from the South African Library

PRINTED AND BOUND IN THE REPUBLIC OF SOUTH AFRICA BY THE RUSTICA PRESS,
NDABENI, WESTERN CAPE
D7497

CONTENTS

FOREWORD

Why does the *Drum* story refuse to go away, over forty years later? The obvious answer is the quality of the *Drum* writers, which still seems as fresh and original in the reprints and anthologies as when it first appeared on cheap newsprint. It still jumps out of the page after many of the events have been forgotten, because it reflected the authentic life of the townships, its comedies and tragedies, and its explosive dialogue and repartee. But another answer is that the prose reflected the extraordinary creativity of an age when writers, despite or because of the miseries and humiliations of apartheid, felt impelled to maintain their human spirit and values with a compassion and ironic humour which defied the encroachments of the police state.

It is this spirit which Sylvester Stein so vividly records in this remarkable memoir, which reads llike a racy comic thriller but conveys all the more poignantly the suffering behind the laughter. For Sylvester bravely edited *Drum* magazine during those painful years when the staff were coming up against impossible frustrations, escaping into alcohol or exile, and dying young; and he does not try to evade the dark side of the sparkling story.

Of course the *Drum* editors were only catalysts or funnels for the writing they assembled and presented. The black talent in Johannesburg at that time was overflowing, and the editor's main job was to ensure that it flowed into *Drum* office, and on to the pages in some kind of shape. The fact that the magazine maintained such a continuous and consistent character under three editors who were so thoroughly different showed how far it had acquired a life of its own, and how powerful and infectious was the style of the writers. I had the good luck to be the first of them as an inhibited young Englishman with no experience of journalism, which compelled me to listen and make the most of the writers who knew much more than I. Sylvester my successor was a much more experienced South African journalist accustomed to white newspapers, but he bravely seized the opportunity to plunge into the black world – even briefly disguising himself as an African – and to launch new campaigns, most notably for equality in sport. Sylvester's successor, Tom Hopkinson – later Sir Tom – was already a distinguished British editor, with an imaginative and fastidious eye for good photography and layouts, who gave the magazine new standards. But the writers and photographers learnt more from each other – as creative people always do in the camaraderie of lively groups – than any editor could teach them. And through all the editorships it was the brilliance of the reporting and pictures, and their portrayal of the vibrant township life, which brought the magazine to life and gave it the distinctive character which re-emerges so sharply when it is re-read today.

It was the proprietor Jim Bailey, as Sylvester generously acknowledges, who first insisted that *Drum* must avoid 'the white hand' and allow urban Africans to have their own clear voice, and who enabled the magazine to flourish and take risks – until it was eventually sadly taken over by more cautious and conformist Afrikaner proprietors. The complex and lively personality of Jim Bailey deserves a book to itself; and each editor had his own different and difficult relationship with him. For myself, as an old Oxford friend, it was probably easier than for others, as tensions and arguments could be resolved with counterblasts and laughter. Sylvester, steering the magazine through more dangerous rocks and shoals of politics in the late 'fifties, had more fundamental disagreements with Jim about the magazine's responsibilities and risks – which form part of the climax of this book. But Sylvester leaves no doubt that Jim 'was the one who kept it alive for so long, who provided and persevered with the true vision.'

Sylvester contributed his own unusual qualitites to the magazine, including a tireless adventurousness, curiosity and a quirky humour which could depict the horrors of apartheid in terms of black farce – like many African writers – which shines through in this book, this 'historical caprice' as he calls it. He had a love of dialogue which enlivens his own comic novels, enabling him to relish and capture the vigour and nuances of African talk – an ability which has evaded most white novelists writing about South Africa. In this book we can hear the black jokes and badinage as vividly as in a play, and we can also get an idea of the kind of township talk which was so miraculously distilled into the *Drum* writing.

He does not skirt round the uneasiness of the relationships across the colour—bar, at a time when they were more difficult and delicate than today: as he explains it:

> *It wasn't easy to fool one another, even by leaning over backwards – all that did*
> *was make it obvious that one was trying to hide something! We dared not dig*
> *into the unstated truths floating about in our minds, we still had half-strangled*
> *and distorted racial doubts and suspicions about one another, despite all the*
> *years working together in combating racism. They thought that we thought a*
> *black wasn't as good as a white and we thought guiltily that maybe they were*
> *right and we did think so.*

But he had an awareness of African sensitivities which enabled him to share many of the fears and anxieties on the other side, as the black staff faced much greater ordeals and dangers than the whites, and as a good listener he could convincingly record their feelings. He describes for instance how, when he was himself in exile, he heard the news from Es'kia Mphahlele, another exile, of how the hard-drinking genius of Can Themba was confronted by the stricter demands of his successor Tom Hopkinson – who seemed more interested, as Sylvester describes, in cleaning up the paper than in preserving its raw strength and bite. 'He's got a problem with Can, has Tom, and he's being a bit of a blighter about it'.

When Can was fired by Tom, the paper lost one of its last great writers; but it was the constraints of censorship, and the silencing of all serious black opposition, which dealt the death-blow to *Drum*'s independent spirit. It was only after most of the writers had died, prematurely and often in the loneliness of exile, that their work was

properly revived and appreciated as never before. As Sylvester elo-
quently puts it: 'They died long ago and far too early, our men; yet,
with a fine kind of irony that would have appealed to them, they are
more alive today than those who killed them'.

Anthony Sampson July 1999

PART ONE

TOP:
Drum staff "at work".

LEFT:
Mr. Drum – Henry Nxumalo.

1. HAPPY, HAPPY AFRICA!

Five o'clock in the morning, New Year's Day. 'Hello?' asks the telephone by my bedside, 'is that Stein?'

'Huh?'

'Hello, hello? it inquires again. Mr Stein, are you Mr Stein, Mr Stein?'

'Mr Stein?' For a moment I'm not at all sure myself. Am I Mr Stein? But eventually I get the point. 'Ja-a, ja, oh yes, Stein'. I recall that it is me, five hours since the stroke of auld lang syne and no more than one hour since the final working through of certain alcohol-related uxorious arrangements under the kaross coverlet ... but what the hell, I think defensively, give me a chance, give me a chance, this voice so early in the day is very bloody grating, it puts even the telephone receiver on bloody edge. 'Ja, yes. Yes, it's Stein.'

'Nou ja, Stein,' grunts the caller heavily, 'look here now, Stein, this is the polisie: Sergeant Bezuidenhout, Western Native Township. We've got one of your boys here, hey? This boy Henry Nxumalo.'

I'm really angered. Oh blast, so on this occasion it's Henry Nxumalo who's been picked up, must be for being out after curfew, it must be him this time that's got to be bailed during unsocial hours, five-o-bloody clock in the a-bloody-em. 'One of our boys!' It makes me mad, I'm almost driven to cursing the policeman, 'Christ, man, Sergeant – Henry Nxumalo! You're talking about our chief reporter, you fucking illiterate *piesang* (banana); and he's got a special pass; there's not supposed to be any curfewing for him. Come on, man. Bloody Jeeesus, man!'

However I don't say any of it, I don't level any of this *Drum*–style talk at him, I want to be seen to be reasonable, I don't want to give offence by showing how angry I am, just because I *am* angry. I don't want the police to put me on their suspect list; I won't call the guy an illiterate banana, I'll keep my anger stewing quietly away on the back plate, for private enjoyment later. Meantime, my wife Jenny, lying half-asleep on her stomach and wanting to go back to being fully asleep, wiggles her porky backside against me, nudging me to get on with it; and the sergeant, fearing that communication has ceased entirely, goes on sending over a lot more peremptory hello-hellos, to check on why-so. So I finally reply, 'Yes, fine, you've got Henry Nxumalo there. So, what then, Sergeant.' I'm now being my normal crisp and businesslike self.

'Ja, Mr Stein, that's right and I need you to come down here, yes, okay? Yes, hello, hello, hello? You with me there still, Mr Stein?'

I sit up in bed to show the sergeant I'm really on the job now, but this only causes the wife to tug the covers back off me in a wilful way and on to herself again. 'Well now, look sergeant, it's not necessary for anyone to come over specially,' I start to argue, to explain to him that Henry Nxumalo is our senior writer, an important person, a world-famous person did he but know it, if black, who could safely be released on his own recognisances, having a special pass anyway, but I'm interrupted.

'Okay, now, Mr Stein, okay, *stadig, stadig* (slow, slow), steady hey ... but I want you to come along down to the station and identify the body, ja?'

Cold, cold horror.

By the time I, Henry's white editor on *Drum*, had driven the five miles into and through the centre of Johannesburg and the 10 miles out again to Western Native, the sun had made its debut on the New Year summer scene and had already dyed the cart-ruts that represent the main road in the township a sickly, eroded yellow colour and had caused a good deal of heat to radiate off two sheets of corrugated iron that were propped against one another in a lengthwise inverted V over the body of Henry, with the aim of shielding his twisted, carved-up anatomy from the public gaze and further doses of sun. In one of the road ruts beside this makeshift iron tent was a nicely-polished brown shoe. The sergeant scooped it up and chucked it over beside Henry, whose right foot was missing a shoe – come off in a desperate scuffle no doubt.

'Oh, Henry!' I wailed. 'Well, my God, Henry!'

I blenched. 'My God, ach, horrible, *horrible!*' I very nearly retched. What a devastating sight! Horror! Henry knifed to death! 'Oh, God! Horrible, horrible, horrible! ' I repeated. Though a handsome man in life, Henry Nxumalo, he was no good-looking corpse at all, like the men on *Drum* all joked might become their fate; not at all as good-looking a corpse as he might have expected to bequeath us, poor bloody Henry, a score of sharp-edged gashes across his neck and chest, mouth hanging grotesquely open and blood caking his face. I shook myself roughly: 'Come along! What are you up to, writing Henry's obituary already? Now's the time to hold steady and start to get to the bottom of things.' But I couldn't help but be swamped with thoughts of Henry's person and his life, of what a dear *skelm* (rascal) of a man he was and of how with his own thrust and energy and his deep feeling for liberty, truth and equality, and how with his cheek – yes, cheek, that almost forbidden quality for a black man in this white society – he had *made* the magazine. It was his Mr Drum bravado: his exposés of the police, his adventures in the sinister mine-recruitment organisation and his exploits on the Boer forced-labour farms, that had first called world attention to the iniquities of apartheid, at the same time making famous the name of *Drum.*

Slowly, slowly over the generation or so that was to follow, the world roused itself against this crime on humanity, Britain taking 40 dragging years, until after Nelson Mandela's release from gaol, before it finally came clean and withdrew its support for apartheid – but right then and there, with Henry's daredevilries, the first cracks had started to appear. People of influence slowly became enlightened and concerned and started to enlighten others in turn. And Henry has to be given much credit for having first trickled awareness into their thick heads.

I had to stop to ask myself, all that long while ago, were the British in fact *thick*, or wasn't it that as usual they were being very *shrewd*? Wouldn't you say the interests of the mineowners in the City of London were best served by a tough apartheid government doing the job of beating profits out of the blacks? Yes, well-informed people like you and me can perceive that today, but at the time all that kind of political analysis was still struggling to reach the surface of my mind. But whatever the true position of the imperial power, and whether it was indeed slow and stupid, or cynical and self-serving, it needed the death-defying assaults on its opinion by people like Henry to stir it up. I mourned for the loss of a hero in this fight, not just of a most valuable chief reporter on my staff and of a dear family friend. I was hammered insensible, grief and rage overcame me, and I determined to find his killer and avenge him.

To think about Henry and his deeds like that churned into a turmoil my always volatile emotions, and instantly turned me tearful, so that I could barely control myself before the man who accompanied me, the very Sgt Bezuidenhout who had telephoned. He was a burly chap but had tiny feet that afforded him a surprisingly nimble way of moving about. As we stood there a makeshift hearse speeded up, blowing the dust about before coming to a cautious standstill beside the body. The driver and his helper summarily dumped him in their vehicle. The blood was showing a particularly violent red against his matt black skin. They chucked in with him the brown shoe and his brown hat that must have been knocked off in the scuffle and had been lying on a half-alive bush beside the track. He'd worn that hat day and night, working at his desk or loafing with friends.

I sat beside the sergeant during the dusty drive back to the station in his police wagon. 'Who did it, who could have done it?' I asked sorrowfully, head in hands. 'No, who could have did it!' echoed Sgt Bezuidenhout, in a clumsy attempt to show sympathy. 'Ja, jus' some other drunk kaffir probably, no, not so?' The policeman felt he really had to counter all this blubbing, this sentimental over-reaction of mine: 'No, chummy ... jus' black-on-black, jus' an ornirarry black-on-black type of case. We get 'em every night of the week, specially Saturdays. Ach man, Saturdays, you should see! Ja – and even worse at New Year! No, yes, just some ornirarry bleddy *tsotsi* (thug) what want to try out his knife on the next person he see. Ja, wragtig (truly).'

Yes, a *tsotsi*, another wayward tragic death by a roaming, knife-mad *skelm* from the outskirts of society. I signed the formal statement of identification, then transferred back to my own Chevrolet, but before setting out home I motored back inside the township again to sneak another look at the spot where Henry's body had been discovered. The sergeant was surely right, Henry had got in the way of some villainous township *amalaita* (street thugs), just drunkenly laying into everything in their path without any rational motive, and there'd be no witnesses and no evidence left behind and nothing to go on. But I'd got to make an attempt to help to find and apprehend that abominable culprit; rather weakly I felt that at the least I'd got to make it look as if I was making an attempt. If I went back to the office next day after the holiday, they'd expect me to have done some digging around.

Man, but what could you possibly turn up on this worn-out bit of veld? I shuddered at the sickening prospect of going back there to stir up the dust where Henry had lain and bled. For a while I wandered vaguely around the discarded sheets of corrugated iron, not knowing what might be a clue and what might not; anyhow wouldn't the police surely have picked up any kind of item they spotted? *Domkops* (fools), probably not.

I collected a few odd things: the broken-off bowl of a used pipe, two tram tickets, a dried-out peach pip and the shiny-bright button of a uniform – hey, wait, wait a minute, a S A Polisie button, of all things! After a little thought I threw away the pip, which obviously had been lying there through the whole of the early summer drought. Was the police button from Bezuidenhout's own spotless uniform? Ha! What about that! That sent an electric current through the brain.

I got down to the job more earnestly. I examined the sandy untarred main road of the township for evidence of a scuffle. But bloody goodness, you couldn't tell whether the shoe marks and barefeet marks were normal signs of people walking around or signs of some particular agitation, or whether this foot was imprinted there first and the other trampled over it immediately after or even days after. Or bloody what! The Bushmen, so they say, could read the whole story of a meeting between two or three people from the marks shown on the ground. Truly remarkable. On the other hand, I mused, wouldn't a Bushman find it quite as remarkable that a person like me could drive round and round Clarendon Circle in a heavy Chevvy among hundreds of similar whirling vehicles and not one of them even graze his car? Give us some credit.

Out came my handkerchief, to wrap the tram tickets, the button and the remnant of pipe, heavily encrusted with carbonised tobacco, virtually no room in the bowl to pack in even enough *twak* (tobacco) for one decent burn-up. Then I threw the useless things away in disgust at my antics, everything but the highly polished button. I stood by my car, thinking deeply about why it was Henry had been murdered. Surely there was a reason, a motive. There's a reason for everything in life, one of my fundamental beliefs, there's no such thing as chance, or luck or magic, there's a rational cause for every action. Suddenly this was all too much for me, theorising coldly about a real woeful happening to someone close to me. I was overcome again by tremendous emotions sweeping through head and heart: love of Henry, hatred of the system that held the life of a black person so cheap, and, firming up all the time, a determination to get to the bottom of the crime despite the obstacles.

I accelerated away from that dangerous, slummy part of the world and drove out past the police building, the only way to approach the township exit, right past Sgt Bezuidenhout, who was leaning against the main door, staring ahead of him. I decided not to give any sign of recognition, as it wasn't legal for a white man to swan around without a permit in a black area, though in fact he could hardly have missed me.

My mind rambled along among some daydreams. If the button really was Bezuidenhout's, did it simply drop off while he was there examining and turning over Henry's body – or, hey, how about this, before ever Henry died, was it torn off Bezuidenhout's uniform by Henry trying to escape his clutches. Now here's a scenario: were the cops simply investigators or were they themselves to be classed as suspects, or maybe accessories before the fact?

That wild notion seized me. It was the kind of thought always lurking below the surface in one's life – yes, of course it was Bezuidenhout, how logical, was it not indeed more than a silly dream, yes, Bezuidenhout acting under instructions from his superiors, the Special Branch, say? Was there after all any bigger embarrassment to the government and the national party and Hendrik Verwoerd, the architect of apartheid, than Henry and his exposés that were serving to bring South Africa's 'idealistic' apartheid theory into disrepute? What simpler way to get rid of him than sending orders for him to be blotted out, as they had done before and as they were to do over and over again for the next three or four decades: the hundreds pushed out of eighth-floor police cells, Steve Biko murdered in a van, the dirty tricks masterminded by contract spies. ... Was then Henry's murder also authorised, ordered, was it a contract killing?

This idea, although soon fading a bit, brought a smug smile to my face for its ingenuity, though it was also responsible for a mutinous shadow crossing it. Complicated emotions: on the one hand my conscience called on me to follow up my resolution there and then, pursue my clues and suspicions and confront Bezuidenhout; on the other hand, personal safety recommended that I should not risk my life by doing that, and convenience dictated that I put the whole business off for the while, for it would mean abandoning my journey back to Orange Grove and home comforts. If I was to do what conscience dictated I really ought to get going before the trail went cold, say by seeking an immediate audience with that rather sinister character Mpedi, who often sent us story tip-offs as he was a bit of a know-all witchdoctor, keeping a finger on everything going on – and what he didn't know, inventing, while weaving some plausible magic around the facts to make it appear plausible. Well, that's how all magic works, of course. Anyway through this personality that he'd constructed for himself, people were always rushing over with their own suspicions, scandal-mongerings, accusations and imaginings - 'on his tongue continual rumours rode'. He'd perhaps be able to check on the facts and smell out any other funny business. Something could just possibly be turned up by all the furore. Whereas if I did what personal convenience and self-indulgence advised I would put off any more fossicking around for a while.

Conscience lost this debate to convenience and common sense, so I kept my steering wheel set in the direction of my house near Orange Grove. Henry Nxumalo was dead and there was nothing that would bring him back immediately, I argued with morbid conscience, offering the excuse that anyway it would do better to sleep on things until after the holiday. So now I could give attention to something equal-

ly urgent, if more personal: the curling of myself around my bedfel-
low while I chased after my lost sleep.

Still I shivered again, caught up by the feeling of horror at what
had happened to Henry – devastated at the loss of this most special
and likeable of my closest colleagues. Henry! - the insouciance of the
man, the sweetness of his ways of extracting reactions from the white
official sources who regarded him as nothing better than an unclean
animal, his ability to work when dead-drunk, his ability to find more
drink so as to stay in that state, and his capacity to keep going under
all handicaps.

I recalled my first meetings with him after the war. He had been one
of the few blacks in the South African forces, where they were only
permitted in the ranks as cooks and drivers. Neither General J C
Smuts and his government nor the white voters would consider arm-
ing them, not so much because they believed they might turn and shoot
at their bosses but because it seemed to every 'civilised man' a quite
indecent thing for a black to be allowed to confront, kill or in any way
humiliate a white man, enemy though he may be, the Nazis included.
So they were recruited as non-combatants. Nevertheless they served
in the desert battles, 'went North', as it was described, and were
deployed right up to the front lines where they were fully at risk even
though unarmed. Fighting for democracy worldwide, though, in truth
black South Africans were not promised even the first elements of
democracy, not *them*; democracy in South Africa was for *people*.

Henry, after the war, joined the Springbok Legion, a liberal organisation set up for and by returning servicemen, and there in the late
1940s he, a humble auxiliary, and I, a former naval officer, could meet
and become friends. An easy, open sort of fellow, with perky ways,
with a wry curl of a smile always on the ready. And he turned up in
my life again shortly after, when I started my career in journalism on
the cub reporters' desk at the *Rand Daily Mail*. Henry, by then a
sporting writer himself on the local house-propaganda gazettes put
out by the gold mines for their black labourers, became a sort of backdoor, freelance contributor to the *Daily Mail*. He would sneak in and
hand the sports editor Paul Irwin, an unusually liberal character
imported from the British press, a handful of results from township

football. All that was some eight or ten years before Henry and I had become colleagues on *Drum* in the mid-1950s.

I continued on my way back through the empty New Year morning scene to Orange Grove in white Johannesburg, dreaming away the long drive in sad memories: recollected images from the professional life I'd shared with Henry, shots of him arriving back from an assignment, that gangster hat pulled low over his head, brisk and no-nonsense, or feet up on the desk, glass in one hand, bashing away one-finger style on his typewriter; then shuddering to myself as I summoned up imagined scenes of that last brawl that ended in his death. Now I scrolled through to a reconstructed scenario of how Bezuidenhout might have reacted a few minutes ago when seeing me drive past a second time so unexpectedly. What must he have thought? Did he put me down on his list of suspicious characters so that my life too would be under threat now? Or if he was indeed the culprit himself, unlikely though that might be, would he then try putting me up as a suspect, to divert the heat from himself?

As I finally fell asleep I came up with a little conceit, a vignette of how he might have gone about things in unreal South Africa, this low-grade police officer with a yen to display his detective skills. A real-life fantasy script – horror fiction, though based on possible fact:

Scenario

'Hey, come here, Fanie,' Sgt Bezuidenhout beckons his senior constable after I speed past, 'hey, where do you think this kaffir-lover been farting around? Whole bladdy hour or so! You know where? You know where, chummy, around in the section, I'm damn convinced, boetie! That's where he's been, I can see the dust his car kicked up coming back. No, man, now what's all this mean! No, jong! What can it mean, hey, jong. Scene of the crime, ja?'

Constable Fanie du Plessis, his assistant, is already strapping on his holster and picking up the keys of the station V8.

'No, what's this now?' asks the astonished Bezuidenhout. 'Wait, wait, look here, excuse me, hey, what's this now then?'

'I'll go arrest him pronto, Sgt Bez. Contravention of Native Areas Act (1955), Section 7 of sub-section 31.'

Bezuidenhout throws up his hands at this sign of low intelligence from a man who's been through the very latest stuff at police college ... but then mind you these days what can you expect? 'You crazy, Du Plessis? And put him on his guard?'

'It won't help him nothing to put him on his guard, I'll sommer (simply) arrest him, just like that.'

'Never mind arrest him, we might as well cut off his borlz rather. You just hold fire. Put away your sub-section stuff.' Bezuidenhout can begin to see something bigger here than even the breaking of an apartheid law. He explains to Du Plessis what is in his mind: 'Black-on-black nothing. Nothing so simple, this is something else again in the way of murders. Listen ... ' He outlines his idea to Du Plessis, whose eyes begin to take on a shine, as if someone has put a drop of oil in his brainbox.

Was it like that I wondered, tumbling more deeply into sleep, inside my little thatched house, not experiencing a conventional dream of falling through the sky, but was this a real nightmare I figured in?

The wake for Henry was arranged immediately. And there something curious, rather suggestible, surfaced. It was something that surely needed to be pinned down under a practical finger. It reached me by way of a hoarse stage-whisper while I was dancing with the delicious Dolly in the Nxumalo brick-and-iron shack, furbished up for the big wake festivities – nothing but a genuine curiosity could have pushed its way into a man's thoughts in that situation, wrapped inside Dolly. Dolly! The most voluptuous of women, whom Nature had treated so generously when parcelling out its gifts; splurging on her just the right amounts of superfluous flesh ... in the very places where it counted! And Dolly knew so well how to make it count. However, that was not the point at the moment, the real and fearful point was Henry's murder.

2. THE UNIVERSITY OF DRINK

That disturbing little suggestible suspicion had come whispering its way over to me midway through the big, big wake. It went on worming itself deep into my mind, in which restricted space another surmise was already seething. As a result, the two barged into each other, setting up a cerebral shockwave that threatened to spoil the fun of the party and caused me to dance uneasily in Dolly's arms.

This first misgiving had been tickled up in me by the behaviour of the police and legal authorities. They were doing *nothing* about the murder; they were simply ignoring the whole business. The CID had set in train no investigations, the coroner acted as if someone had switched him off at the mains, and the local police at Western Native, when we rang them on the following day from the office for a statement, had put on a deadpan act – 'No, look, hey, get his people to come fetch him and bury him up quick.'

Black-on-black, who cared? Was it just that, the cheapness of black life – or, more sinister, a hush-up from high-up?

Even Johannesburg's white press showed little curiosity about the murder, notwithstanding that beyond South Africa's borders Henry was possibly the country's most famous journalist. The British and American papers had reported the *Drum* story of how Henry had got himself thrown into gaol so that he could come up with a nice exposé of conditions there. Ja, the warders had dished it out to Henry and his fellow inmates with their usual happy abandon, unaware that *Drum's* photographers were scooping up pictures of them at this business, using a long-range camera atop a high-rise building aimed into the prison yard. All front-page stuff when syndicated overseas. Nor was that the only dangerous Mr Drum game in which Henry had starred. Today those things are part of the legend.

Of course, when they heard of his murder, the foreign correspondents swarmed around to cable their stories home via the teleprinters in the

Rand Daily Mail building. All done with the gracious hospitality of the *Rand Daily Mail* and yet the *RDM*, the Star and the rest of the local white sheets printed barely a line. After all, merely black-on-black.

It nevertheless seemed very odd; was there no more to it than that? My own efforts and influence didn't help. I'd once been political editor of the *RDM*, the 'liberal' morning paper, so now I attempted to tip-off my old colleague, Monty Williams, the news editor. But no, forget it, not Monty. He had never willingly sent a reporter after a story of a black man, nor ever a staff photographer. No sir, no pics of kaffirs in the news pages, whatever they might do in the sports section. Paul Irwin, the Sports Editor was one exception – from time to time he'd accepted those sticks of freelance copy from Henry on black soccer. Monty advised me to spike my wishy-washy 'liberalistic' suspicions, or shove off back to the kraal myself.

So it was all paradox for me, upon arriving at Henry's wake. On the one hand a smother-up by the cops and the press while I wanted to hunt down the murderer, on the other this further disturbing hint, an insistent, hoarse, whispered message threading across from the direction of Pinocchio, above the burblings of alto and baritone sax, above the pulsing of the rhythm section, and the shuffling and scraping of a hundred merry hooves. Pinocchio was hinting that it might be worth looking into the connections of a certain young lady not at the party ... she may have been Henry's 'girl friend'.

Was it right to bring up such scurrilous stuff now? It made such an irreverent and doom laden contribution.

In black Orlando township, part of what was later to be called Soweto, SOuth WEstern TOwnships, Henry was a famous newshound and a major social personality. So this was certainly going to be one of those wakes that black Johannesburg was famous for, beginning in solemn tears and ending in tears, but between times full of loud music and lawlessness and hefty laughter, planned to go on all night but in fact lasting all weekend, not to say spilling over into the working week that followed. No, *not* to say that, I worried, no don't say that – no, no! – not like when Johnny Mau Mau, the *Drum* driver, crashed and died, and because of the extensive funerary ceremonials we almost missed the deadline for the next issue, two weeks down the line. Frightful passing thought: in our little community, two men had now died violently!

Things at Henry's wake had started off traditionally slow and solemn, the first mourners to show up being the very young and the very elderly, sitting in stiff respectability on upright chairs around the cement floor. They looked earnestly down past their toes, examining the pattern of grain left by the concrete shuttering around what passed for a 'wainscot'.

We sat there, three or four of us, talking in the same quiet, respectful mood. Teaspoon, a *Drum* hanger-on, said in my ear, putting heavy meaning into it: 'They tell me he wasn't on his way *home* last night.'

Dan Chocho, one of our reporters, a strait-laced character, rather rare in our crew, overheard him. 'No, so what, man, so what! – that's not nothing at all.'

'It's a clue,' said Teaspoon with some relish.

'No, it ain't a clue, it ain't nothing. You're just trying to make something from nothing. Henry was at Percy Hlubi's place late in the afternoon, and he was jus' going out nearby there to do an interview for a big story he's supposed to work on, and Percy said he should better come back there afterwards to stay with him for the night, would be safer than trekking back here so late to Orlando.'

'Safer!' sniffed Teaspoon. Chocho gave him a reproving look.

All this didn't advance things much, though Teaspoon's bit of gossip did add an element of fact, if merely commonplace and explicable, to the undertones of supposition in what Pinocchio had hissed at me. Two different lines, leading off in how many directions?

Teaspoon, in a lugubrious voice, kept low so that Chocho could not hear this message, growled into my ear: 'I'm going to do some sleuthing, find out about this story he was working on, it was to show up some crooked stuff, some abortion business – and if I find out I'll come tell you.' He sidled away again and Dan and I were left on our own for a moment or two.

We continued to sit there pondering the matter. Things at the party were still very respectful and to be truthful, time was dragging for all. Then a big brawny youth in a white shirt who had entered on his own threw a look of little pleasure at this low-key scene and decided to do something about it. He propelled himself in an energetic dance across the room, solo, whereupon two other boys began jiving around too, lad and lad, men-only fashion, then two schoolgirls wafted in, to do a dreamy sashay in each others' arms, lass and lass, accompanying themselves in song. One of the youths slipped between them and grabbed one for himself, which meant that the leftover partners had to reassemble in a second boy-girl pair. Then all were upstaged by a group of older heroes who dashed in with girls in one hand and drinks in the other, winding things up still further as they chuckled together and shouted badinage across the room. Laughter and whistling began to spread.

Soon the party was a party, with everyone warmed up, even the three-year-olds having a go now, their little chubby legs twinkling out the *kwela* (pennywhistle) beat in perfect rhythm, and even the 70-year-olds taking the floor with a lively number 'something like the way we done it in the earlies', and at length the band itself arrived, for no particular reason ignoring the open doorway and crashing in via the single window of the prefab Nxumalo house, instruments in hand. They were already lit up by liquor, these guys, the Six Merry Blackbirds; and in their prudent way they'd remembered to bring along some spare half-jacks of hot stuff in their guitar cases.

I worried at all this liquor let loose, and Henry Telephone's old father and mother worried too. My concern about over-partying was to do with the good of the paper, theirs with its effect on God's peace of mind. Henry Telephone, was not, of course, Henry the Great, the dead man, he was another Henry on our staff, a placid, moon-faced fellow from the office who worked at reception and operated the switchboard whenever able to spare a moment from earholing my own telephone conversations. His parents were of the same placid breed as him, same moon faces. They were members of the black Church of Zion Redemption, though, and, in that, not placid at all, being ardent and tumultuous against sin and drink. They shook worried, angry heads at me to express their feelings. It wasn't the first time that they took up a position like this and it wasn't to be the last, of which more later.

To accommodate the musicians and the hordes of family and friends, of *Drum* workmates and *Drum* fans and local sporting and political celebrities as well as the general population of unemployed and those of the gatecrasher faith, the party, having started in Henry's place, No 983 Orlando, was obliged subsequently to spill over into the homes of neighbours in the adjoining breeze-block prefabs, Nos 985, 985A, 986 and so on.

The thousand-morgen (850 hectares) veld of that locality was smothered in these identical oblong concrete shacks, which had been moulded on the spot by construction gangs and plopped down in rows like eggs deposited from a moth's backside. They stretched criss-cross along the lines of latitude and longitude. And yet there was limitless open scrub where they could have been spread out more comfortably.

But now we're talking politics; we're talking native housing. That might appear unseemly in the middle of such terrible tragedy but it will help to put the scene of the wake into perspective.

Behind that mass building development operation had been the 'Liberals'. The Liberal council of the Witwatersrand was the mouthpiece of the rich whites who owned the factories where the blacks sweated to make them richer. The council spent a little of the ratepayers' money providing the workmen with smatterings of education so that they could read the Europeans Only notices, and passed byelaws to allow black labour to 'influx' into their town, two giveaway signs of being liberal. Not that the council would allow them in too close to white residential areas, native housing had to be situated far, far away and it had to be cheap-cheap, not too much of a drain on the rates, more a drain on the blacks' transport money. This selfish, liberals view paled when compared to that of the Afrikaner opposition councillors, who swore by the *voetsak* (get lost) policy, kicking the natives out altogether, back to where they came from or further.

The council being liberal, the housing contractors wisely turned liberal too, to cement their behind-the-scenes deals with the councillors. To build cheap-cheap they had to lay their little sub-economic housing eggs by the merry thousand on patches of land they had thoughtfully bought up beforehand, even cheap-cheaper. Further, to make enough profit to tap-off some into the councillors' back pockets ... what had to be the outcome? An economy drive: no doors in doorways, no floorboards, no piping, no ceilings, a maximum of two windows per house and no panes of glass in them.

These thoughts of greedy goings-on did not mar the great wonderful style of wake that could be held in those tiny tinny houses. All
the while the knowing and sinister sibilances of Pinocchio filled my
mind.

However, hold it once more! The great love-girl Dolly Rathebe
had arrived by now to grab me; she had a plan in mind it seems, the
great sexy Dolly who'd become famous for her star part in the first
home-made African film and who we'd kept firmly on the road to
fame by promoting her to cover girl and using her to host our *Drum*
Lonely Hearts column. It was entitled 'Dear Dolly' although others
ghosted it, notably young Casey of the crime desk and, if he was in
clink himself for a day or two, then the office driver. Every little
provincial reader absorbing Dolly's advice believed it to be absolutely straight-from-the-shoulder words of wisdom from the famous and
experienced glamour-girl, as she'd played in that hit film *Jim Comes
to Joburg*, and they counted it as the pure confidences of one like
themselves, originally led into difficulties by wicked menfolk.
'Advice me, Dolly,' they'd plead, not greatly worried about spelling,
'how can I deal with this man who I believe has two other lover-girls
at the weekend?' 'Advised' Dolly, in the words of the man who handled the column, 'give him a baby, that'll keep him with you.' This
was in the event profound and extremely sound advice. The lover-
man wanted not just a night of love to hold him, but proof that he had
made a baby, a necessary advert for his masculinity.

Dolly herself was no ingénue; she was knowing and worldy-wise,
though passionate with it, in the mould of all great jazz singers. She
took that evening of the wake to be her chance at last to get me in her
toils, to make me a 'real African' through a little love-making across
the race laws. An attractive and seductive proposition indeed, but
luckily for me and my family loyalties it was the wrong moment she
chose, for it was the moment when I set out on the murder trail.

I asked Dolly, to keep the temperature down, what were her suspicions of the murder. 'Well, it wasn' me did it, darling,' she said in her
husky casual tones.

Did she believe it to be murder? 'Well, it wasn' Henry did it himself,' she replied.

I couldn't regard this as very helpful when I was looking for clear-cut signs and clues and hoping to pick up hints from out of the wood-work. It was not appropriate. I asked her what this guy Pinocchio must have meant when he'd whispered across to me: 'Find out who was the "girl friend", check out the "girl friend".'

I jokily pleaded with her in the way of the readers: 'Advice me, Dolly! Give me advisement! How could the girl friend know who the unknown *tsotsi* was?'

'Ask your wife,' sniffed Dolly.

She was there, Jenny, dancing with Jim Bailey, the owner of *Drum*, my magazine. I suspected that Bailey had secretly egged on Dolly to attempt a breaching of my virginity, to baptise me as a true, rumbus-tious, inhibition-free African, like my staff. For that reason probably he was deliberately diverting Jenny's attention, just as he'd loosened up everyone else with liquor. It was a night of conspiracy theories.

Who was Henry's 'girl friend'? Find that out, Pinocchio had whis-pered, and you have a story. Pinocchio, however, would not dare to say anything more directly off his own bat. A timid little man, but a tool of greater men, and thus what he did let out must carry some weight.

I spent the rest of the time that we were there quizzing everyone tactfully about this talked-up lady-killing of Henry's, but got no two answers alike. Some said no, you talk rubbish man, some said yes and they knew who, 'strue's God, and some said which of the half-dozen do you mean? And Teaspoon said, sidling past me in his furtive way, 'Never mind the girl, I'm getting somewhere, I say look for Mr Big'.

Rumours, rumours ...

It was Jenny who told me later the name of the woman being band-ed around as the most likely girl friend. People told her things. The widow herself, quite unsolicited, had confided it to her, Jenny explained to me on the drive to our Orange Grove thatched rondavel. It was Comfort M'luleke; a person unknown to me, and getting me no nearer to a story with substantial meaning, nor casting any light on the identity of the murderer.

But to return to the funerary party, still continuing at full throttle.

Casey by this stage had got Jenny bottled up in a corner and was test-ing her out by pinching the nice bits of her backside, and occasional-ly of her frontside, while himself swaying with the drink. There was rare music, great dancing, grand singing and then a police scare that evaporated when it was made clear that the cops were simply coming along to pay *their* respects (and get their sample of the hooch, too).

Can Themba found a semi-sober moment to talk to me during the noisy night to stop me being too emotional about the death. Can was my number two on the paper, the Associate Editor, and felt a certain amount of responsibility for my education. 'Look,' he said, 'relax a little bit under fire, Syl, 'cos you may be taking on board more than you think. Do you know, it's not the first occasion like this, Syl. We've lost other good men, too, now how're we going to replace them, Henry and them, that's more to the point, no?'

'No, yes,' echoed little Casey, Can's attendant henchman. Casey was swaying more perilously by now. 'Yes, no,' he repeated, 'it's not first time for us losing a good man. Johnny Mau-Mau went too, a fast cornering in the office car, a tyre got bursted, he's sent explosing out into the road, head's cracked to bits ... and no damn hope from hos-pitalling. They pick up Bob Gosani who was riding with him, basi-cally unhurt 'cept for some sense knocked into him through his head – he says Johnny was drinkin' at the time.' He shook his head tear-fully. 'Waste of a good man. Still, nothing too suspicious. You couldn't say suspicious. Nice car crash, that's all. It would only've been an act of suspicion if Johnny Mau-Mau *wasn't* been drinkin'.'

His very dismissiveness of 'suspicion' roused suspicions in me, in the mood that I was in. Was there another plot lurking behind all this? This *other* man from *Drum* who'd met death; of course, of course, as I'd thought to myself already, Johnny Mau-Mau, that must set it in context. But yet, what was suspicious in that, and looking at things coolly and logically, it was enough to put the girl friend whispers on hold in my mind, just one of a series of great hypotheses bubbling up, new trails opening that were leading nowhere.

At home later, on tucking her roundness up into bed, Jenny hooked together a number of leading oddities. 'Was she married, Comfort?' 'Why does Pinocchio come into this, anyway, he's a bit of a rat and a *tsotsi* himself, isn't he? Do you think *he's* the one who stabbed Henry and is blowing up bits of false and fancy evidence to make things deliberately murky?' 'And how did that nice Mrs Nxumalo know her name anyway?' It all seemed wonderfully nonsensical to me. A remarkable, intuitive mind she had, our Jenny, though mind you the intuitions were as often wrong as right.

I lay awake trying to work it all out, turning over in my head other garbled talk. For instance, at the party Cecil Eprile, my fellow white editor, suggested suicide; Henry was suffering perhaps from cancer of the penis and wanted to end it all? ... Had I thought of trying for a picture of that at the morgue? This sounded to me like his usual slimy, tabloid fantasising, his lubricious mind always seeing the point of a news story in the shape of a penis. But am I hearing it coming from him or am I dreaming it? I am clearly falling off to sleep. As I half-unconsciously turn over, one hand slips around the wife's warm bottom and I fold my ears into the pillow for comfort.

More theories burble up through the stream of consciousness: Henry was murdered to stop him squealing about other murders that he had stumbled on ... or a reporter from the white press had become insanely jealous thinking Henry had stolen a scoop of his ... or it was an inside job, or Jim Bailey looking for more publicity for his magazine, and other such complete tripe ...

I begin a 30-year search among all this bag of rumours for the identity of that murderer. I will track him down and wreak vengeance on him. It will be my life's work.

STREETS ARE SAFE

when you can see

Be ready for anything with EVEREADY light!

A torch is a faithful friend. It leads you from danger — and chases danger away from you. Be safe in the streets tonight with EVEREADY Light. A torch filled with EVEREADY Batteries will keep you safe from harm. EVEREADY Batteries are longer-lasting batteries. They give you stronger light for longer — and so cost you less. Look carefully at your torch before night comes. See that it is filled with good strong light. See that it is filled with EVEREADY Light. Don't go out tonight without a torch — be ready for anything with EVEREADY Light!

ONLY 1d. EACH

EVEREADY
TRADE MARK

EVEREADY GIVES YOU STRONGER LIGHT FOR LONGER!

AFRICAN SERVICES CLUB
(PTY.) LTD.

Because we "CONTROL" Our Membership You Are Sure of "PERSONAL ATTENTION"

PROTECTION
SECURITY — KNOWLEDGE

Let your troubles be our troubles — Our Directorate headed by a University Graduate.

READ WHAT OUR SENIOR MEMBERS WRITE
(replies can be seen in our Offices)

"This Club tops all others" (Swaziland). "The Club has been better a Father to me" (Cape). "I am so proud of the Club" (Pretoria). Club has done wonders for me" (Germiston). "Thank the Club for improving my English" (Bapedionisiai). "My eyes are open since I joined Club" (Durban). "Your Lectures are wonderful" (Rhodesia). "I thank the Club enough" (Hendriksdal).

PROTECTION
- LEGAL AID: We appoint, and pay Lawyers to defend you anys
- DEBTS: We help you by arranging, where possible, that you pay your debts in small weekly amounts.
- BAIL: We assist with Bail, so that you do not lose your jo
- ADVICE. Expert help in all Business, Financial, Personal, Marr Hire purchase, Holidays, Buying, Housing and Education.

SECURITY
- INSURANCE. If a Member dies, his Family will be paid by the Dove Insurance. This costs you no extra.
- FAMILY BURIAL. The Family of Club Members receive a stupes funeral by paying only 3/6 extra a month.
- OFFICIAL AGENTS for Federal Building Society and Insurance Corp.
- BONDS AND INVESTMENTS: We help you to raise mone freehold property, and we help you to invest your money, a make your money work for you.

KNOWLEDGE
- CLUB WHOLESALERS: You can use the Club Wholesalers save money.
- EDUCATION. You get free monthly written courses of instru in subjects which are useful to you. Senior members also rece complete course on English.
- NEWS LETTER: Free monthly Club Magazine, full of information.
- BURSARIES: A limited number of free courses (from a C pendence College) are available to older members.

WRITE TODAY.

Please send me POST FREE full details of th way in which you can help me and my family.

NAME ....

ADDRESS ....

Send to, or call —

AFRICAN SERVICES CLUB (Pty.) Ltd
BOX 9124
7/10 Glencairn Bldgs., Cr. Joubert & Market St
(36a Joubert St.).
JOHANNESBURG ———— Phone 23-712

Feel younger
on Dr. WILLIAMS PINK PILL

Whatever your job is — you'll do it better if you feel fine! So give yourself new vital energy. Build up your blood with iron. When you're run-down and worn-out, you need a course of Dr. Williams Pink Pills. Just two, after every meal, for three weeks — will help to make your blood rich and full of new life. Help yourself to health — you'll look years younger!

3/6
per bottle from your chemist or store

Dr. Williams
Pink Pil

Sold in the red and white box

3. *DRUM* - A MASTERPIECE IN BRONZE

B y the Monday after the grand wake the daily urgencies of bringing out a magazine had intervened, cutting clear across my ruminations and preoccupations with the murder hunt and inevitably downgrading the priority of dedicating it as my life's work. There was the need particularly to start work on a major story for next month's issue, scheduled to be the big story of the year and ironically Henry's own annual Mr Drum exposé. Henry the brave was to have been sent to sunday service at white churches; brave he'd have had to be.

That would be the second big Mr Drum coup under my editorship. It was something of a challenge I'd inherited on taking over the magazine a year or so before – to work up a feature with world impact from time to time.

It was not the only thing I'd inherited. On the credit side I was able to step into a fully-fledged operation, a going concern. When I arrived at the offices in Main Street in February of 1955 I found a magazine barely three years old but already a mature and mighty little urchin. I took over from Anthony Sampson, who presented me with a blueprint for the new job, some 300 closely typed pages. This was in fact the manuscript of his soon-to-be-published book, *Drum*, and in the 40 years that have elapsed since this first youthful work, he has gone on to bring out books by the score, from *Inside Britain* to Nelson Mandela's biography. It was a happy convenience for me, that advance glimpse of his ms, as I knew immediately the complete history of the paper's early struggles, I knew just who was who on my staff, and a thing or two about how to manage the proprietor, the formidable Jim Bailey.

Bailey was labelled an eccentric. Probably everyone on the staff was something of the sort, by a process of natural selection. Jim dressed the part, hair too long for the prescripts of the day, clothes too casual. That and a rather buffoonish laugh did not equate with his Oxford accent and an Oxford curl of the lips, and it puzzled polite society – he'd gone native, what? But he had the character to go with his role of proprietor. He had judgment, energy, determination and a conscience that didn't fetter him too greatly in the handling of his ingenuous staff or still more ingenuous readers.

With Sampson's book I had also a general handbook of tricks and know-how to give me a running start. It was just as well, because the day I started, I effectively lost most of the editorial staff, Bailey marching them off under his wing, like a corporal escorting a detachment of recruits to the quartermaster's, to the adjacent office, to man the tabloid Sunday paper he'd decided to launch at that moment. A heady idea – to expand, to be an important publisher in the land. In fact it was but a few months since he'd tried to follow up the success of *Drum* with another monthly, a magazine called *Africa*, offering a profile more feminine than *Drum*'s. It was struggling, and soon to fail, yet he persisted with his onward drive.

He persisted, what's more, with a weekly, a project four times the financial burden and risk of *Drum*. But a weekly, there was glamour for you! The *Drum* writers were of that mind too, delighted at last for blacks to gatecrash the big white world with their own wideawake Sunday news-sheet. They wanted to expunge the image that the white world still had of them as illiterates, tribesmen, barbarians – well, barely that even, not evolved as true humans yet. There'd recently been a visit by a pair of Afrikaner reporters to the *Drum* offices; they'd stood with their mouths open at seeing black men clattering away over their typewriters. 'Magtig!' they appeared to gasp, 'bobbejane!' (heavens, baboons). You could see the thought go through their heads, the old cliche must be true then. If a dozen bobbejane typed away for a thousand years they'd be able to turn out all the books in the British Museum – that surely was the principle we worked on.

To be fair, at that time it wasn't just the Afrikaners but the whole of white South Africa that was so immensely uneducated about their own country; virtually none had ever met a black who was not a kitchen hand or shoveller of rock in the mines. Tiny powers of imagination, these whites possessed, leaving them unable to conceive of a black man with the intellect to pass beyond grade 2 in school.

With the arrival of *Golden City Post*, the new and brash weekly, the staff largely deserted *Drum*, and I was left to do 10 men's jobs, with only the young sub-editor, Arthur Maimane, left behind to help me, he doing the work of another 10 men. What it did do was, speed up my learning process as editor of a news-picture magazine. Previous to that I'd merely been a newspaperman, a writer, a political editor, ignorant of magazine strategy, layout and design. Now I had to become skilled in every aspect of picture-feature journalism, from making the tea to laying out jolly photo-spreads on river-duckings by the Baptist Church of Zion. Later, I managed gradually to woo back most of the best members of our staff.

Drum was – almost – the first black man's magazine. It developed out of the wartime flexings of the intellectual spirit in South Africa, which had brought forth a sturdy coterie of indigenous literary and political magazines, notably *Trek* and *Forum*. Arising naturally out of this scene in 1951 was Bailey's takeover of a magazine launched for the non-white reader. It was titled, with a certain self-conscious priggery for those days, *The African Drum*, and had the appearance of being a donation from on-high, from the white man to the worthy 'native'.

At the time, as an underground intellectual operating in the practical world of newspaper reporting, I readily bought and read the first issue. It appealed to me – aesthetics and social anthropology at a level I could relate to. There were profound essays on the ethnic origins of the peoples of South Africa, appreciations of tribal customs and hand-painted crockery, and tasty documentaries on primitivism in art.

These offerings were shaped and coloured by the liberal sentimentalities of the founding owners, but before long Bailey's natural business sharpness took control, following in the path of his father, Sir Abe Bailey, one of the least admired of the Rand's gold-mining magnates and least liberal of its press moguls.

It was Bailey family money that enabled Jim to assume control after the first owner's mistakes in the positioning of *The African Drum*, rewarding him with slumping sales and a slump in his finances. The pumped-in Bailey money, mind you, was soon flooding away also. The panga had to be wielded; costs must be slashed and a few directors cut loose. Once done, strong and gifted publishing could be applied.

Bailey had divined the trouble: no one was buying the paper save for liberal-thinking whites and a handful of white-thinking blacks. In a melancholy moment it might be thought that the total circulation was made up of himself and me!

By the second or third issue he had pinpointed the reason for its lack of pulling power with the ordinary bulk of blacks. He polled influential black politicos, churchmen, teachers and civic under-administrators and, more importantly, black sports personalities rather than whites, and black jazz musicians and 'socialites', not omitting a friendly group of thieves around a pot of prohibition hooch in a black tavern. The diagnosis was easy for them to make. *Drum*, to them, seemed designed for whites not blacks. And it was *for* whites because it was *by* whites.

The subject matter in the paper was academic, for academics. It was not aimed in any way at the people. 'Make it more like *Zonk*,' was one startling comment, 'and you'll sell'. In fact, *The African Drum* was not the first black magazine, it did not spring out of abso-lutely nowhere, though it was the first publication of quality and able to command respect. *Zonk* existed as a vulgar, kitschy, commercial monthly, displaying for the semi-literate black population pictures of their township football players and song–and–dance stars, and their own suburban shanty-town socialites and soft-porn stars.

Drum had been born as literary and refined. Soon, in a desperate bid to hold on to the last few Bailey millions, and under the influence of the churchmen, the comrades and the crooks, it became less refined, though it never descended into being another *Zonk*. There was not only football in the re-named *Drum*, but politics too; not just tribal art but social causes; not merely popular music but the great and original Township Jazz; not tame Europeanised writing and senti-mental photography alone but true African talk and rough-house genre photography – plenty of *real* zonk.

'And let's have crime!' Crime as an issue and crime as drama – as melodrama, as tragedy, as day-to-day reality in the lives of blacks. 'And let's have good old scandal, good old gossip and good old sexy pin-ups.' Then, they promised, it would sell. And so it would, as a modern student of the media would know.

Swiftly, within months of the launch, the first owner-editor, Bob

Crisp, a hero of white South Africa, a famous pre-war Springbok cricketer and dashing wartime tank commander, well suited to the Johannesburg establishment, a body embodied in common speech as the Rand Club, was jettisoned. He was superseded by a young Englishman, a friend of Bailey's at Oxford, and distinguished author-to-be, Anthony Sampson. Although more or less acceptable to members of the Rand Club, Sampson was not tainted with their inborn colour prejudices and patronage, which for him would turn out to be a great and necessary advantage on the black playing field.

Then there were the new reporter-writers; not the university toilers, white and black, whose measured stuff had been run in the first issues, but men living in the real rough world of Africa. Honoured men of Africa! – the soon to be famous Todd Matshikiza, Henry Nxumalo, Can Themba, Casey Motsisi, Arthur Maimane, Zeke (to become Es'kia) Mphahlele, Bloke (who had been William) Modisane, Gwigwi Mwerbi, Nat Nakasa. Nor should we omit the one or two white outsiders, Sampson and the photographer Jurgen Schadeberg, who were ready to plunge into the black community. They were shanghaied aboard in all sorts of ways. Some were shipped in by Father Trevor Huddleston from his St Peters School, some were nominated by township worthies, some dropped out from Fort Hare university, some just came jiving along the pavement, knocked at the door and barged in.

Can, Casey, Nat, Todd, Henry, Zeke: these were the Fifties People, and today 40 years later, still alive and making a name is Arthur Maimane, who repatriated himself from Britain after Mandela's election to become managing editor at *The Star*, the Johannesburg daily; Zeke/Es'kia is another who survived premature wiping out; while another late joining youngster, Lewis Nkosi, is today a professor of literature in Wyoming, US. But these others in later years must surely have become leaders of Africa, too – managing editors and managing directors; managing captains and managing kings.

Drum made its second debut at a frolicking and walloping pace; with the zest, personality, kerfuffle, obstinacy and cheek that the new staff introduced, most especially with their cheek. And remember that to be a cheeky kaffir was not to be merely cheeky, but heroic too, inviting cuffs, slings and prison sentences. Even to have the gall to go out dressed in a suit might call down trouble; you were meant to be seen only in servant uniform, white kaffir-duck, with half length sleeves and legs, bordered by blue piping.

Yes, cheek, bravado, daring and courage were something special that the staff brought along to their work ... not for them the humble acceptance of the town domestics, singing in chorus: 'Yes madame, Ja master'; nor of the good-boy academics who in the end dared no cheekier songs than that.

Speedily they talked up *Drum* into a noisy, opinionated journal, courageous and cheeky, which is what finally gave it its world repute – the thought that those bound-serfs of Africa dared to answer back. To be cheeky was a political statement in itself. Nevertheless to those working on the paper day-to-day, more important than politics seemed matters of football, crime, sex, social, music, magic and mumbo, and freakballs.

The words and the pictures. The *Drum* -style photography was created by Jurgen Schadeberg, a tousle-topped, argumentative, rather wayward immigrant German youngster, who was picked up by Bailey sitting on the pavement outside an Indian curry house in Durban, with a camera slung over his shoulder. Here was a lad, impervious to the colour bar, an unlikely but necessary lad; here was one who thought a man was a man, for all that.

Jurgen became chief photographer and picture editor. His contribution to technique was to bring picture processing into the office. His contribution to moral upliftment was to introduce the pin-up. They spirited Dolly, the great sexy lady, to the top of the City Deep mine dump, where beached on the waste sands of acidic precipitates she might languish in a bikini away from police eyeshot to show off her mighty curves. This scandalous vision they emblazoned on the cover! Where before had Africa found the opportunity to goggle at its own loveliness? Never in print, though one must concede that in the backveld a million tribal girls roamed around naturally naked and nubile. As young men we had gone out surreptitiously to snap them up on camera. Can I forget those firm-breasted Dianas of the veld, who swung along the donga paths behind their long-horned cattle?

But could the real living thing ever be as glamorous or as shockable as its image in a magazine?

Jurgen trained the lanky photolab assistant Bob Gosani, a staff family connection, to be the number one photographer. Jurgen trained other casuals too to bring back pictures, plucking his most famous apprentice from the ranks of the office drivers – Peter Magubane. Out on an assignment with the current staff photographer, Peter, a silent, practical man, would take a small Box Brownie and come back with his own images. Soon he had to turn to it in full seriousness when the duty photographer failed to appear, being needed at some other urgent mission (or urgent drink session). Peter became famous, boasting credits from *Time*, *Life* and from a dozen books of camera art.

Over the years Jurgen gave boundless encouragement in the photographic calling to the whole black nation. He continued to produce many marvellous pictures, both unauthorised news-shots of state secrets and posed profile portraits. He or Bob would be the ones to go with a writer to interview bigshots of the black world for the magazine's monthly prestige feature, Masterpiece in Bronze. Among those selected as masterpiece men were future Nobel prizewinners such as Chief Albert Luthuli and Nelson Mandela, or the painter Sekoto, the writer Peter Abrahams, the cricketer Basil D' Oliviera, plus many jazzmen, footballers and boxers.

On one occasion when I sent off a writer-photographer team to profile and ennoble the ANC politician Mandela in this way, they'd no sooner returned than the subject himself phoned me: 'Now Sylvester, man, please don't use that photo of me in boxing shorts.' It was a happy if slightly comical off-duty shot of him. An amateur boxer and a burly man in those days, not slim and elegant as he was to be in the 1990s, Mandela'd been caught by the photographer sparring in the gym, shorts pulled over his track trousers to help him sweat off weight. The redundant pounds bulging up under the tight gear added something endearing, though certainly comical, to his appearance. His concern was for his public image. 'Nelson!' I remonstrated, ' Mr Secretary General! How could I bow like that to political pressure?' 'I beseech you, Sylvester!' He feared for his gravitas. I surrendered and tore up the photograph.

Gosani was an easy ambassador for the paper on these diplomatic missions. A good-looking, languid youth, of loose and limber elegance and good-natured too, he displayed excellent natural manners – a likeable fellow. He was unpretentious, what's more: not strictly a 'native', he was born more of a 'Coloured', a bit of an advantage socially, but he had gladly opted for the black side, unlike most of his relations who preferred to stow away as whites.

Like any black, Bob was obliged to act the 'good native', keeping resentment of his enforced inferiority bottled up behind a smile. All our great heroes, in truth, played it on the surface like this, they had to: Henry, the fierce Todd, the soignee Bloke, Can, Casey, Arthur and Gwigwi, all presenting themselves as good natives, not only to the police, where it was an essential part of personal safety, but to ordinary whites in the street, for who would dare insist on his right of way on the pavement lest a lynching should follow? So did they present themselves to anyone in authority, not least their boss, Jim Bailey, or me, their editor. Deep down maybe they cursed us, together with the whole white race, and deep down we recognised it. Inside they knew we knew, and inside we knew they knew we knew. We could still all be friends together, though, and enjoy the passing hour and put on a big show of hail fellow and very well met. It was only when their guard was down that you knew of the bitterness.

Although Bob Gosani had chosen not to depend on his light colouring, he would still sometimes play things both ways, slipping across at will from one race to the next. White manners, black habits, coloured vices. He was at home in English, Afrikaans and Sesotho and in the *tsotsi* lingo, with its coded gangster vocabulary. He had each race's strengths and weaknesses as well as particular ones of his own. They were written into his life story: strong drink and weak lungs; fast cars and fast women; plus that slow poisoner, the cigarette. Yet always a brilliant member of Jurgen's photographic team.

So Jurgen worked on, in his logical German way, in his disputative German manner, in our common effort to bring the best out of the photography, layout and drama of the paper. He and I studied the world's best news magazines, *Life*, in those days a powerful weekly, *Paris Match*, powerful too and beautiful, *Look* and *Picture Post*. We were conscious that we were living through a historic period, on a paper that was carrying out a historic role, living history itself.

So we schemed and argued between ourselves. And in conference with my number two, Can, a man of personal leadership and profound reasoning power, with *his* number two, Casey, a laconic man of sharp yet kindly satire, and with everyone else on the magazine joining in, down to the dour Henry-of-the-telephone and to the newest tea-boy, David Sibeko, we debated and wrangled and shouted and worked away on the paper. It was a symphony performance: Can Themba as virtuoso soloist putting over a long, provocative proposal, the rest of them as the orchestra, baying away *tutti*, while conductor Stein kept time with one hand, mopping the sweat away with the other. A loud and lusty *indaba* (conference), from which, without fail, the wisest decisions would emerge to be tabled.

Then did death visit us again. A terrible and untimely death of a third young man. This was a considerable time later, but it jolted one into thinking ... this is more than coincidence surely? Yet it wasn't another murder, you couldn't lay the blame on that same *tsotsi*, there was no common motive and there couldn't be any connecting link at all with Henry's case. Isolated tragedies – yet for as many as three men to die, and all only in their twenties and thirties, within one small social group, there must be a reason.

The only way it could be related to Henry's case was that the victim was a distant young in-law of Henry's – but then this was no matter of violence, its immediate cause was pneumonia. Could you set pneumonia down to the account of any *tsotsi*? And for that matter where could Henry's alleged girl friend have come into it, and so long after? What outside agent could you blame for the raging pneumonia that was the cause of the third death?

In this quite unlooked-for manner had death reappeared. A saddening further death among our young men. The seemingly conventional circumstances of this death merely served to confuse the trail, to frustrate the murder chase after the unknown *tsotsi* and to damp down the pace and intensity of my investigation.

Flash photography is easy!

with a **BROWNIE** camera by **Kodak**

Six-20 Brownie Flash B Camera
Price £2.17.6. Flashholder £1.10.6
extra

Brownie Cresta II Camera
Price £2.2.6. Flashholder £1.10.6
extra

Day or night, indoors or out, a Brownie camera can give you pictures to be proud of, pictures your friends will want to see again and again. Just think! The happiness you have today, or tonight, can be kept forever, just by pressing a button. Your Kodak Dealer will help you choose the Brownie Camera that suits you best.

Six-20 Brownie Flash B Camera

Has a built-in close-up lens, and a filter to make clouds stand out. Can be used with the Brownie flashholder.

Brownie Cresta II Camera

Takes twelve 2¼" x 2¼" pictures. Has built-in filter and a close-up lens. Can be used with the Brownie flashholder.

Kodak Verichrome Pan Film

for better pictures in any light
IN SUNLIGHT, ON DULL DAYS, BY FLASHLIGHT

Kodak, Brownie, Cresta and Verichrome are Registered Trade Marks

---

The stylish Baronet Rambler Hat.

You're <u>headed</u> for success in a **BARONET HAT**

Whether it's business or pleasure you'll find the successful man wearing a Baronet Hat. It's not surprising because Baronet Hats are ahead in styling, ahead in quality and ahead in value!

Get yourself a stylish, comfortable Baronet Rambler. It could be your first step to success!

Baronet Rambler has these advantages:

· **FANCY BAND** · **MULTI-MIX FELT** · **PRICE**

At good stores everywhere!

BARONET HATS *from the house of DORIAN*

WRITE TODAY FOR FREE ILLUSTRATED LEAFLET

DORIAN HATS (PTY) LTD., P.O. Box 10, Booysens, Transvaal.

I asked myself again, could you at the time it happened have really laid the blame on the *tsotsi* gangster or for that matter on any mysterious, sweet and frilly girl friend of Henry, or a Mr Big – or even Sgt Bezuidenhout, to air that other fanciful idea in my head - for a third *Drum* death as well? The Johnny Mau Mau death maybe, a motor accident cunningly contrived, but this third one ... pneumonia! Could you, a resourceful and inventive person no doubt, have been able to lay at the door of any commonplace murderer the crime of inoculating with a deadly germ our graceful virtuoso of the Leica, the youthful photographer Bob Gosani?

For it was he, Gosani, none other, who was to die, dear Bob Gosani. It was he who was slain by the evil giant double pneumonia.

There had no doubt been those with a reason to do away with Bob, in spite of him being such a long, loveable, creamy brown, soft-looking and inoffensive man. But would they have been able to dispense a dose of magic *muti* pathogenic enough to stab a man with pneumonia?

No, after all, the real causes of morbidity could quite logically, quite categorically, be read between the lines of his death certificate. They were the weaknesses that we well knew to be possessed by Bob, along with his strengths: smoking, drinking, long hours, irregular diet, zero exercise, wayward germs ... wayward doctoring. Looking backward, it was clearly those wild properties of Bob's that did for him. Had we looked ahead, with a Cassandra's insight, we should have been able to anticipate its coming. Careless, reckless, arrogant inside his outward disguises of gentleness, respectability and humility, *Gosani was sure to die*. Once before, and in spite of his wish for that favourite, violent James Dean-type of ending, his wish to leave 'a good-looking corpse', he'd missed his date with death, on the day Johnny Mau-Mau was flung out of the car. Bob wasn't flung as far, for which he'd apologised to Johnny Mau-Mau's mother.

Consumption, lung disease, cirrhosis of the liver, renal insufficiency, pneumonia ... these were what a modern-tongued Cassandra would correctly have foreseen. And at whose door were they to be laid? Could that possibly be my mission to discover?

Communing within myself at the time of the burial I summoned up a personal memory of Bob, built around the enchanting scene on the day that I met him. I had started at *Drum* that same morning and hurried over to direct a photo session set up some time before to shoot the monthly science-fantasy story. We were to get pictures of three live monkeys, stage-managed to look as if they were personally 'driving' the huge, clumsy newspaper press that printed our magazine.

This was one in the series of spoofy, spooky stories that greatly intrigued our readers. The journalists believed that the readers accepted these fake pictures as genuine. I suspect some of the journalists almost did too. We would conjure up trick photography of 2.5 cm men climbing over the *Drum* office desks and in and out of Castle beer bottles; or of football on the surface of the moon. Incredible, but didn't it look perhaps true, yes, no?

On this occasion we had these unruly blue vervet monkeys, borrowed from the University of Witwatersrand (Wits) laboratory, being encouraged to pull on levers, work the paper through and feed out red ink from the Stop Press box.

Readers were to think, "Well, REALLY, so that's how *Drum* is printed?" For those of us in the office it was meant as a leg-pull of our printers, a satire on those backward white men who reckoned themselves such highly-skilled artisans and grumbled at having to 'work for kaffirs'. It was a humiliation for a white worker to be classed below blacks in the intellectual hierarchy. This was one reason we had to have a white editor, to give the formal orders, to point authoritatively at the column in the compositor's forme where a story was to be dropped in.

And here were veritable monkeys measuring up to the skill of our printers with great insouciance. And here was Bob, even more insouciant, and almost as gracefully monkeylike, there with his Leica, clicking and winding on 20 times a minute, scrambling up to a vantage point at the peak of that pile of machinery, which was massive enough to have graced a ship's engine-room, or lying full-length on his back on the concrete down below to snap a worm's eye view – in the end hoping to catch at least one realistic shot of a monkey swarming over the equipment yet not in a blurred fidget, astride the mighty cylinders in commanding manner, with small fist pulling down on the levers.

They were the devil to deal with, even with the press stopped, but it was a lovely sight to see those tiny, nimble primates and that willowy photographer chasing each other over and around the heavy machinery, like Peter Pan and the pirates. It was certainly more fun for a monkey than being at the laboratory having its brains decanted spoon by spoon while Professor Joe Gilman of Wits measured at what point it began to lose interest in its feeding. We printed the pictures, of these earnest little wage-slaves rolling out the next edition of *Drum*. It challenged belief – incredible yet true. What could one say but *hau*!

Bob died but his pictures lived on; he stamped his likeness on the future. A thousand thousand people were to see his photographs reproduced a thousand thousand times over, not in Drum alone but in scores of newspapers around the world, in books and in dozens of films and television documentaries, the camera panning slowly across the stills. That body of work was to speak for Africa in the days of revolution ahead and help to shape a future where Africans would take their rightful place in society, and where a Bob Gosani might be honoured in his own world.

Why had he died in the middle of life? That was a question for us, his friends.

But, to return to Henry's death in the early hours of New Year's Day 1957, and the events of the weeks immediately following, after the memorial party we had been debating constantly how we could track down the vile *tsotsi* killer. At length, 'Hey, never mind all the talky-talk,' Todd Matshikiza cried, 'let's have some action!' Todd was not really the action man of the team, mind you, he was a creator of music, fingers flying freely over the keys and, as our jazz critic, a creator of music in words too, brilliant, fancy words that rushed around in their own arpeggios and flew off his typewriter in their spicy *pizzicatos*. But not a toughie, no, a man who worked with his fingers not his fists. Yet now he was right, we needed action.

'Man, that's just more pretty talk too itself,' sniffed the unflattering

Casey, however.

'All right,' interceded Can Themba, with his usual authority and calmness,'here's what we do. It's the way a magazine can act. We run our own in-magazine investigation.'

Everyone could see it immediately and loved it and I brought it to a practical proposition at an editorial conference: we would mount a 'private prosecution', *Drum* itself would attempt what the police refused to tackle. We would use our own columns for a public inquiry.

This started in an appeal to readers for information about the minutest circumstances of Henry's death. Someone must have seen a violent *skabenga* (bandit) act strangely or heard him drop a hint and perhaps boast about his doings. There was a flood of response, most of it quite wild and useless, in visits, phone calls and bagfuls of letters, highly speculative and observing in their style none of the rules of fact or grammar. Of course, it did turn out to be a sensational circulation-booster, a satisfying pay-off for us as journalists.

There was one potentially significant communication, a laconic and peremptory message via a third party from Mpedi the *Inyanga* (medicine man), summoning Casey to an audience at his country hideout, a secluded kraal at Bandoliers Kop, tucked away in one of the Northern Transvaal's so-called native reserves. Casey was our normal contact with the old magic man, being one of those urbanised young blacks still half under the influence of his peasant family and still half sharing their superstitions.

An absolute rationalist myself, who didn't believe anything unless I could actually stub my toe on it, it was hard for me to swallow such attitudes in members of my staff, not least in such a slave to the hard-bitten Yankee literary genre as Casey. It depressed me too because it showed I wasn't altogether one of them and could never be and could only scorn those still tied to tribal customs – paying *lobola* (gift of cattle) for a wife, for instance. Yet one might have been more forgiving, remembering Casey's family dilemma and the fact that he still lived with parents. No, *lobola*, no wife! Philosophical beliefs apart, he'd have to toe the line if he wanted help from them in coming up with the necessary.

So Mpedi had, after all, netted some meaningful underground whispers. I berated myself for not having sought him out immediately, on the morning after the murder. Casey was sent off in the battered old office car. Meanwhile, other vaguely plausible leads were being followed up in the *shebeens* and among hangers-on of the Rand gangster mobs. We were keyed up, perhaps we would happen on something valuable. There was further chatter from Teaspoon, still unsatisfyingly short on hard fact, about the story that Henry had been following up.

At the same time we had to get on with life, to return to work and fortune, to plan the next issue of the paper. As I've said it was time for the annual Mr Drum story, our prestige effort of the year, but now alas to be done without the star Mr Drum, without our chief reporter, without our heroic Henry – Henry the Brave, Henry the Suave.

Who would be the new Mr Drum? A crucial decision had to be made, for we were about to embark on a project that would influence the lives – and deaths, perhaps – of two more men, the men that would be needed as stand-ins for Henry.

We had chosen the particular subject because it had to be something weighty, and it had to support the position that *Drum* was by now a world wonder, a very 'masterpiece in bronze' in its own right, a prophet of its times - and, in the way of prophets, honoured in any land other than its own. This year's theme was intended to achieve this in boldness and grandeur – Mr Drum walking unafraid into a white church. 'Brothers in Christ' it would be entitled.

Before I could settle down to this, though, a short diversion had to be dealt with, a new development in the murder puzzle, pointing a troubling finger at ... at who? I had complained to Cecil Eprile, my pink-faced and blubbery-lipped fellow white editor about the white press having ignored Henry's death so completely. 'Laddie, lee- lee- leave it to me,' he commanded, this self-satisfied fellow with his irritating stammer. He sat before me, blinking owlishly while wallowing in thought, ruminating, an actual chewing of the cud, an unattractive way he had of dealing with the bits left over from that day's breakfast. This was a signal that, although a man of action, he was a thinking man too.

In due course he spoke: laddie, he would see what he could do to interest the police in our dear colleague's death, and for his trouble he would at the same time use the opportunity to dredge what he could from police sources in the way of a news story for his own paper. Knowing Cecil it would certainly be dredging he'd be up to, dredging in the dirt. He was a creepy man – slimy, to be completely frank – resembling a Charlie Chaplin who'd taken the wrong turning in life, retaining just the clipped black moustache and oiled black hair. Cecil was an early tabloid editor, with an itchy blue pencil, dedicated to the slaying of immorality wherever it might be found, in the process dealing morality a death blow.

He was back from his ferreting among the garbage 24 hours later. He looked embarrassed when he sat down before my desk, and needed a further spell of rumination, chewing over that day's fried eggs and bacon, before he could talk. 'The boys're following a sus- sus- sus-, they're following a sus- sus- suspicious sp- spoor,' he said at length, the stammer spoiling his attempt at laconic murder-story mode. 'And better you know about it.'

'Whose spoor?' I asked. 'It's a different suspect?'

'Maybe you can guess who,' he answered meaningfully, sinisterly. But he wouldn't amplify this, irritatingly; he told me first of what was currently engrossing the police mind, the enjoyable practice of Black Velvet, as they called it. This was the pay-off the police extorted while policing the shadier depths of crime. Pouncing on a white man and a black girl found enjoying 'illicit sex' together, the police would arrest the man but free the woman, in return for a taste of her blackness in the back of the police van.

Cecil's source for this information was Bertie Stallibrass, crime man on one of the white dailies, who spent his days riding with the CID in their squad cars, so as to be on the spot when a story broke. As a result of this style of life, living in the *konstabels*' pockets, he had degenerated into a through-and-through konstabulary character himself. And fair exchange – he paid his way by tipping-off the police about anyone acting against apartheid, fellow reporters included.

So, while pumping Bertie about the Henry murder and what he'd managed to pick up from Sgt 'Sampie' Bez, Bertie's closest and sleaziest police companion, who was the very same Sgt Bezuidenhout of Western Native Township, Cecil learnt two things. First, all the

scabrous details of the new police 'whoopee', Black Velvet; second-
ly about an alleged practitioner of illicit sex that they were after –
nobody but myself, S R Stein.

I iced up, breaking into a heavy sweat in the same moment – being
guilty of love across the colour bar was one of apartheid's gravest
crimes, almost a capital offence, 15 years at the least and beatings by
the cops first, then by your fellows in gaol. And to be accused was
virtually to be found guilty.

'And what's that got to do with Henry?' I roared a bit quaveringly,
trying to act forthright and severe. 'And where'd they get on to such
a lot of balls?' I comforted myself: what had I done in reality, but
squeeze up to Dolly?

Cecil nudged me in a conspiratorial way, a sort of a winking and a
licking of the lips at my supposed cunning in bringing off such a nice
bit of lechery. He half believed the story and was part way to accept-
ing its corollary, an even more heinous allegation, that I had been
responsible for the murder of Henry, in the light of an arguably plausible motive trotted out by Sgt Sampie.

I froze again, now in a cold sweat. 'Rubbish!' I shouted. 'What
motive?' I demanded.

All right hang on first, protested Cecil, hang on, he'd been told he
could break the story in next Sunday's *Post*. 'No w- w- wait!' he said,
seeing the look in my eye accusing him of gross disloyalty. 'W- wait,
why not, just think about it calmly, it would be to your advantage if
we did that, laddie, it would be better for you than for it to come out
first in the white papers. Those chaps would put it very negatively ...
r- r- roast you.' Really, of course, Cecil was torn by the hope of a big
scoop; nothing would stop him pursuing a scoop, just as nothing
would stop the police pursuing a conviction, evidence or no.

While I was shrieking at him for being a bastard, Cecil explained
how Sgt Sampie Bez had seen me behaving suspiciously in Western
Native and slowly his brain had ground out a working theory, complete
with a logical motivation for murder. It was this, he hypothesised:
Henry had been procuring me black girls for my own enjoyment, but
had then turned nasty and blackmailed me for the very offence of
Black Velvet. Thus I'd had to get rid of Henry to save my own skin.

It really looked as if Cecil was taken in by this idiot fantasy - my God, almost envied me for it, and only wished he'd had the courage to pick off a few flirty African ladies. Meantime, he smirked apologetically, didn't I think after all that it was quite a story and wouldn't it be a feather in its cap for the firm if his paper beat the whole white press to it?

I shouted more violently and threatened him with excommunication, castration and being handed over to the staff to be eaten alive, before slamming off home. Shortly after he rang me to say: oh no, he hadn't believed it for a minute, it was just one more theory that had to be examined; he'd had to test me. Like the absurd rat that he was he then put up a show of great contempt for Bertie Stallibrass, and his police chums, at having the poison in themselves to believe such rot.

I set it down to tabloid sickness, a kind of galloping hack's hysteria on Cecil's part, though it seems hard even now to credit his actions. Years later a great secret about Cecil was exposed in the press, of a deed rotten enough to make that little attempted scoop of his nothing in comparison. Just as Bertie had been playing the informer's card it eventually became officially acknowledged that Cecil had been doing the same all along. Quite unsuspected by us he had been working on the side as a paid spy for the Central Intelligence Agency in the United States. What's more he continued to do so for the rest of his life at open and official level once he'd left South Africa in the 1960s and travelled via Britain to America, where he was to end his days in the early Nineties.

All the same, he came back to the point, I'd better watch out for Bertie and the cops, for he wasn't sure if he could defend me from them, though he'd go back and tell them they were barking up the wrong tree. But nevertheless, not to worry, he said, not to worry.

But I did worry, worry after worry. So there was another suspect – and it was me! Worry left me bereft of sleep, which had a bad effect, taking my mind off night games on the domestic playing field, leaving quite unexploited for days on end the nubbly parts of the female body I shared with its owner. It took my thoughts away from work too.

However, 'alibi!' I suddenly yelled to myself the next morning, driving to the office. 'Man, how could Bezuidenhout possibly suspect it was me? He himself had telephoned me at home 20 miles away when Henry was found stabbed. Agh, ja, magtig, the perfect alibi, what!' I felt a sight more relaxed. But then, almost immediately, I had a bit of a relapse – a complete downer again: supposing he had it schemed out that I was Mr Big and had been luxuriating in bed in Orange Grove at the time my *tsotsi* hitman had gone to work at the other end of the Reef with his knife?

It was very speculative and merely circumstantial all of this, nevertheless, and thus some of the fear was taken away from the mind of a nervy fellow; and now I could worry professionally instead, planning for that big story, 'Brothers in Christ' starring Mr Drum. A complication was that Bailey had heard of this plan and now poked his nose into editorial affairs where it wasn't wanted. We should go instead for some other big story subject, he ordered. He'd got the wind up, fearing that we'd be closed down if we did this one, just as he'd been scared in 1955 when Henry, Can and I had given the year's big Mr Drum special a different twist being more directly political than in former years, with a provocative sports piece demanding that South Africa should allow blacks into the Olympic team. The mere thought written down on paper would send a blast of hatred through government minds and have me shot and the paper banned, Bailey had claimed then. Which, I wondered, would concern him more?

I determined to work my way round his objections on the church story, just as in the end I had managed to do with the sports piece two years previously. The obstacles that arose over the sports issue and how they were handled will demonstrate the 'Brothers in Christ' story, and how it will dovetail nicely into the *Drum* investigation into the circumstance of Henry's death. This means advancing the story by marching backwards to when Henry was alive and on his mettle and working up *Drum*'s Olympic feature of 1955.

TOP RECORDINGS OF TOP AFRICAN ARTISTS FOR ONLY 2/6 EACH

(or 3/3d. each for post and packing to your home)

JOIN THE SENSATIONAL

FIVE STAR RECORD CLUB

All you do is send your Postal Order for 10/- if you are going to collect your records in Johannesburg, or 13/- if you want them posted to you. This is all you pay for 4 78 r.p.m. records plus a completely FREE one the moment you join. Top quality 78 r.p.m. hit records are pressed specially for Club members by top stars of the Townships. What records—hit tunes by hit stars—unbreakable—more than two minutes playing time on each side. Here's a wonderful way to build your record collection.

YOU GET THIS COMPLETELY *FREE* 78 r.p.m. RECORD THE MOMENT YOU JOIN
'HOT PHATHA-PHATHA' by 'The Shooting Stars' and
'SHELTON JIVE' by 'The Comets'

The First Month's Record Hit is:

'ISITIMELA' by TOKA and the Satellites and
'JABULANI JIVE' by 'The Shooting Stars'

If you want to FETCH your records it will cost 10/-.
If you want us to SEND your records it will cost 13/-.
The extra money is for postage and packing.
Fill in ONE of these Coupons and tell us what you want to do.

FIVE STAR RECORD CLUB

To: The Five Star Record Club,
P.O. Box 2848, Johannesburg
I want to FETCH my records

NAME _____

ADDRESS _____

Please make me a Member of the Club. I will FETCH my records and I enclose a Postal Order for 10/- for FOUR records. As soon as I get my Membership Card I will FETCH my first record at the address you will give me. I will also get ONE FREE RECORD.

To: The Five Star Record Club,
P.O. Box 2848 Johannesburg
I want you to SEND my records

NAME _____

ADDRESS _____

Please make me a member of the Club. I want you to SEND my records to the above address. I enclose a Postal Order for 13/- to pay for FOUR records and postage and packing. When you send my first record you will also send my Membership Card and ONE FREE RECORD.

5. SPORTING MEMOIRS OF 1955

Ayear or two before Henry's death I had given him the main responsibility for our great sports story. He was an expert on sport in the black world and, as already mentioned, as early as 1948 I'd bumped into him from time to time as he handed in sheets of results for the sports pages at the trade doorway of the *Rand Daily Mail* offices. His three, close-written pages of prose might end up as no more than a one-line listing:

Orlando Pirates 0, Goliaths 2

Still, that little was gulped down by thousands of black readers, whose needs were otherwise ignored by the white press because its owners, its editors, its journalists, its printers, even the poor-white grandee who acted as commissionaire at the entrance, largely choked at the thought of black readers besmirching their paper by running their eyes down its columns. However, Paul Irwin, the sports editor, whose mind was not so closed off, being newly imported from England, managed to slip in just that stick or two.

Thus Henry had some working experience of the subject, and when *Drum* got going he became its Sports Editor as well as Chief Reporter; and being a man with a clear political grasp it was natural for him now to be given the chance to lead off this ambitious two-issue politico/sports special.

We started with a polemic – Why can't our black sportsmen go to the Olympics? The Melbourne Olympics were due in a year, but the South African Olympic Committee treated it as an utterly irrefutable axiom that no non-white should be allowed in the team, no matter that there were black countries in the line-up and no matter that there were South African blacks who could have qualified. One or two did duly find their way into those Olympics, being adopted by other national teams, such as Britain and New Zealand, and even won medals for them.

I had long felt a strong and obstinate urge to handle that sports feature; yes, it truly was more political than what we usually tackled, but

I was a more politically motivated man than Bailey, more even than most of the blacks on the paper. And sport, in my opinion, certainly related closely to politics.

Those protesting paragraphs of Henry's story became the first rumblings through South African sport on the question of the black man taking part. This disturbance was to continue and grow and become a hammer-force over the next 35 years, during which time it spilt into every corner of the world beyond South Africa, was to influence very greatly the course of the apartheid war, and later to play a leading part in the steps for reconciliation and peace that came after that war was won.

Absurd and irrelevant though the issue appeared in those early days to a white sportsman or administrator, it was a hot personal cause for the ordinary person in black society. The whites were strangely innocent and unaware that there was mighty interest among their servant class in sporting affairs – in football and boxing on the Rand and in cricket and rugby at the Cape – and that there were very able black sportsmen. To the whites it seemed unsavoury that their tame blacks should be taking up white man's games, while the thought of cross-competition among the races was complete anathema. It lasted into the early 1990s; even after Nelson Mandela had begun his triumphal walk to freedom, there were schoolboy rugby players in the Transvaal who wrinkled their noses in disgust when asked to play against blacks and absolutely refused.

So sport for all was then and always a burning issue among our readers. And in spite of the fact that most *Drum* writers were apolitical, they were passionate about freedom and passionate about sport. Thus though we covered these sports topics in an avowedly subversive manner, they were quite ready to tackle the project, if in their own creative, very idiosyncratic, way.

After the initial polemic, we moved on to the planned follow-up feature, the politics of football. Our office news conference on this topic was adjourned at the end of a couple of hours to Can's local shebeen, the famous Back of the Moon. A couple of shots of the madame's best *skokiaan* brew were needed to give clarity to the ideas, argued Can. This home-brew was packed with magical calories to impart extra heat and light to the debate. Do not think though that we

came up with nothing but moonshine! No, highly booted-up meetings like that produced the finest debate and controversy – we shouted up our uninhibited thoughts, demolished slack arguments,
punched everyone's noses for emphasis and from all the sound and
fury there emerged the soundest of strategies.

Football was the natural day-by-day sport of the blacks in the
townships. We would here be looking at its political and social
aspects, having previously stuck to the plain business of kicking the
ball into the net. Our case would be this: we wanted local and international recognition for black football – and why not financial aid,
too? Not one tiny piece of co-operation did government or local
authority give to African and Indian footballers or the slightest mon-
etary help to their threadbare associations, yet every prosperous white
school, club and national team tucked into a fat official budget.
Spectators too: at the public stadiums blacks were offered nothing but
a generous kick up the backside – it was only the most inhospitable
areas, tucked well out of sight of the action, that were not marked
Europeans Only.

Opposition needed to become more articulate. We would do our
part by giving major coverage to the issue. I assigned Can Themba,
with his side-kick Casey, to handle the opening conference on
apartheid in soccer in big-story style. Can, however, a questioning
man, a sceptic, an existentialist, wasn't so very certain that sport had
a serious place in history and before he got going he offered me these
few private lines, a parable to illustrate his point of view, I suppose,
for my private autograph book:

How to pass the time cheaply

*At each end of the scale in South Africa you have people with
nothing much to do – you have on the one hand the unemployed, mostly black, all very poor and many who can hardly
even afford to starve. At the other end you have the upper
classes, who have not much need to work, and are usually not
too poor and generally eat well enough ... too well?*

They have the time to spare, both these sets. What can they both do that is absorbing, that will keep them from the need to be constantly entertained and that does not interfere with other people's pleasures? They can join the Special Project. This is something that anyone can belong to and that each and every person of both sets can put their hearts into. It has the extra advantage that it requires in the beginner no special language skills – the English, Afrikaans or African languages will all do – no great expenditure on equipment, and little call for initiative.

Rules of the sport: Take an hour-glass, preferably one with a 20-minute cycle, and up-end it on the centre of a table, observing carefully as the sand runs down from the upper glass through the neck to the lower. Then reverse it and watch the sand go from the lower glass, now at the top, through to the upper, now at the bottom. When this has been done, you will have used up 40 minutes.

Repeat as necessary.

6. EQUALITY IN SPORT

Hurrying along the uncared-for road to the first soccer parliament, with his short-statured crony Casey J Motsisi scrambling to keep up beside him, Can Themba was out to tackle the story of sport from a neo-political and essentially seditious angle.

Following unobtrusively a pace or two behind were Dan Chocho and myself. I was going along, not to lean on Can and Casey at work, but to pick up some of the background feeling for myself. We could hear Can confiding to Casey details of his current romance, one of those that he put into short story form later and, still later, was published in book form. And from that book much, much later still, 40 years on, one of those stories was brought out in dramatic form as *The Suit*, staged to acclaim in theatres around the world.

Can seemed to be anxious about a letter from a girl friend that after several weeks had still not materialised – if in fact a letter ever had been written, or if written ever posted to him. He was slightly desperate. How could he survive without one amorous word?

'My friend, you can't make love to a letter.' Casey J, ghost writer for Dolly's Heartbreaks column, dismissed this slushy nonsense drily and authoritatively, 'I know that for a fact. There was this guy did it once; he told me afterwards it wasn't no good.'

Can sighed, an uncharacteristic reaction, a way of acknowledging to Casey his lapse into sentimentality. Here he was, a renaissance man by reputation, he Can Themba, worrying over a girl! He, an expert on existentialism! He, an expert on pan Africanism and on philology (speaking English, Zulu, Afrikaans, *Fanagalo* (a pidgin English-Zulu language) and *tsotsi*-taal and able to chat in French above menu level), a theorist on Afro-Asiatic roots, a critic not only of bottled beers and brandies but a connoisseur of the vintages of *skokiaan* (fermented home-brew), *KB* (Kaffir beer) and pin-upple, here was he almost blubbling. He, an authority on police corruption, an adept bushveld hand knowing where to seek the wild *madumbies* (a starchy tuber), a virtuoso among modern *panjandra*, was to be found wasting his talents on a bubble, on nought. An enthusiast on cricket and football who should be at his football studies this very minute, here he was – where? He pulled himself together: 'We'll make football the big issue of the moment!'

He sped along the dirt road before us with his problem, leaping from the ridges to the humps, each of which Casey J's little legs needed to tackle as a separate hillock, panting up the one side then twinkling down the other. 'But look ... ' Can still needed to talk on; he appealed to Casey J, cocking a sideways look to check the effect his words were having. He noted that his friend's little face was bunched from effort, causing the crewtop hairdo to tilt downwards over the nose – Casey J's one glory was that crop of bushy hair; his one vanity, that afro-topiary. 'But look man, Casey J, before we go on, I've built important decisions on this letter. It will tell me whether life is worth living or not, or whether to sensibly stick to liquor.'

Fortunately, at this point we arrived at our destination, the gothic hamburger-shaped building, standing out from all others in Soweto, where the great soccer talking match was to be held. Casey J rubbed his short stubby nose with the heel of his hand, to conceal his heavy breathing, squashed tidy the edges of his crewtop between the ends of his fingers and thumbs, then went over to buttonhole Abel Konko, the manager of the dilapidated building, who was also the conference host, sponsor and chairman, prosperous taxi-owner and boss of the Red Sox club. Konko, a man of rich, round shape, whom Casey was hoping might let drop in casual conversation a tip for a growth-stock share on the Johannesburg Stock Exchange, a share that could only go up and never down. Worldly-wise in most things Casey J had an innocent faith in Konko's forecasting powers, equal to that he had in Mpedi's, even at moments when Konko had just pointed in the up direction and the fancied share had chosen to hurry off down.

The conference was called to order. I lurked at the back of the hall, not to inhibit things by my white presence. Another white, Harry Bloom, the anti-apartheid lawyer, was also there, but near the platform. He represented the black soccer movement in its dealings with authority.

Ushers were shouting that all should get seated on the rows of dainty wedding-party chairs that had been 'borrowed' for the occasion. Konko as it happened also owned a large lorry, had hired its services out to move these chairs from one smart suburban *bar mitzvah* party to another, and had managed to poach a little free usage for this soccer function. Amid guffawing and hand-shaking and the hitching of hulking bodies atop the thin gilt stilts that supported the chairs, this inaugural assembly of delegates from all soccer walks of life settled down to discuss international recognition for black teams, which in turn might force the government to give them national recognition, a paradoxical reversal of the normal way of things.

Willy Rip, president of the Cape Soccer Association, made the keynote speech. Willy, one-time goalie-skipper, of lengthy design of body, who had famously relied on this lengthiness for keeping the ball out of the net, set out his views. We were there to initiate a movement to break down the race barriers in sport. Fair Play for All. That would not only have great sporting but also political significance. 'If you can only get two people making football together not war, you have a good start,' he said.

'Twenty-two still better,' chipped in a barracker.

The laughter following this set a happy mood for the conference, although, the delegates and observers having been selected to represent all shades of opinion, there was plenty of controversy, even fighting talk. There were those who simply wanted to get on with their local football, Pirates versus Goliaths, and forget the politicians. And there were those sporting bolsheviks who saw no reason why whites and blacks should not play in the same teams. And why should not South Africa be represented internationally by such mixed teams, selected from the best of all races?

At this, 'Keep politics out of sport,' shouted B J Champion of Eastern Province, one of the traditionalists. It would simply give the regime a stick to beat them with, he said.

'That's not good enough, keep sport out of politics,' countered Drainpipe Tembo, a man from Natal. 'It wasn't us started it.'

Konko put in a word from the platform to support this point. 'We are all against apartheid, we have to make a stand and oppose the regime's apartheid policy, *as such*, or it will have serious consequences not just for our votes and our other rights but for our own beloved game of soccer.'

Here there was great cheering, as there was every time a speaker invoked the sacred word soccer. 'Hear, hear!'

A left-winger, name of Klaaste, stood up: 'Let us take our cause to the outside world. Let us get soccerites all over the world to give us support. One soccerite to help another. Let us go to the world body of soccer, the esteemed FIFA, to take up our case.'

'FIFA, FIFA!' came a united bellowing, as of an *impi* on the march. This seemed at last a strong and very practical step, and was accepted after a short debate. There was carried a motion that Bloom the lawyer, who had a valid passport (whereas none of the non-whites would be permitted to leave the country), should attend the FIFA conference in London the following month and smuggle out to them a request for representation for blacks from South Africa, not whites alone.

'Now you're talking football! That's football!'

And that was the football story we ran, backing the delegation to FIFA. In the end FIFA, although on our side, weren't able to persuade white South Africa's footballers to give up their apartheid dream. But FIFA did become one of the first world sports bodies to ban South Africa from international competition and remained one of the fiercest supporters of the South African blacks.

7. HUSH-HUSH TACTICS

Our sports series was done – researched, reported, set up and all but printed. Can had turned out a powerful version of what he'd seen and heard at the soccer parliament, which in parts he'd improved on. Big-story treatment indeed.

Now to argue it through the Bailey barrier. Bailey and I had gone through the should-we-shouldn't-we debate on printing the highly-charged material many times already. The arguments had been repeatedly paraded with diligence by the one side and repeatedly trampled on with utter indifference by the other. There was not a great deal new to add and no chummy compromise to be reached.

'It's just the sort of stuff *Drum* needs, mounting a campaign for non-racial sport and getting its readers behind it,' I argued for the fourth time or so, with what I thought a canny touch, appealing to the business instincts of the proprietor.

'It's the sort of stuff that will get the government behind it with a *sjambok* (whip),' countered the proprietor, concerned with the very survival of his business.

'Nevertheless, we should publish,' I insisted, a bit shrilly.

'Publish and be banned!' Bailey quipped, in tight-jawed mood.

Casey, that taciturn fellow, intervened now to put his case for running the story. No giant of dialectic, Casey J Motsisi, but a useful man with the satire. 'Tell you what, let me go speak straight to the horse's mouth himself, what say I take advice from the minister for sport,' suggested Casey J. In truth he wouldn't be able to get as far as the minister's second secretary's lavatory-cleaner without having his front teeth knocked out, and his ornamental middle initial along with them. But we did in the end, with Casey's sarcasm and Can's sophistry, manage to soften up Bailey and it was agreed that we go ahead with the series. It's true that when it duly came out there was some jolly sniping from the government-supporting press, offering to have us deported in wooden boxes and our magazines roasted alive, but we coasted over the bumps.

There were highly significant sequels to both the football and Olympics stories, which in particular became the manifesto of a movement that established the world boycott, the boycott that truly tried to take politics out of sport, and that beset the sporting world everywhere for more than a generation and, in consequence, the political world too, until white South Africa was forced to give way to the will of the majority.

The public ventilation in the magazine of the whole unjust business had helped to put heart and belief into black sportsmen, and a committee was formed there and then under Dennis Brutus to take up the cause. That militant committee was to become Sanroc (South African Non-Racial Olympics Committee), the boycott organisation. As it turned out I was co-opted onto that movement's executive committee 20 years afterwards, improbably enough a veteran competitive athlete in my own right by that time.

But let's be careful not to race too far ahead of ourselves for it's necessary now to make the move onwards again, from that pre-Melbourne 1955 feature to the time after Henry's death two years later, when we will look for enlightenment on Mpedi's oracular pronouncements in helping us to seek out Henry's true murderer, and when we will tackle the proposed feature on white churches.

Unfortunately, here again with this subject of the Christian churches and the blacks, we would be stirring up Bailey's fears, for in government quarters it was as unmentionable a topic as sport for the blacks. Likely, therefore, to be in conflict with Bailey again on a political story, I decided to sidestep his possible grumbles by saying nothing, by simply ploughing ahead unobtrusively, slyly perhaps. Later, for a third time and terminally, he and I were to tangle head-on over what *Drum* might dare to publish; again over a sporting matter, a cover picture of Althea Gibson, the black 1957 Wimbledon champion, being embraced by her runner-up, Darlene Hard, another American but white. Oh horrors, a black girl and a white girl kissing! But I will return to it and its immortal consequences in its proper place.

For now we are at the starting point of the first Sunday's attempt to launch the 'Brothers in Christ' assignment. We sought out a nice traditional church for Mr Drum to attend – uninvited – a handsome old-fashioned place in the parklands of the English-speaking northern suburbs. Two photographers were to be waiting to catch our man being thrown out on his ear and I would be there too, in case something more serious threatened. Finally, to handle the background colour report, we had selected the genial William 'Bloke' Modisane, a man with an eye for picturesque and poetic detail.

SORE THROAT? BAD COUGH?

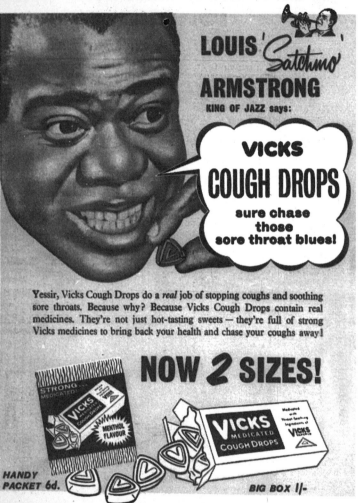

LOUIS *Satchmo* **ARMSTRONG**

KING OF JAZZ says:

VICKS COUGH DROPS sure chase those sore throat blues!

Yessir, Vicks Cough Drops do a *real* job of stopping coughs and soothing sore throats. Because why? Because Vicks Cough Drops contain real medicines. They're not just hot-tasting sweets — they're full of strong Vicks medicines to bring back your health and chase your coughs away!

NOW 2 SIZES!

HANDY PACKET 6d.

STRONG... MEDICATED VICKS Cough Drops MENTHOL FLAVOUR

VICKS MEDICATED Cough Drops

BIG BOX 1/-

VICKS COUGH DROPS
STRONG! MEDICATED!

P 2058

Get HEAl and **POWE**

This was me a short troubled with backache, eak. Not enjoying wo

My friend Ben said De Witt's Pills. They clear out of your body and ma

So I got this

New Tri

RESULTS IN A FEW

With my own eyes, I De Witt's Pills worked kidneys and my urine cle

All my pains gone now, full of POWER for wor thanks to De Witt's Pills, the wonderful tonic medicine that makes you fit and keeps you well.

Stop BACKACHE JOINT PAINS ACHING MUSCLES KIDNEY & BLADDER TROUBLES with

DeWi Kidney & Bl PILL

for POW

8. BROTHERS IN CHRIST

The golden Transvaal highveld – Nature's plateau, sunning itself a mile and more up in the heavens, whose very elevation has brought it close to God in his heavenly mansion.

It is closer still to the astronaut, floating in his own celestial cabin some way down below God. On a cloudless day he can pick out one mysterious feature, a display of heliographic dots and flashes spread across 20 miles – the city of Johannesburg.

That is what the gods and astronauts see. At a yet lower level the airline pilot observes a city, no, two cities? Another riddle? Yes, one city from which emanates the mysterious flashing and shimmering, but beside it a sister city with a dull surface, barely distinguishable from the surrounding veld. What is it that reveals the one, conceals the other?

The city that the Church knows sends its adoring light aloft from the glassy walls of modern buildings, where commerce and mining and industry reside; it reflects brightness from elevated roadways, it mirrors heavenwards those strange signals, that turn out to be reflections from a thousand swimming pools. This is the luxurious radiance of Johannesburg.

The sister city, not visible in heaven, is a place of dust and daub and lowly breezeblock. It is the home of some million people, many more than in the other city, yet it knows not industry, it knows not gloss and grandeur, it knows not illuminated boulevards, it boasts no thousand swimming pools ... it boasts but two! It is Johannesburg - yet not Johannesburg. It is the dormitory of the workforce of Johannesburg, it is Soweto. It is thought to be the biggest city in Africa, yet not plotted on the map were God to look for it there.

The observer at ground level perceives that these cities, though adjoining, are not joined. There is veld between them, polluted and worn, yellowed and sour, scorched by lightning; it does not connect, it divides. Those peoples live in sister

cities yet brothers they are not. But to God surely they are
equals, hath he not love for both?

The way we'd decided to present this *Drum* story
with its Christian theme was to ask that very question of God
about his servants and his people. And to ask that question of his
servants about their people, all the people, were they not all Brothers
in Christ?

We'd been steered towards the theme by innumerable reactions
from abroad. Our postbag was permanently filled with fan mail from
the rest of black Africa, from politicians, churchmen and ordinary
people battling for their own political freedom, delighted at the way
these militant black newspapermen were stirring it up in South Africa
and ecstatically proud of those unknown heroes, Henry, Can, Zeke
and others. There was articulate support from churchmen, white as
well as black, in Britain, the US and almost everywhere else – except,
of course, in South Africa. Here, although there were some soft
mouthings from on high and the valiant exception of Father
Huddleston, at that time not one Afrikaner churchmen, and but a tiny
few of the English, would offer a single benign word to the blacks.
The Afrikaner church could barely convince itself that Africans were
even formally covered by the biblical definition of humankind.

Let's show them up to the world, I thought. Let's test the sinceri-
ty of their faith. Do these Christians accept their labourers as
Brothers in Christ? Will they, as a start, even allow them into their
houses of worship?

Not a chance, we thought, for right inside the Church apartheid
flourished and fermented. Blacks were permitted to be Christians, so
long as they kept strictly to their shanty-hall congregations. Some
Afrikaner-dominated Dutch Reformed churches choked at that
thought even.

We would be sending our courageous Mr Drum along to church, to
observe if he'd be allowed to worship his God in God's own 'European'
church, permitted to take up a small space in a humble back pew.

There was a minor moral difficulty for me in masterminding this
challenge. As a Jew was it any business of mine to jeer at Christians

for not upholding a religion that I personally didn't adhere to? I took the problem to Trevor Huddleston. He'd been my counsellor on many a matter. I'd met him in my days as a reporter on the *Rand Daily Mail* in 1948 when he already had a reputation as one who fought for the blacks. 'Here,' Monty Williams had sneered handing me a cutting about Huddleston – I was still on Monty's reporters' desk then - 'here's another of your kaffir-lovers, inciting his black pals in Sophiatown against what they didn't know was even wrong. But you better get a story from him – go on, but just a par or two, just a short stick.' It transpired that editor, Rayner Ellis, had obliged him to diarise the Huddleston interview.

Why not, said Huddleston, settling my problem, why not. And after all weren't the Jews themselves in some measure among the out-casts of white South Africa? True, I beamed, and I'll send Mr Drum to a synagogue too.

We had to hurry, a week or two had been lost already in the dark aftermath of Henry's death, and there would be only a few Sundays left for our series of churchgoing expeditions. Now, who was to be Mr Drum in place of Henry? I assigned the role to Can. Henry the Intrepid would have strolled coolly into God's and his servants' hous-es and been able to do so as a professing Christian. Can had the courage and presence, but he lacked the commitment, being by faith an existentialist. Nevertheless he'd have to take it on, only he among the staff had the toughness, self-confidence and experience.

Can was fearless and calm. He was a big man, with a strong and handsome face ornamented by a buccaneer's scar, and he had a way with him. He was my number two on *Drum*, associate editor, and the leader of our staff. A natural chief, Can, by force of personality, and intellectually a giant. I put him down as a coming man of Africa. Can could be a charming talker at times, spouting and spouting away and drawing wonderful themes and fancies out of his head like a silk-worm spinning a cocoon, but at others he could clothe himself in a positively magisterial silence. Mouth shut, he would lure others into filling the embarrassing space and spluttering out their confidences. People would react to him, and be ready to take his orders.

Once an 'uncle' of his – Can's family situation was unclear – told

me, as we were gossiping in a shebeen, that you could have forecast
a great future for Can at two years old; where he went the lesser babes
waddled after, impressed by the authority that he radiated. Was the
uncle not right; are leadership qualities not settled already by one's
birth? The confident infant has a firm idea of what he wants and sets
out his demands to the world, expecting others to fall in with him.
'Ja, is true what you say, and a person can't teach themself confidence,' philosophised the uncle, expatiating on the subject in the
warmth of the family shebeen, whose comfortable madame was serving us whisky in lemonade bottles, or *was* it whisky? 'He can't
instruct himself in confidence, no, is true, man, is true as anything,
and same time nobody can't never teach *another* guy confidence, or
teach him to have guts. If you say so, you talking complete drizzle ...
just drizzle, man. Ja, and same time you can't teach having brains.'

So we were waiting for Can to arrive and stride into the place of
worship in Parktown, a high-church congregation in a middle-class
suburb, a building of blond Cotswold stone, imported to remind the
English burghers of home. I was waiting for Bloke as well and for
our stand-by photographer, quite beside myself with impatience and
irritation. Brought up to be punctual, I couldn't quite forgive these
Africans with their 'African time'. I knew one had to consider our
very different circumstances of upbringing, yet it was embittering to
a go-getting newspaperman. My own home life was so bourgeois and
settled. 'I'll see you there at one o'clock,' my old parents would say
to one another, 'and if I'm not there 10 minutes early it means I'm not
coming.' That was my own training too, whereas my dear colleagues
had come from homes where no one owned a watch – could barely
read one – and where time was marked off by the new moon, and if
you went to catch a train you made sure to arrive the day before and
huddled down overnight on the grassy platform until the choof-choof
rolled into sight.

Now it was two minutes to curtain-up and I was beginning to worry
seriously. Our one photographer, Jurgen, was lurking there with hidden camera, but what was he to shoot and where was the back-up
man? Only then did I see the bandy-legged Bloke making his grand
entry, running the gauntlet of the waiting gentry, smiling and bowing

left and right at them – at the very moment the vicar emerged to shoo
in this flock. Bloke smiled and bowed and scraped at him too.

'God, Bloke, you're a bit late,' I admonish him.

'Wait, wait. Until you hear why!' Bloke responds.

'Never mind, excuses later,' was my cross reply, 'let's get on quick
now, and where the hell's Can?'

'Wait,' he says again, 'look, man, Sylv, no look, man, Casey's back
from Bandoliers Kop, from Mpedi's, he's onto something, that's
what's my reason for being late. Something big, boy.'

Now I was in a fury and a confusion, on the one hand what can this
big development be, on the other we have to get on with our story.
Director and camera crew on stage, but no star, no Can Themba.
Well, here was another thing that the uncle and I both knew about
what Can had taken in with his mother's milk – a weakness for alcohol. Many a time, after a heavy jag going on for a day or two, he
would simply fail to arrive for work. A grave fault in his genes and a
maddening thing for his editor.

It was more than that, a calamitous thing now. We could not afford
to waste a single Sunday of our shortened schedule and the congregation had already filed in. I was desperate. Not a minute to spare. After
a final, vain glance down the road, I was forced into an emergency decision, I ordered the amiable but untried Bloke to take over the lead role
and follow me in as soon as I had taken up a strategic position.

At first thought Bloke might have seemed very appropriate for this
project: he was at least Christian born, with the culture and graces of
western society and a very European mind; he'd often been called a
white man in a black skin. But for courage, I fear, he's merely a
sheep in sheep's clothing. Yet it's got to be him, there's no one else.

I hastened to take a seat, sidling in and wondering for an instant
whether one put one's feet or one's bottom on the little red velvet
stool. I settled down while the vicar ascended his throne, and looked
around for Bloke to make his entrance.

But nothing. Nothing ... no Bloke.

The vicar cleared his throat, and still no Bloke. And I was trapped in
a ruddy Christian church service. I sat it out for another minute or two
and then summoned up courage, and squeezed embarrassed out of the

pew to haul Bloke in. Perhaps he hadn't understood. But he had, he simply hadn't been able to pull it off. 'Sylver, they'll chuck me out,' he pleaded. I shouted back: 'Of course they'll chuck you out; of course they will, I hope they will, that's why we're here, to see you chucked out and capture it on historical film and land a killer punch for black Africa.' Whimpered Bloke: 'Maybe they will chuck me, but maybe they'll shoot me, or they'll call the cops man, how d'you know they won't man!'

Bloke simply didn't have the raw guts, he'd wilted at the very thought of offending the bourgeoisie, let alone having them boot him out. He felt safer outside. In the end we had to trail off with no story.

Back at the office there was still no Can but there was Casey waiting to tell us about Mpedi, making the laconic most of it, just a dry half-smile on his face, sitting in the centre of an expectant and excited group of colleagues. He looked as if he had something vast and significant under his hat, which he would reveal only when we were all gathered.

What he told us thrilled some of the people there, but had yet to convince me. It was a mystical, delphic message, spoutings from a shaman, no doubt conveyed to Casey along with a ritual throwing of the bones.

This is what Mpedi had told him: he had been vouchsafed some celestial words from a little *tokoloshe* (evil spirit) in Tembuland, to the effect that we were looking in the wrong place, for the wrong person, for the wrong reasons; when we looked in the right place we would find many persons, but only the one reason. In the end we would find a very big secret of Africa hidden there.

'H'm,' I sniffed.

'And Mpedi said that the *tokoloshe* from Tembuland had prophetised that more gotto die still,' he added. 'He said that *many more must die first*.' I sniffed again.

'No Sylv, my son,' Todd Matshikiza put in, 'don't sneer at Africa's Sherlock Holmeses, we must look for value in this stuff of Mpedi's, it's going to have some meaningfulness. Mpedi has a seer's intuition, which is worth as much as your cold science. He doesn't *know* it's true, the bones and the dried roots and the preserved snake's testicles don't really spell out any facts, but in a state of trance his trained intuition sniffs up genuine possibilities from the air.'

Zeke, a serious man and as much a sceptic as myself, but a man of unencumbered creative impulses, seized on this: 'Look, can it point to the possibility of another suspect entirely, with another motive entirely? Not the *tsotsi* at all, maybe?'

'Maybe the cops ...!' Bloke, in awe, made this suggestion, by no means a nonsensical one, in view of the government's well-known and very practical way of dealing with its more effective opponents.

'A cop?' I asked, thinking in particular of my own suspicion of Sgt Bez. And though I didn't say it aloud, I had to run it through my head again, as a corollary, another chilling suggestion also, the sergeant's suspicion of *myself*.

Bloke was wrestling with a still more complex speculation. 'Or maybe it was the *tsotsi*, but he's there merely as an agent of the true killer?'

'The agent for the girl friend!' I whispered, momentarily taken with this scenario.

'Ja wait,' Bloke went on, inspiration really flowing, 'ja, no, wait, and I got an even classier idea, where does the murdered man's wife figure in this?'

'And there really may be a Mr Big like they say,' put in Todd. 'Esme,' – Todd's wife – 'Esme said that they say there's a Mr Big. Something to do with the story Henry was working on that night – you know, the illegal abortions.'

'Tell you what, Sylv,' offered Dan Chocho, that steady fellow, 'I'll take up that story where he left off and see if I can find any clues that's got themselves left behind.'

'Yes,' I accepted rather ungraciously, 'and see if you can get a story out of it for the paper while you're about it, not just playing clues and detectives.' I was grouchy, because it was all too much, rumour, speculation, mysticism – my sense of order and reason intervened and I closed the discussion sharply. To dash a draft of cold water over all the loose witchcraft effort I ordered Casey to go back to the police again, officially, and to get some fresh statement. I knew he wouldn't like this, and in truth he did get a very rude-brush off and no statement, and in the end we were no forwarder.

Next day it was back to replanning the church story. Can had shown up at the office. I didn't attack his dignity, I didn't shout at him, how could you at so masterful a man, one's own number two? I simply set him up for the job a second time. To make up for lost time we decided to schedule a pair of churches for the same weekend, one on the Saturday and one on the Sunday. This was made possible by including the Seventh Day Adventist Church, by definition a Christian sect that kept the Saturday holy – and very providentially for us.

Shortly before the Seventh Day service was to begin, Can Themba, respectably dressed and respectfully demeanoured, moved in to take his seat, one not too close to the front. I followed separately, to drop into the row behind – just keeping an eye on things. Near the door lurked Jurgen, camera concealed behind his jacket, to snatch the pictures.

The congregation, aware immediately of the horror that had settled into their midst, screwed their heads around to stare behind and began to set up an angry buzzing. It went on for a minute or more, this ugly sound, though no one went as far as to create a scene in God's house, despite their fury at its desecration.

But reaction was swift. Two burly men, heading a posse of six or seven, walked down the aisle to Can, silently yanked him up between them and silently walked him outside.

Here was our show, at last. Jurgen got busy, skipping around the little firing squad with his camera. This was exactly what we'd anticipated ... let's say hoped to set up.

Can was frog-marched onto the forecourt towards a black Buick 8 car. The back doors were opened and they piled him in, the two burlies cramming him between them on the seat. Suddenly, my mood changed, I blanched ... our little story seemed to have got out of hand. If ever I'd seen an invitation that was not to a wedding feast this was it.

Not all that bold a man myself, I nevertheless had to rush over to the car to remonstrate. Seventh Day eyes turned to me now; 'OK, this bugger's with him,' said one, 'come on, *bamba* (catch) him too.' So I was caught and bundled in between another pair of burlies in the front seat.

It was clearly no party. We spotted that the crowd around us had twigged what Jurgen was up to, and a hue and cry of 20 or 30 warriors for Christ started after him. We saw him fly away, clinging to the straps of his camera, finally arriving all but dead at the offices of a friend, who whisked him away into sanctuary.

The car sped down the road with Can and myself, no one speaking. When we'd left the city behind, they began to whisper icy words to each other ... bloody *kaffir* this, bloody *kaffir* that and bloody *kaffir-boetie* the other.

In what part of the veld would they find a handy tree, one wondered? They drove and drove, out past Turffontein in the grim southern suburbs and on into the peri-urban area. There finally on a dusty street they stopped the car, the man on my outside got out and tugged me after him, the driver shoving me from the other side. My instinct was to grab on and not leave the safety of the Buick, but they prised me out easily and tumbled me onto the pavement, where I sat up. Can had landed there too. The church thugs dusted off their suits and clambered back into the Buick; we watched them drive off, without having ever addressed a word to us. They'd managed to leave their mark on Can; from being dragged over the rough ground, his trousers were torn and you could see underneath the grazed skin of a black knee with red blood oozing out of it. 'Nothing,' he said, brushing it off with the back of his hand.

We made for the office. 'What about going to the police,' I worried aloud, 'we've got to report these guys.' I knew this would be pointless, though, and anyway I wasn't keen to arouse their attentions – was Sgt Bez not just waiting for me before trying to stick an 'immorality' rap or even a murder rap on me?

Can ignored my panic. He said laconically as we trudged along: 'More Holy Ghosting tomorrow?' Of course, he was right, we needed to get on with the story.

So we did in the morning at a Dutch Reformed Church in Westdene, and that was really to challenge the worst. The DRC was nothing but the Nationalist Party at prayer, quite drugged by the apartheid doctrine and always able to find a biblical quotation to support its stand. Its basic tenet: the role of Ham was to draw water and hew wood and otherwise shut up and *voetsak* (push off) the hell out of here.

They were ready for us at Westdene! The previous day's incident had alerted the secret police, for within minutes of entering the church it was surrounded by wailing squad cars drawn up in *laager* (circular formation). The congregation, hearing the *gewaldt* (row), turned round and, seeing us, thought that here was the devil being finally run to earth and smoked out; it was truly a wonderful thing, which everyone should get involved in.

Tiptoeing in a ladylike way through the door in leather high boots, at the head of his troops, was the chief of the Special Branch, the fat and infamous Colonel Spengler, there to pick us up personally. He relieved the man-handling burghers of their two prisoners and we were stuffed roughly into a car, a khaki-coloured police Ford V8 this time, and were soon back on the road to the open veld.

This was merely to give Spengler a chance to frighten us. He began immediately hectoring me, addressing me by name, and warning me of whatever kinds of penalties. He shouted me down when I asked to see our lawyer. What law had we broken, I asked, what contravention of the statutes was it to walk into a church? 'You better watch out for yourself,' he spat, 'you and this native, you gonna get yourself caught for the anti-Communism Act, that's the laws of the country.' That could attract the death penalty. At that point he ordered the car back to HQ.

With our motor-bike escort we drove into the centre of the city and were shovelled out at Grey's Buildings, the Special Branch's seven-storey block. It was no out-of-town lynching after all, or were we being offered a chance to 'throw ourselves' out of the top floor window as many an awkward anti-government prisoner was alleged to have done? The one thing Spengler did was take my camera from me, open it up and 'confiscate' the film. Then we were released.

Jurgen they missed, and again he was back with some excellent action pictures, though next day he went down with a nasty headache, developing into a month-long case of meningitis, his meninges having quite cracked up in the exertions of his flight from the Adventists the day before.

We certainly had our story and we printed it. The big pay-off came unexpectedly, many months later, elevating Brothers in Christ to the status of another nail in the coffin of apartheid. I had a visit in my Johannesburg office from the world diplomatic head of the Seventh Day Adventists, a splendid fleshy, monkish fellow. He came from

America with an apology – branches of the church all over Africa, where it had a widespread existence, and many branches in the US, the headquarters of the church, had felt themselves hurt and insulted by what those white Johannesburg Adventists had done, and he was here to put matters right. Would we accept his compliments and congratulations and the apologies of the movement, and would we like to know that he was preparing a severe wigging for the Johannesburg branch? We did, and we published that too, in some triumph.

This little adventure had certainly needed Can. Through it all, one must say, he'd preserved his usual sang-froid. A little personal habit helped his composure, he was always to be seen picking his teeth with a bitten off matchstick; it did for him what chewing gum did for others.

There has been no one I have admired more, in a lifetime of mixing with the great and the little, than Canadoce Dorsay von Themba, and no one I've hoped more to see fulfilled. A man of great reading, a working philosopher, a witty and wise companion, a gifted editor and writer, he had the one serious fault. This was, of course, his weakness for drink, partly to be excused by reason of his adopted philosophy – existentialism. Glass after glass of 'KB' (as kaffir-beer was known in euphemistic circles), *shimiyane*, Pin-Up (pineapple gin) and that doubtful whisky served in a lemonade bottle were his refuge from the frustrations of life on the wrong side of the colour line. In spite of the law, which prohibited blacks from buying or drinking anything other than that watery kaffir beer (mildly alcoholic maize beer bought at a municipal hall), Can, like every one of them, was always able to get hold of strong drink when needed. The first drink made it the more needful to find another, and so on, and it was often not until a three or four-day drinking session was over that he would be able to return to sobriety and to his job.

How could his editor handle this? I never learnt. I would threaten him with everything: with my displeasure, with pay cuts, with the sack – but when it came to it I would not mean it of course, especially not the sack. He was the heart of the paper. Perhaps he thought underneath that he was the one who deserved to be editor and perhaps underneath I thought the same, and if he couldn't he might as well spend his time as he liked. All to be attributed to frustration with the system.

Sir Tom Hopkinson, my distinguished British successor, never learnt how to handle this either. He threatened and he threatened, and one wondered if the day might come when he would paint himself into a corner and be forced to carry out the threat. It seemed as if Tom longed for an obedient and punctual replacement for Can so that he could turn out a tidied-up paper – yet a cleaned-up *Drum* would be an emasculated *Drum*, a contradiction in terms; and a slung-out Can would be a man with less meaning in life than was justified even by his own unsentimental philosophy.

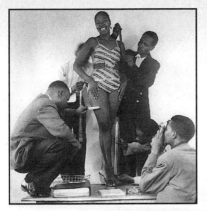

PART TWO

TOP LEFT:
Beauty Queen.

TOP RIGHT:
Arthur Maimane
with the mail.

LEFT:
Can Themba being
tumbled out of
church.

... this life exposed me to a rude introduction to the South African police, they made me realise the brutal, dominant presence of the white man in South Africa. I saw my mother insulted, sworn at and bundled into the kwela-kwela, the police wagon, so often it began to seem – and I perhaps accepted it – as a way of life, the life of being black. Listening to the young constables screaming obscenities at Ma-Willie emphasised the fact that we were black, and because my mother was black she was despised and humiliated, called 'kafir meid' and 'swart hell'. I was hopeless in the coffin of my skin and began to resent the black of my skin, it offered no protection to my mother from the delinquency of the police constables who saw only the mask representative of a despised race; but Ma-Willie was not black, she was my mother, and if I had been white the whiteness of my skin would have protected her honour. I wished I was white.

from *Blame Me on History*, by Bloke Modisane (Thames & Hudson)

Jaunty, jokey, and sensitive underneath, Bloke 'Debonair' Modisane was well fitted to do the colour and humour pieces in the magazine – he was essentially a writer rather than a hard-news man. After he'd crumpled up under fire on that miserable Sunday at the church, little Casey of the spare phrase had put him in his place at the editorial conference: 'You're a Pulitzer.'

'How's that?' asked Bloke, wary of this compliment.

'Only a Pulitzer. You're jus' only a Pulitzer.'

'Aw, come on!' Bloke reacted sourly, not pleased to be pigeonholed like that, diminished.

'War correspondent you ain't,' Casey rubbed it in, firing off one of his Runyonisms.

'And Checkhov you ain't,' Bloke snarled back.

Casey said no more, he'd drawn blood. He was a scrumptious small chap you could have eaten up, crew-cut hair, runny nose and all, but he had a cutting edge with his pen and with his tongue. He spoke true, however: unlike the rest of the case-hardened crew of *Drum*, Willie-Bloke was eminently a soft, smiling, gentle, civilised man, and a man who had the genius to live the civilised life quite against the odds. Before I recruited him for the paper he'd had a job at Vanguard Books, run by Fanny Klenerman, a matronly figure though a fierce and fanatical Trotskyist. Even in her dedicatedly radical establishment, however, he was not allowed at the counter, where he'd be visible to the white customers. Wrapping up the goods in the back room and running errands was his experience of the literary life.

He lived in Sophiatown, that once white suburb that had in the past generation deteriorated to a slum and thus become legitimatised for black habitation. In a majority of the houses, mostly falling to bits, you might find quartered as many as eight or nine families – up to 50 people. As for the garbage spilling out into the yard ... dear God, some of the garbage turned out to be human too.

Threading their way past these odorous ruins, Bloke's visitors were delighted to enter the nice middle-class display he'd contrived inside his one-room establishment ... the brass bedstead, the gents robe of Japanese oak, the almost walk-in refrigerator and the ultimate modernistic gramophone, housed in a double-storeyed wooden cabinet, shelves for records (a cupboard for cocktails below and turntable above), with electric 'auto-coupling' equipment that could eject a 12-inch shellac record and slap on a dozen more in sequence to replace it. As these magnificent furnishings quite filled his room the washstand had to be banished to the stoep ... But here was grandeur, here was paradox for you.

Except for him, Can Themba and Si Mogape, our black staff were not privileged to lead such 'European' lives. Banished to vast farms of iron and concrete pods 15 miles away, they had to do without running water or sewage, without laid-on electricity and without tarred roads, let alone the cars to drive along them, and without the ordinary necessities of a newspaperman's calling, such as telephones and postal services, not to mention early-morning deliveries of the daily papers! It was easiest of all for white-man me, of course, living on a town bus route, as well as owning two cars plus an Italian motor scooter, being a paterfamilias and boss of two servant maids and a gardener, and ensconced in a sprawling set of thatched *rondavels* with additional outhouses for the black staff. Plus a sabre-toothed ridge-back dog to chase off any prowling blacks.

But Bloke actually had running water (in the yard), Bloke had an electric cooker as well as that fridge, and Bloke had even applied for a telephone, though it never arrived during the two years that elapsed before he was to flee the township. However, Bloke the playboy, Bloke the debonair, Bloke, civilised and courteous, joking at the impossible vision of himself as a 'native', Bloke had the charm but not the cheek. It was perhaps this sensitivity of his, his 'Pulitzer' discretion rather than his valour, that saved him to live on beyond the span of those who valued their lives less and were snuffed out early.

Bloke knew he would have to leave Africa in the end to save his life and stay out of gaol, and also because he wanted so much to see the rest of the adored civilised world. As if to prepare himself, he took a correspondence course in French; it's no easy way to learn a language, but where was there a class in town that would have accepted him inside that uncultured skin?

However, here at this moment in our lives, smiling and joking, he was throwing himself into the hunt for Henry's murderer. He would let them see who was a Pulitzer. He came to see me alone in my office, bustling in with that bandy-legged swagger of his. 'Look at it like this, boss,' he said with no introduction, taking up the theme he'd started the other day, 'I'm not saying it wasn't a *tsotsi*, I'm saying it *was* a *tsotsi*, but who was he acting for, who paid him?

'Okay,' he went on, not giving me any chance to answer his question, 'I'll tell you ...'

'The girl friend?' I interrupted, to show my quick take-up, 'she'd turned against Henry?'

'No, man boss, don't rush me, hang on, no, here's your motive, she's been forced to blot out Henry. It's the girl friend's *boy friend* forcing her!'

'Wozzat?' It was a chilling thought, though I couldn't work out exactly what he was getting at. His point was that this boy friend was no doubt a big gangster, one of the many township crookeds wanting to get at Henry for exposing their evil, violent and parasitical practices against the ordinary folk of the place.

'He forced her to take up with Henry *in the first place*, get Henry's confidence, and lull him somewhere so the *tsotsi* stooge could kill him. All she does: pays the *tsotsi* two or three quids for his handiwork, what he likes doing anyway, it's his hobby.'

It was muddled, but was there not some logic in it?

'And I've got my hands on a piece of evidence,' he added conspiratorially, 'something for a definite fact.'

'You've got?' I asked excitedly.

But at that point Bloke went too far, went over the top, wound up by my excitement as well as his, allowing speculation absolute licence: 'Or then just as likely, stand it all on its head, try this alternative scenario, it's maybe Henry's *wife* who hires the *tsotsi*, because she's found out about he's got this girl friend dame and has got it in for him for that.'

'Oh no,' I expostulated, 'Oh no, what tripe,' knowing the gentle, respectable person that Mrs Nxumalo was – a nurse by profession. It made me recover my sense of normal scepticism immediately and I forbade him to go on like this and set him instead to turn out a rich, hot, jazzy piece on the American singer Lena Horne, a heroine of the townships and one of his own idols.

Nevertheless, what Mpedi's mystical pronouncements had done was stir up everyone's ideas and open up the case again. We spent further time thinking about the death of Henry and we were persuaded to broaden the list of possible situations and suspects to be considered. We began to tick off other possible motivations there could have been for Henry to be polished off like that in the middle of the night:

1) He was a sore embarrassment to the government;

2) If there *was* a girl friend that he'd been messing around with, well perhaps she was his best friend's wife? This hypothesis could then become a motive not only for the best friend turning murderous but also for Henry's wife turning that way, if one wanted to

offer twopence for that idiot theory;

3) He wouldn't pay his owings to the Chinese gambling syndicate;

3a) Or his bill to the Indian shopkeeper;

4) He stood in the way of professional journalist rivals;

5) He'd bullied the tea-boy to desperation;

6) Or quite simply he'd got himself ambushed by a casual late-night *tsotsi* pickpocket in pursuit of the few handy shillings that Henry might have been carrying;

7) And, yes, we could not omit ... it might have been a follow-up visitation from the Spoiler Gang gunmen who had invaded the office one day in protest at being exposed in print by Henry, and had also put the frights on Cecil, the white editor of our sister paper, so that Cecil had crept off home and whimpered for a police escort for *himself* not to worry about one for poor old Henry;

8) Or what about that abortion story and a Mr Big?

These were truly bizarre suspicionings; beyond and above them, however, were more philosophical mysteries, which I did not dismiss so readily, but which I did dwell on deeply, wondering if there was not wider meaning in Mpedi's message, asking myself what was wrapped up in those secrets of Africa. *Many more must die!*

Yet slowly over time the murder trail went cold. And it was a long while before something did happen that stirred us into activity again, something very dreadful, and yes, it was another death. And then another, and as time passed, slowly but remorselessly, there was another and then another; yes, and more and more deaths, spreading away into the future. Is that what the oracle had foreseen? With what big secret to be revealed?

On each occasion the positive identity of the killer was a mystery again; was it the same original agent of death, and if so what was the motive?

Before we chronicle these deaths, though, we must examine what was a common factor in them all, the death of dear, unlovely Sophiatown, our spiritual home. Here we knew the identity of the killer, its brutal murder was ordered by state law and carried out by state troopers, and its tearing down, which enforced the diaspora of so many bewildered thousands, was the direct cause of the break-up and dispersal of our own brilliant crowd, and that, in turn, became the common factor that was to precipitate the demise of so many of them.

Let's get an inside view of the passing of Sophiatown by looking at the text of an imaginative feature that was submitted to me by Henry Telephone (written under his blotter when he should have been attending to callers), describing Can's last days in Sophiatown.

10. SMASHING UP SOPHIATOWN

From Henry Telephone's unpublished manuscript:

'Canadoce Amatikulu von Themba is at home. He's waiting there at home for the government bulldozers to bulldoze down his part of Sophiatown. They's still 17 streets away. I'm in the *Drum* office, waiting for Can to answer the phone, so I can give him the message from editor Syl that he's got to turn up for work. No, genuine, man, we need him at work, we need him bad.

His part of Sophiatown is Lucy Street. He lives in one and a half rooms in a tumbledown house in the good end of Lucy Street. In the worse end some of the houses got tumbled down completely. The rooms there in those worse ones were ... *meaningless*, they doesn't exist. Those places long ago started to come down by themselves, even before the bulldozers got on the job. The people went on living anyway in them, even in some bare backyards, in their own home-made *pondokkies* (shacks). The ritzier ones in this section had a proper piece of wall left where they could lean their tins and cardboards up against, but the slummier ones wuz satisfied with leaning up against each other, just one *pondok* leaning on the next. One thing, you got more people in a yard this way than if a house wuz taking up the space.

No, they paid rent just the same, walls or no walls, rooms or no rooms. Some mysterious people is the real owners – the fah-fee Chinese or the Indians, the store coolies? Or is it the Boers really, ministers in the government actually, as a lot of people always say? Our reporters tried to find out exactly who, 'cos it would make a good story in the magazine. They's rich people anyway these mysterious owners, but whatever kind of people, and even if they been pro-government, they still didn't have enough pull with the government to stop the bulldozers coming onto their stands and smashing up their property – smashing them to buggery. Rent-paying tenants and all. The lot!

Well, you might say, it must make sense, no, that bulldozering business? Slum clearance? Isn't the government trying to make a bit of social and economic sense of this nice little township, which is littered with stinking shanties full of out-of-work blacks and profiteering Indians and all sorts, and choked with disease and crime?

No, that isn't the story.

No, the story is like this. The place is right next door to Lerouxville, which is as Afrikaner as hell, and the Lerouxville residents doan' like people to think they live near a lot of *kaffirs*. It isn't safe for their daughters. Same time it isn't good for property prices. No, shame! So the kaffirs has got to go ... and then the Afrikaner Boers of Lerouxville can bring in their poor-white cousins to live there and they soon get rich and they will make sense of this place Sophiatown, they can give employment and Christianity to some of the blacks in their kitchens, and some other blacks can go back to their own *kraals* to hell-and-gone in the *hamadoellas*, the reserves, among their own kind, and work for themselves, and pay themselves good money. That's logic ... what they like about it. But of course, really a complete fantasy.

Canadoce, called Can – Canadoce Amatikulu Themba, he liked to call himself C.A.T. – he hadn't got any kraal, he isn't coming from a kraal in the first place even. So it doesn't apply, you'd think. He come from Lovedale College, where he done his studies at Fort Hare with Gatsha Buthelezi and the two doctors Ngi that later married each other, and Professor Matthews' grandson, and Professor Jabavu's grandson. And where he had met Nelson Mandela for debatings. And all kinds of chiefs' children mainly, all having a go at college together.

Canadoce wuz waiting for this crazy government to try to bulldoze down his house with their police bulldozers and take him away 18 mile distance to start up again in Soweto, bundled off in a big open lorry with a big steel barrel to take his goods in and to use for a house when he first would be settled. It would be all his, each family got one. He counts as a family because he's got a job. Here he's got the only house with a telephone because he works as editor. But he wouldn't have one in Meadowlands, that part of Soweto, he couldn't have such a thing in Soweto, there's no telephone poles going so far out, except for the police.

Can is a tall man, with a strong face, little bit of a scar across from the lip and upward. Short kind of hair, nice stiffy hair, he sometimes keep his pencil stuck in it (sometimes a cigarette, but that could be risky). The other thing he always got is a pin, an ordinary pin which he uses to think with, he picks the teeth with it when he wants to think. He is light-complexioned, maybe Xhosa? But nobody knew, *he* didn't know. Did his mother know?

He looks really as if his father is a chief or from a chief's family. Canadoce acts like one. People doan' like to answer him back. Some more ignorant ones even doan' like to walk in front of him in a room, like they doan' in front of Gatsha Buthelezi Amazulu, who's a very big chief. Even his councillors has to bend and crouch when they comes near *his* sight, not to get in the way of where he is looking at. That's how they behaved when they come to visit our news conference here once.

Can's got slitty eyes in his big broad face – Xhosa again? A bit of bushman in the ancestors?

Now at the point what we is starting my short story at, Can is waiting for the bulldozers, still 17 streets away. He's training to get himself ready for when they come for him. His training is to sleep in late there in his room, through as much noise as possible, like the old woman who works for him, Tan' Essie, banging on his door to get him ready for work in time, or the telephone ringing for him. So that's why he isn't ready and so he doesn't hear me ring to find out where the hell he is again instead of being at work. Number two to editor Syl, and missing again!

Never min', the bulldozers themselves is thinking, never min', we got plenty time, we can wait. They knew they could wait, although they doan' realise that they'd miss Bloke if they waited, Bloke would slip off, on the run to England. But not Can, he'd be there till the end.

The bulldozers is tuning up now, far away other side Lucy Street, in Penelope still, or Good, working on the rows of houses there, then stopping and picking the mud out of their pushers before they move on.

And Can ain't at work in Main Street, near the corner of Jeppe, in the *Drum* offices, where the others is waiting for him, including also

the two men all the way from United States, Mister Adlai Stephenson
and Mister Norman Cousins and their whole team, who got themselves
organised to sit in on his story-planning conference. I'm waiting there
too, tapping in on the switchboard now, and trying to remind him.

They can go on waiting until Nineteen Fifty-Voetsak, Can himself
is thinking probably. Because he's busy for the moment.

Can is in his bed, not alone this time, but I can't say who exac'ly
he got there with himself. I'll get into trouble with Can if I tell that.
So that's where I got to end my story, this true story I want to put into
Drum.'

Signed

Henry Telephone

So it ended, this unsolicited ms from Henry Telephone. I was sour
about it, not only because it was totally unsuitable for publication,
being all about our own internal affairs, but because it didn't help a
great deal in summoning Can back to work, to meet the distinguished
Illinois governor, Adlai Stephenson, who was travelling the world
getting to know it, en route to his election campaign and his hoped-
for assumption of the US presidency. But Henry Telephone didn't
manage to communicate my summons to Can, who was too busy on
his own affairs. Nothing much ever did bring him to order.

I guessed who it was that was engaging Can's attention in Henry's
story and in truth it was another reason for my being sour: jealousy.
For this very same girl would then by the very same act have been
two-timing *me* – thus my intense and unreasonable jealousy! My suspicion was confirmed when Can wrote up a second-person bit of fiction based on his first-person life and handed it in for publication.
This also was unsuitable for use in the magazine at that time, though
it is presented here, in Can's words, Can writing about Can, fact trad-
ing as fiction:

From Can's manuscript:

'Thing is, putting it prototypically,' Can ruminated, 'you can
clasp your two hands around her one leg above the knee and
slide them up steadily until they're embracing the very highest
part of her thigh. To go further it may be necessary at this

*stage to divest the lovely lady of her black silky broeks, to get
the exact feel of her in two separate split-up halves. Um, problem. Still, there's a net gain in that to both parties ...*

*'Can was working away thinking like this, musing aloud to
himself like this, busy at work really on* Drum *magazine that he
worked for, business before pleasure with him. He was getting
ready to make up a short story based on what he was doing.
"The firm flesh of our girls", he liked that a lot: when you
pushed into it, it came out again instantly like elastic, and went
plink! Though he liked also the long, soft, flowing hair of the
white girls, that's how he wrote up the girls in his stories, more
glamorous for the readers. They needed those thoughts to work
up their imagination.*

*'This thinking work woke him from his dreams. So he woke
the little lady too, again, and made nice love to her. When she
co-operated with him, she felt very lovely towards him and
wouldn't leave him when they finished. So every time they did
it that night he ended tangled up in her arms. That made things
so he couldn't sleep properly, and then he woke up again ... so
she woke up again, to find him on top of her. Zow!*

*'Then he wrote it all down on the paper on the floor next to
him and got it off his memory.*

*'Can lies there for a while more with her black broeks
crushed in his palm, thinking in philosophical vein of their silk-
iness: "It's marvellous how they can so easily take on an
entirely different presence from this tiny compressed bundle ...
next they may be found enveloping and moulding the lower
torso of a member of womankind as a linen bag does its load
of washing or a giant iron bucket a half-ton of solidified
cement. The torso of this big desirable schoolgirl here will be
contained within these broeks ... starting from the bottom part
of her trunk and finishing at the tops of her legs, with the out-
line of her labia nestling against the joining bit."*

*'He begins to find her less desirable the more times he has
her and now he has decided to go to work. He was annoyed
with himself now – and her – at the thought that he might have*

missed the plenipotentiary and eminent Americans and the chance of an invite to a party in the embassy as big as any ever offered a black man in South Africa, and must be the only official chance of offering such a man a drink or two.

"How little a schoolchild understands of the affairs of the world", he sighs reprovingly as he leaves for work.

'In due course – overdue *– Can assembles to meet Adlai Stephenson, who has come out to study the situation while training to lose his election battle for the US presidency. With his mate, editor Norman Cousins, he is given permission to meet real blacks and sit in on* Drum's *managing editorial conference, which consequent to the little lady's intervention, gets going two hours late.*

'Can tries to persuade them of his faith of the moment that there's only inconsiderable differences between the blacks' position today in Southern Africa and the industrial dwellers in the UK a hundred years before – or those in New York. Or in Rome, as you could read in Horace (Cousins went back and duly has these same thoughts in his Saturday Review, *we discover one day).*

'Then there's a return party away from the embassy, with shimyane, *nice strong moonshine hooch, rather than shop liquor. The singing and the* shimyane *gets Casey going. He accuses Adlai confidentially of being a pulitzer and a busybody, talking philosophy from one end of him and at the same time farting endless rubbish from the other. Adlai must have been pleased of this information, for not many people gave him the cold home-truth.*

'There's more drink and more deep thoughts and talk but eventually says Adlai to his aides: "Tell Mike Hunt that we must be going".

'Casey looks horrified. "Tell who?" he asks.

'Mike Hunt.'

"That's what I thought. How're you spelling that, Ad?" asks Casey - "my cunt or do you mean my kant (side)"?

"Look at your hands," Casey warns them, as they finish

laughing and say goodbye, "in case the black comes off on you."

'Cousins tells him they know all about blacks of course, they got them in parts of New York. Casey answers back to him he hasn't read about no blacks in Damon Runyon.'

Ends extract of Can's manuscript

11. SOPHIATOWN, AN OBITUARY

The razing of Sophiatown ranks as the second greatest mistake made by the blind and brutal government in all its 40 years of violence, second in callousness and ineptitude only to the massacre at Sharpeville. Those were their two fatal mistakes, together certifying to the world outside that the whites of South Africa were truly mad, crazed with ethnophobia, and that the blacks were entitled to the most profound sympathy – and here you have what led, in the very long run, to the defeat of the ruling extremists, the line-up against them of censorious forces outside and of angry forces inside.

For the inhabitants of the wretched, decaying suburb itself the demolition of Sophiatown was the ultimate bum's rush, hustling them by bulldozer out of their homes and almost 20 miles across country to 'bantu' ghettoes on the veld.

For the educated ones, the enterprising, the aspiring, the sophisticated, it was cultural murder, since Sophiatown was the last town area open to blacks, a charmed enclave of civilisation, their only access to the modern world and to hopes of betterment.

For *Drum*'s own people the loss of that environment really signalled the end of everything ... there was nowhere else that we could continue to meet as equals, white staff and black, in our social, drinking, sporting and political activities, at Bloke's room or Can's or in the speakeasies. And life beat breezily there, whereas in the locations of Soweto, where the people were summarily dumped, the heart of black society was slowed to a faint pulse, the machine-made homes being dispersed over bare square miles in a cold, mechanical pattern, potatoes planted in a field, with no focus, no critical mass to them.

It was there in Sophiatown that Can Themba had matured in intellectual strength, and it was there at his home base, the House of Truth, where we blacks and honorary blacks gathered to debate a thousand topics ranging from Sartre philosophy to the vintages of hooch, that the discourse was at its most brilliant. And the partying too, for there we were blessed with that elaborate chain of *shebeens* where one could see and be seen. Sophytown, beloved Sophytown.

And it was there in the martyred town that Bloke had built up his salon, there he'd been 'one of the Four Hundred'. He stuck it out through years of waiting for the threatened eviction, listening out for the demolition teams, but eventually he would have to flee, not being one with raw courage.

The brave would hang on longer, though steadily over the months as the herd of bulldozers moved inwards from the boundaries, trampling down house after house like elephants rampaging through the mealie-lands, these bitter-enders found themselves penned into a diminishing centre, rats cornered in the last unflattened patch of mealies.

Can was one of those to hold out longest, a defiant gesture per-haps. Nevertheless, go soon go late, all were in the end flung out of their homes.

It's necessary here to deal with a puzzling question: why did the whites so very wilfully force through this eviction; whence came the burning hate that drove them to it?

It was the very civilising influence of Sophiatown that offended them, the opportunity it offered for blacks to comport themselves like human beings. The impudence of it, to think they were people, to classify themselves as human! That was the poison that roused the white man's ethnic passion.

Look dispassionately behind those drummed-up ethnic tantrums and you'll find the true reason for suppressing and diminishing the blacks; you will find hard economics, the raw economics of colonial-ism, which some call greed. There was more than enough of nature's gifts for everyone in South Africa, but the whites wanted to feel abso-lutely secure about holding on to their own comfortable share. They weren't going to spare any room beside them at the feeding trough for the black millions, and to make this appear morally right to them-selves they had to blank off any sentimental thought that a black had entitlement as a human being. A complicated internal adjustment of their motivations – yet some still call it greed.

Such a morality, even the calling in of biblical support, to class the blacks as sub-persons, ruled the sub-conscious of all that pig-headed white society; it was no monopoly of the Afrikaners. It embraced the political spectrum as far even as the groups trumpeting about justice, who valued the concept of human rights as dearly as life itself – yet human rights, by definition, were surely for humans, not for natives.

So Sophiatown had to go.

A year or two back when the evictions had begun, everything that Softown meant for black life and for *Drum*'s own existence had already begun to slip away from us and the process was now to accelerate.

Before it was quite over I took the opportunity to live for a fortnight as a black in Sophiatown. To go native in that way, I believed, would help me to feel my way into the black skin that my colleagues and my readers lived in permanently. Disguised as a 'native boy' I would be able to taste the buffetings by petty authority, or the summoning – 'Here, Jim!' – by any casual white motorist wanting his car given a shove. I'd see what it was like to be banned from the ordinary simple and good things of life: sitting on park benches, dwelling in towns, riding in white trams, splashing around in swimming baths, eating in restaurants, attending the theatre, travelling in white ambulances or white taxis, working where you liked ... or any other normal thing. Or consuming alcoholic drink. Or receiving a decent education, or having any sort of career. Or being allowed to change your abode, or being served in a shop. Or whistling at a blonde. Or answering back when told off for coveting those things.

I put my plan to Can Themba. We kept it secret, so that I could get an open and objective reception in the black community as well as in the white. He found me a room and bed near to him with a pal of his: I was introduced as a visitor from East Africa, an Asian. It turned out I had to become Asian, not true African, because my blue eyes and prominent nose were too ridiculously wrong to aspire to an African look. Jean, the English girl who was everybody's sweetheart, carved me out a stiff crew-cut and stained it with black hairwash, dabbed on a rakish Valentino moustache and darkened me up with permanganate dye to the skin, then clapped on a pair of necessary sun-glasses. I passed as a Kenyan commercial traveller, Rani Moolah. At the back of the room in the dim light of the shebeen to which I gravitated on my first night even Bloke and our other friends didn't see through the camouflage.

I had a more than interesting time. It was no new experience to taste
the illicit hooch, but it was intimidating to sit there among gangster
elements without the natural protection that my white skin would have
given me. And, on the contrary, it was where I could converse at ease
with my constituents, without *their* being defensive before a lani, a
white man. It was where I could tune in to the wise, uncensored pub
talk of Can's uncle. Or overhear what biting comments Todd and others might have about their white comrades, not excluding me.

There were surprises. It wasn't the police that assaulted me on the
first night, it was the bed-bugs. In my soft upbringing I'd never
encountered one before. This first occasion they mounted a grudge
raid to make up for that. They stormed me from the woodwork, they
dive-bombed me from the ceiling, they bit me, they sucked at every
pore of my virgin body, they scrambled over my head. I tickled and
I scratched, I slapped at them as they crossed my face, I thrashed
about. But they won hands down, or so I thought as I gave up the
attempt to sleep, yet ... yet, in the morning, I could see that squads of
those kamikaze bombers had been squashed dead under my back or
on my face, their blood smearing the permanganate of potash until it
ran mauve in every direction.

Ironically even in death they could claim victory: it meant my disguise was ruined. I had to hide from my host until I could paint
myself up again and even then the colours didn't match, so I now had
a piebald look that quite amazed him when he returned from work
later that day, though it didn't absolutely blow my cover. Sunburn
from sightseeing all day, I lamely explained.

Lying in bed that night awaiting the next enemy offensive, I kept
myself awake by musing deeply on racism and its victory over natural justice. I ran through my own attitude to other races, reminding
myself of the distance I had travelled since childhood, gradually
throwing over the normal prejudices of a white lad and accommodating to feelings of understanding for the blacks and goodwill towards
them, and, most important of all, acceptance of them as blood brothers, which would entitle them to the same rights and the same status
as everyone else.

In fact in the 1920s in Durban one had thought not at all about them, the 'natives'. They were just there, part of the fauna and flora of Natal. One could walk right through a group of them and see no one. The only reaction might be at something that offended, as the smell of a tribal Zulu woman dressed to kill, on her way to visit her husband in town – dressed not in clothing as such, only in an anointment of sheep-fat, which gave off a musky, in fact, ahem ... very rancid ... scent.

Natives? No, it was a rare 'European' who ever used this polite form of address. They were niggers to the vulgar, *kaffirs* to the gentry. Slowly over a decade or so there did occur a general switch to 'native', though to most at first it sounded pi and awkward, and later to 'Non-European', which covered the kaffirs as well as the 'coolies' (a third of Durban's population was Indian). It was only in the late 1930s that a handful of progressives finally graduated to uttering the term African, and this also came over initially as very bogus in the ears of the ordinary classes. You'd feel a fool using that term when speaking to your colleagues or friends or even to a simple black servant. Meanwhile officialdom was graduating to the use of Bantu and Non-white (*Nie-blanke*). Only much later did black become a possible alternative.

Now all are South Africans...well, perhaps we are.

When young, I gave no thought to blacks as a competing species even; it was the gentiles who were cast as the other race. Smell was a bit of an indicator in this case too; I believed I could detect in my own non-Jewish schoolmates an unappetising Christian whiff, though this might simply have been from the bacon in their diet, the fat of it vaporising off their skin and wafting over to my Jewish nose.

They seemed to be all anti-semites, anyway, using ugly terms for Jews in your hearing and socking you one over the head with a knotted handkerchief in extreme cases for crimes against Jesus Christ of some long standing. Even a friend with most moderate views might quite unconsciously remark to one: 'Hey, you know that Bongo Robinson? He's trying to jew me out of my marbles.'

The campaign against anti-semitism was a constant of Jewish life. Yet what did we suffer really ... name-calling, blackballing from smart clubs? Could that compare with the lot of the black?

The Jews, due to that exaggerated chip on their shoulders but also rightfully intimidated in the late 1930s by fears of Nazi treatment at the government's hands, were driven to react against racism in their own self-interest; in the end it moved many of them to take up arms beside the non-whites against intransigent white power. Historically it can be seen that without the aid of this Jewish minority it might have taken far longer to break the power of apartheid. They were able to act as a Trojan horse, having access to facilities and powers inside the ruling society. They would become almost the only ones to accept briefs as lawyers for the ANC, to be journalists and academics with a pro-black stance, to provide the revolutionaries with jobs and funds and safe houses and to become the necessary go-betweens when it came to political and military stand-offs.

So did I lie awake analysing things. It was in the shebeen, however, where my practical observations were carried out, political and social. I chose to spend my time at 'Fatty's', Mrs Shabalala's place, as her bootleg liquor suffered the least watering-down and this was where the *Drum* people hung out. Here I could hear that wide, wild laugh of Todd Matshikiza, a huge laugh from a small man. His was a round bustling body, spilling over in cheeriness and jokes; it took some years of knowing him before one realised that under the Matshikiza skin a deal of bitterness too was pressing to escape.

At that period Todd was enjoying a soaring success. A maker of African jazz, he also wrote high, fun jazz into his journalism, with the result that he'd become famous among the black population for both his song hits and for being our music critic. At the time of my Sophiatown visit he was already working on the score for *King Kong,* the musical masterpiece that would make him famous among whites too and would tour the world – though it would be his doom.

Here at Fatty's Casey too turned up one evening and sat beside me on an upturned box, quietly drinking himself into a suitably cerebral state for the evening's philosophies. He had, it seemed, his next agony column for *Drum* stewing away in his head, for he came out aloud with a one-liner preview of it: 'Romance is beauty, romanticism is crap ... yours sincerely, Dolly Heartbreaks.'

'Ah,' sighed Can, ready to strike up and contribute to the fun and being as usual in a lovelorn condition, 'ah, romance! ah, woman'!

The undersized sage, Casey J Motsisi, was ready to deal with the unstated personal problem posed here: 'One trouble with people like you, my friend – you only feel for a woman when she gets you all jealoused up. You bounce along from Tossie to Tandy and Tandy to Tinzi, all the girls playing along nicely with you and you not being quite committed in love with any of them ... but as soon as one lady comes along who refuses you, you get quite heavily in love. Kerpoof! Only when you can't get it, that's when you suddenly want it. You are worried that maybe someone else is having her and jealousy eats you up. And that's what you think is love.'

A disagreeable diagnosis to swallow, it kept Can sounding off about that no-longer current girl of his; nostalgia was all that seemed left to him. 'It's an odd thing, Casey J, when I met this girl the first time, I instinctively resented her. We started off with the mutual bristles.'

Casey J was equal to this point too. He thought for a moment, tugging away at his short nose, which emerged from under his crewtop obedient to his call, ready to take part in the problem solving. Here was their verdict: 'You was frightened she was too damn good-looking. You once said your own self that she was much too beautiful. When you guys who is a bit short of self-confidence first cast eyes on someone like that, you feel "Hell, this person is in another league, man, far above me, she's so beautiful she could have anyone – my chances are nil." So you shut out the idea completely and go in for the sour-grape act; you behave like an infant who thinks it's been rejected by its ma, so it gets jealous of its own pa and resents the one it loves. It's what they call resentmantile rejectionism.'

'Resentmantile rejectionism, eh, doc?' It was news to Can, but it seemed an impressive enough name for his symptom. Casey J must have been studying hard and wide for his Dolly role. A wise lad.

Truly short-changed by Nature on length of leg, yet Casey J towered mentally. His brainbox verily bulged with muscle, giving a distinctive top-heavy shape to his head; and one could see peering out from inside the skull two brown and beady eyes alert with higher thought. On top, protective packing for all this equipment, was a tight, tiny, shiny set of curls, kept in bloom with frequent oiling.

Can now threw in a somewhat cryptic postscript: 'I may be coming to you with a rebound problem very soon, doc, touching a new
and different kind of romance,' he said, 'and, by the way, would you
be able to prescribe for me a get-out-of-jail voucher for it too, along
with your worthy advice?'

Casey J said nothing, but looked inscrutable, too preoccupied to
deal with such a question, as if busy searching his mind for something
of importance, say a name of the right weight to go with his unallo-
cated middle initial.

I decided as a leg-pull that I would help to keep this jolly question-
and-answer game going, and in a posh Arab accent asked him: 'Can
you advise me, dear Dolly, where there is another nice-time shebeen
like this that I could move on to next?'

'Well, ja,' he said in laconic style, burying his head in his sawn-off
tin can to seek an answer there. He teased it slowly out of the frothy
KB and turned to me, 'Ja, easy, Rani man, no too easy, hey, what you
do is this, ja?' He sat up and waved his hand at the door, 'so, man,
listen – there's a nice-nice one just quite very near, you go out of here,
turn left along Dulcie, then right into Hofstein Street, you get it?; then
right, then right again, right, right, then left, then walk a bit right ...'
He stopped to see if I was keeping up (everyone else was watching
too), 'okay, but watch out for the Skelm Kids here, okay? Then take
a right, a left, left, left, left again and down a bit there ...'

When Casey stopped no one said a word but all looked to see how
I was taking it. My mouth fallen open so wide, my eyebrows raised
so high, showed my perplexity; to see this smart-arse from foreign
parts discomfited like that sent all into bellows of laughter. The leg-
pull was on me.

Daytimes my host and other acquaintances were mostly at work so
I wandered around the streets looking for copy. I strolled up to the
main cross-road corner one mid-morning and together with a small
crowd of other unemployed loafers stood, hands in pockets, looking
wistfully into a baker's window. It was a pathetic sight really: seven
loaves of bread and a display of sweaty fat-cakes spread out over
sheets torn from last year's newspapers. Even the shop flies were put
off at the vision and buzzed at the window glass, anxious to be out.

Suddenly I'm barged over, together with the others beside me. We fall one upon another yelling in surprise slap onto the pavement, not made of paving but of soft rubble luckily, although I do get a nasty bang on the skull from the boot of the man next to me. I have the breath knocked out of my body and the senses out of my mind. At the same moment there's an ugly nasal squealing in what I guessed to be *tsotsi-taal*, as it wasn't the ordinary Zulu or Sesotho I knew.

'*Haait, haait, haait*!' came the shouts as we struggled back to our feet only to receive hard biffs over the head. I yelped with pain. '*Tula*!' I got a thump across the face to shut me up.

Two rough young blacks, in coats twice the correct size for their skinny physiques, were holding guns to our heads. They were already at it, frisking through the pockets of two of my neighbours. They cursed as they drew a blank and awarded the two an extra clout for being so backward and indigent – but what earning power could they have expected from this sad crowd, really? Small-time crooks they clearly were, starting off with low aspirations.

Yet they were none the less fearsome for that. So what was I to do, I gulped, what was I to do? Should I try to flee, then they'd fire after me; should I shout out for help, but there'd be no one ready to stand up to these fiends ... should I try to fight them with my bare hands, some hope, some hope, what could I do? I needed to decide and act quick, and I grasped at a possible solution – there was a way open to me, and only one way. But would I feel right about grabbing at it, such a desperate and rather despicable way out as had occurred to me?

I needed time to answer such an ethical question. I simply had to stop to think and wrestle with my moral conscience and with my professional conscience as a journalist. For the hope, you see, the only hope, was to own up to my true colour, to take refuge in the fact of my race. On the other hand that cowardly step would immediately blow my cover as well as be ratting on the other victims.

Yet it was the way I could save my neck – for paradoxically the truth was that whatever the nervous white population might think, a white man was far safer in a black neighbourhood than was a non-white, as the bad guys would be putting themselves at serious risk if they attacked him, while black on black stirred up little concern among the police.

I swung the argument by reasoning with myself that it would be only fair to my readers to keep myself whole for another occasion. So, pull back my sleeves and reveal the fair skin beneath! Probably the hoodlums would reckon that I was a white detective in disguise doing the job of a human Q-ship, waiting around to be attacked, and they'd sheer off at speed leaving me unharmed, and letting my comrades alone too.

Well, well, come on now, what was I to decide then, show the white flag or not? After all my dithering now was the last moment for positive action, since they were heading straight for me next; didn't I after all offer the richest target for them, in my respectable clothing? I was overwhelmed with fright as they bore down on me, wartime veteran or not, and alas unable to make any sort of decision at all, quite beyond the help of logical thought or speech. 'Hey, koelie, kom hierso,' one snarled, beckoning at me. I cleared my throat pathetically, no words would come.

Then amazingly ... at that instant a squad of police arrived on the scene, sirens howling. More screaming and hollering and flashing of guns as three uniformed constables jumped out of a khaki Ford pick-up van and made for us with curses as foul and fearsome as the gunmen's.

Here was relief! Surely in the absolute nick of time! Never mind the coarse language of these messengers of justice, happy feelings gushed through me and I chortled to myself: Ha, the rascally crooks got their timing wrong! Rescue at hand!

I was sore all over, but at least I wasn't going to become another black-on-black murder statistic, if a quite spurious one, my case being not in truth black-on-black. The helping hand might be that of our old enemy, the police, but I had to be grateful for it nevertheless.

But no, no, no, steady on ... no, steady a minute, hello, something was wrong surely? This wasn't proceeding at all as planned, what the hell was going on? Suddenly everything turned as black and doomful as before.

12. WHERE'S YOUR PASS, KAFFIR?

Everything was going tragically wrong again, and I was in the thick of it once more, along with my fellow window-shoppers. We were being shoved and kicked and pushed around all over again, but this time by the police, the crew of the pick-up van having made straight for us and started laying around them with clubs and *kerries*. They'd quite ignored the hold-up men, didn't set a finger on them, simply shouldered their way past and fell upon us innocents trustfully awaiting rescue.

Why, why was this? Why? Not such a difficult one to answer. That was their job, after all, that was their official mission, these cops, their duty as well as their main aim and pleasure in life: to rid the city of surplus blacks, to round them up if they were without passes and deliver them in tumbril-loads to the courts. So these three were methodically and enthusiastically scooping us in to add to their collection. What they were after was pass-breakers, not mere mobsters or murderers. A pass was the bit of paper to prove an African had a job with a white man and could thus be admitted to the streets of Johannesburg. My ten-year-old son's signature on a slip of paper was enough to authorise our sociologist friend Professor Ngakane to walk the town.

They tore into us, roaring out 'Waar's jou pas, waar's jou pas', while the two crooks were allowed to slip silently away. They harried us and herded us together and banged us violently against one another. Then we were formed into a crocodile, an awkward little detachment, to be frog-marched down the street at the double and all the way back up again at the double while they whipped in a string of other vagrants and layabouts. At the tailgate of the van we were hurled aboard one by one. Guilty-until-proved-innocent, the normal rule of law that applied to the African.

The constables kept their own spirits up meanwhile with singing out a rhythmic 'kom, kom, kom, kom, kom, kom, kom', on each beat hitting at a man running their gauntlet. If they missed a nice knock on the top of the head to go with one of the 'kom, koms' you could see an unhappy little look on their faces, it was quite disappointing for them.

The last man aboard was flicked on the tail by a heavy *sjambok* to speed him up. This was me. They were particularly irritated with me, perhaps because I looked a 'cheeky' type, being well-dressed.

They bundled me in, and I fell flat across the steel floor of the van, then started worming my way forward on my belly, to get away from the centre of attention. But I was spotted by a fourth cop on board the van, the sergeant in charge; *he* was going to decide how and where we were packed in, not me. He was a fat man with a very swarthy skin and crinkly black hair as well as a black, black moustache. Such colouring was typical of some Afrikaners, and in spite of the way it advertised their recent ancestry, these were often the most benighted of the apartheid men. If he'd known it, I myself had him beat when it came to racial purity. This made me ask myself tearfully, while the officer was kindly helping me back to my correct place with his boot, whether I shouldn't own up to my white status, someone who wasn't obliged to carry a pass, or would this then only encourage him to take me straight off to the Special Branch – and then who knew what?

But at this moment the sweaty, energetic, fat and saturnine fellow, in the process of rolling me over and over, caught a glimpse of my face. Aghast at what he saw, ethnic expert that he was, he whined at his men, really annoyed with them, 'what's this, what's this, hey, look here you *derms* (offal), what're you doing, sending this rubbish in here, this one's not a kaffir, he's jes' a koelie, sommer a blerry koelie'. Furious with me too, for wrongfully allowing myself to be arrested, he shoved at me and belaboured me and gave me a final few kicks that sent me tumbling back along the floor of the van and out over its tailgate.

He had no further use for me, for the reason that Indians were not obliged by law to carry passes, despised and penalised though they might otherwise be by our Nationalist rulers. Of course they did suffer other very stiff prohibitions, for it was only in Natal and the Transvaal that they could work at all, not even being permitted to enter or reside in most other parts.

I dragged my way back to my hideout, wishing there was such a

thing as a bathroom in Sophiatown and cleaned myself up in a basin-
ful of cold water. Then I rested up for a day or two.

I didn't report my Sophiatown adventure in *Drum* when I got back,
it was surely against the law to play black or to go into *shebeens*, but
after I'd left the country I worked it up into a talk that was broadcast
from the BBC.

I was back at the office on the Monday. There was several rumours
circulating. Two of the items were to do with the Henry mystery.
Chocho had come up with something on the abortion story ... Henry
on the fateful night was on his way to visit a nurse who could tell him
the name of the white surgeon involved. In those days abortion was
not only strictly illegal and punished with serious penalties, but it was
also very hole-in-corner and grim, and only the sleaziest of doctors
would deal in it. It seemed that this rather gross fellow who carried
on a cash practice among the blacks had been tipped off that the press
were on to him and was said to have offered a fat contract to a known
felon to bump off Henry.

'Well, we can't publish that,' I said flatly, 'all hearsay and we'd be
in the libel courts immediately.'

'Well let's go to the police then.'

'Pah, the police won't believe you either, and besides they're probably getting a regular pay-off from this guy not to interfere with his
practice and they'll hate to have their regular source of income cut off.'

Chocho looked flat.

'All right,' I relented, 'get some really tight evidence and one or
two plausible witnesses. Then we'll take it to a lawyer and see what
we can do.'

The other items were of romantic interest, another story linking a
woman's name with the late Henry and setting up fresh, fleeting
hopes of finding the murder culprit. Then finally a really hot one was
circulating, to do with Can. The gossip was out that he was already
and most unexpectedly into a new affair, this time a quite extraordinary one ... unprecedented! It was with the enchanting Jean, an
English girl. Whew, that was a hot piece of news. Never mind the
mere saucy aspect that she was happily married to Malcolm, as
charming a person as her, but for white and black lovers to be caught

at it was to put them into mortal danger. Punishable by law with many years in prison, there was also the risk that violent white upholders of so-called 'Western Christian civilisation' might take the verdict and the carrying out of sentencing into their own hands.

What advice, Dear Dolly, would you give Can and Jean and could you get hold of jail vouchers for them?

Let's admit it, we all felt violent towards Can, the rotter, there wasn't one of the crowd, not one of us, who wasn't jealous of him for this. All were in love with Jean – she had a way of making you feel that you were specially favoured by her – and now could see that romance with her was a realistic possibility, and if only they'd realised this before, if only they'd known, and if only they'd been courageous enough and quick enough they might have had a pitch at it themselves. For she was not only admirably good-looking, doubly so for being blonde, but witty and wise and a wonderfully talented dancer and singer, able to shake out a sexy *kwela* and coo an exquisite jazz number in the original Sotho, looking in the process so Anglo-Saxon blonde and yet so African somehow! She had such a way of smiling and whispering at everyone, man, woman or child, inviting them into a special secret cuddly relationship with her, that all became sworn to her for ever.

Yes, my nose was put out of joint – though she assured me in private that there was no truth in the rumour, it was still only me. One was too ready to believe it.

This was at a time when I was working over early plans to go abroad with my wife Jenny and our four kids, as the first of our crowd to desert *Drum* and South Africa, so I never did get at the full truth until there appeared eventually a total of four different books based on that daring story. One of them it happened was a novel of my own.

Almost all those wonderful members of my staff had also become preoccupied with thoughts of melting away overseas. We all suddenly took off within a year or so of this as if on a signal, fleeing South Africa, abandoning *Drum* and leaving virtually only Can and Casey remaining loyal to their country and their work on the magazine. This put on ice for the time the following-up of this mystery romance as well as the tragic story of Henry – we quite neglected to go after the suspect hinted at in the riddlings of the wee *Tokoloshe* of Tembuland.

Nor did we harbour any inkling of further pain lying in wait for *Drum's* men – whether or not the *Tokoloshe* had smelled out signs of this and the web of circumstances then being woven that might point to the capture of some of them in its threads and the dragging of them off for an untimely meeting with the Leveller.

Allspice

...new Browns for Summer

There's new flavour and excitement in John Drake summer-weights — exotic spice browns to give a lift to your favourite styles. You'll be the smartest man in town if you team them correctly with your suits — Nutmeg Brown with greys, Cinnamon Brown with fawns, Clove Brown with blues. Visit your John Drake stockist soon — see the new interest in John Drake's rich premium leathers and suedes.

There's a

John Drake

Shoe for every Summer occasion!

FROM YOUR JOHN DRAKE STOCKIST

VGM/600A/1975

for aching, perspiring and tired feet

'TROT' ANTISEPTIC FOOT POWDER

2/6 PER PACKET

Available from all Chemists, Medicine Shops or direct from manufacturers:
ALEX ROBINSON (PTY) LTD.
15 Central Road, Fordsburg
Johannesburg

STOMACH Sufferers— rely on

De Witt's ANTACID POWDER

quickly stops INDIGESTION

Price 3/- large canister (double size) 5/6

IF NOT— WHY NOT?

ARE YOU LUCKY?

Your personal horoscope of Love, Marriage, Success, Money, Friends, Family, etc.

Use your analysis as a guide to happiness from the world's greatest astrologist.

Send only 10/- for The Lucky Talisman of fate; receive also a complete personal horoscope free!

Read some of the many letters received:— "Mrs. L.N. "... I obtained £2,600 ..." "L.S. "... won £1,300 in sweepstake ..." "Miss D.L. "... to my amazement I won £1,900 ..." "W.E. "... won £350 to my surprise ..." "A.G. "... and I may win over £20 ..." "F.N. "... surprising how few facts I..." "Mrs. S.M. "... all you wrote is quite true ..."

Send 10/- cash or postal order for The Lucky Talisman of fate; stating:— (1) Date of birth, (2) Name known by, (3) Address.

Send to: KIRON, Dept. DR
P.O. Box 450, Johannesburg

NEW DISCOVERY RESTORES YOUTHFUL VIGOUR

Sufferers from loss of vigour, nervousness, weak body, impure blood, failing memory, and who are old and worn out before their time will be delighted to learn of a new discovery by an American Doctor.

This new discovery makes it possible to quickly and easily restore vigour to your system, build rich, pure blood, strengthen your mind and memory and feel like a new man. In fact, this discovery which is a home medicine is pleasant, easy-to-take form, quickly begins to build new vigour and energy, yet is absolutely harmless and natural in action.

The success of this amazing discovery, called Higalon, has been so great that it is now being distributed by chemists here. Higalon makes you feel full of vigour, energy and years younger. A special bottle of 48 Higalon tablets costs little. Get Higalon from your chemist today.

MAKE BIG MONEY

Become a QUALIFIED HOUSE BUILDER

In Just Eight Months

Our splendid Home-study course for owners teaches everything - Plans, Bricklaying, Plastering, Plumbing, Carpentry, Painting etc. In a few short months you can be ready to make BIG money.

VALUABLE DIPLOMA
BEAUTIFUL BADGE
FREE BUILDING PLANS
with course

Write for FREE particulars:
THE INSTITUTE OF BUILDING
Box 10521 · Johannesburg

13. THE TWO ASSASSINATIONS OF VERWOERD

A truth from the beyond

His self slithered out of its carcase and ascended a short distance into the ether to remain hovering over the operating table. Upon the marbled surface a team was working on a body that he knew to be his own.

The clanking of implements was heard above the cries of surgeons and frantic nurses. He himself did not feel any concern; in fact a great peace came over him.

He now entered a tunnel of light through which he floated a little way until he came to another world, to meet beneath a polela tree at its border a number of people that could be recognised as Hertzog, Smuts, Malan, Strijdom, another man whose name seemed to begin with a V like his and finally ... Botha! All of these were people of the past, except the last-named, who was shivering at the thought of being numbered there among the shades. Botha nevertheless signed to him and mouthed: 'The man with a V, that is you, it is you, Verwoerd.'

They each reached out to touch him and speak in a kindly way with him. Botha hurried to put in an extra apologetic word of grace.

V was led to an altar to hear an announcement that a new day would dawn: freedom for the volk, no more rooinek power, no blacks in the land.

Suddenly he found himself back in his body again, authorised to return from the edge and lead those still on the other side onward to their victory - hou koers (hold course)!

It was the very worst of times in the long reign of apartheid. Darkness had conquered enlightenment and all roads to freedom were blocked.

For *Drum* and its people there was finally nowhere left to go. It was the last *voetsak*, one by one we had to quit the stage.

Pressure was mounting. Dr Verwoerd was the Minister of Native Affairs. He was hurrying to bring about perfect apartheid, the madness that passed for his philosophy, for his religion – each race in its own separate territory. To appease the whites, mind, the blacks could still come in as "work-seekers" and servants. But they'd have no rights of residence; it was simply the pass system again, another quasi-legal trick in the century-old process of plundering the land and its blessings from the black man.

By the late 1950s the hated Verwoerd had seized complete power. The Department of Justice as well as his own Department of Native Affairs danced to his tune, so that he held the country in his grip even before eventually becoming Prime Minister. He emasculated all opposition by putting on trial 156 blacks and radicals, the leaders of every party that had any standing, ranging from the ANC and the Communists to the anti-white militants. This was the Treason Trial. The ruse was to tie them up in court day after day *for four years* so that their organisations would be left rudderless. In the end there was no genuine case for them to have to answer of course, and they were discharged by the court.

As for the white parliamentary opposition – it offered no opposition, just lay down and presented its belly to be scratched by the government. White business and the white press too. Even Jim Bailey was fearful of poking his head too high above the trenches, believing his magazine would be closed down if he allowed his editor full rein in the thwarting and teasing of the country's rulers.

By now the pressure inside the land was as in a top-security jail; events moved faster and faster, more and more disastrously – most disastrously for the architect of all this, ironically, leading at future dates to assassination attempts on Verwoerd, twice tried, once failed.

So there was nowhere to go for those at *Drum*, nothing for it but a final scramble, a wild, rushed last year or so in the pursuit of destiny. It was high tempo. We worked at speed, we matured at speed and we involved ourselves more closely with the political process, our every action touched with panic. We were defiant until the end, we sang, danced and partied harder than ever, and we cocked a farewell snook at apartheid ... we indulged in mixed social gatherings, love affairs across the colour line, black-and-white theatre groups, European private schools that admitted black kids.

Here is an example from my own family chronicles:

Soweto, a sunny Saturday morning. Picture two little girls of an age, one white and one black, dressed in identical yellow-spotted organdie frocks, standing side by side holding hands. They are the centre of a large, chattering group. Yes, an amazed reaction, this was something unheard of before ... as well as being *verboten*! Black kids had poured out from their shacks to touch their dresses and wonder at their friendship; many had never seen a white child before though the neighbouring city numbered a quarter of a million of them.

The one was my eight-year-old daughter Lyndall, freckled of skin and with wondrous red hair. This was a historic crossing of the colour bar; she had spent the weekend in the black township as a guest of the other eight-year-old, Theresa Mphahlele. The two-roomed house, with no running water, no electric lighting, situated on the bleak veld among thousands like it, beside a rutted dirt road, was something of an amazing object to her too.

This was a family farewell gesture to the colour bar. Theresa was the daughter of my favourite colleague at *Drum*, Ezekiel Mphahlele, and of Rebecca. Zeke's family and mine were rather as images in a mirror. Wives of strong character and children of an age.

Prior to this Lyndall had met Theresa when they called at our house in the suburbs for a get-together of all the family people on the paper, invited to pick apricots off the huge tree in our garden. Jenny and Rebecca had decided the visit should be returned, in spite of the law and the custom. It was an adventurous expedition for our girl – someone coming from Mars.

This story entranced some of the visitors from Britain who called on me at *Drum*, wanting a guided tour of black South Africa. It particularly touched Dame Sybil Thorndike, the actress, and was remembered for long after by John Dankworth, the jazzman, who made easy contact with the blacks through his music.

Then there were the intellectual parties at our thatched house, where the *Drum* writers could meet on even terms other distinguished personalities from abroad, as well as those local politicos, writers and academics of white South Africa who were not too nervous to be seen or caught in their company.

At Bailey's Johannesburg home, a farmstead just out of town, the social affairs were secure from police raids. After the last of the big, rowdy parties of his that I attended, police stopped Jenny and me driving home in the early hours. We were giving a lift back to Alexandra Township to Arthur Maimane, who was seated in the back of the car. They were extremely uneasy about this, our harbouring a black passenger. 'Who's this *Hotnot* (Hottentot) in the back?' they coarsely questioned us to his face.

The long glassfuls of Cape Smoke that had been poured down me at the party funded me with the glibness to trot out the right answer: 'Our kitchen boy, sergeant, we brought him along to make the fire up at a friend's *braaivleis* (barbecue).' That staved off more trouble and after all Arthur like all the others was well used to playing the stupid, deferential native boy when confronting the authorities.

Todd and Esme Matshikiza threw a mixed party at their bungalow in the part of Soweto where they lived, a rare venue and a daring one. It was a good, happy time. How could we not bring that off, with old friends and marvellous singers and musicians in our company, and something of a farewell in the air?

As ever we sang songs from the nations, folk songs, rugby songs, army songs, work songs and the township songs of the day, *Skokiaan*, *Lizzie*, *You Tell such Lovely Lies* and *Jozi-Jozi*, the song of Johannesburg, those present doing a kind of conga round the room to its tune, led by ANC heroes, a leadership triumvirate of Walter Sisulu, Robert Resha and Moses Kotane.

Then crash, a pair of black policemen at the door – however had they tracked down that something illicit was going on here, for not only was it against the law for Africans to take any strong alcoholic drink at all, in any circumstances, it was also a punishable offence for whites to be found in the location?

Todd, the cheery voluble host, was easily able to deal with this – he knew that the cops would tour the place at night looking for any party that might be going on, so that they could blackmail the offenders for a free drink for themselves. Esme opened a bottle of so-called champagne for the occasion. Those policemen luckily were not aware of the identity and great significance of the political leaders they might have caught in their bag if they had carried out their duty properly.

NOW! A LOVELIER, LIGHTER SKIN FOR YOU...

thanks to this wonder
of modern science

NEW

ARTRA®

Skin Tone Cream

with <u>Miracle</u>-<u>Action</u> Hydroquinone

Developed by Doctors!
Laboratory Tested!
*Proven effective by thousand
of satisfied users!*

Now! A complexion cream for lighter, lovelier skin that's both thorough *and* gentle! It's new Artra Skin Tone Cream with Hydroquinone—the miracle-action bleaching ingredient, laboratory proven for effectiveness and safe use on normal skin. Try it! Massage Artra lightly into your skin...it vanishes without a trace of oiliness (makes a perfect powder base). So soothing and refreshing, too. And most wonderful of all...Artra's deep-down penetrating action begins to work at once to help lighten and soften your skin...give you that creamy smooth complexion you've longed for. Follow the lead of thousands of beauty minded women everywhere. Use Artra and you, too, can have that radiant glow...that lovelier, lighter "Artra look." Ask for Artra Skin Tone Cream soon at your favorite drug or cosmetic counter.

Read these facts:

- Contains no ammoniated mercury!
- No time-consuming ritual to follow!
- Vanishes! Use under make-up!
- Use anytime—even before going out!
- Helps keep skin clear and clean!

$1.00

7/6

Can be bought anywh

At *Drum* there was always the monthly deadline, life had to go on. As often before, there was a tug-of-war being waged between Bailey's two editors, Cecil and me, over the editorial staff. We both wanted the best men. It was a natural assumption to me that the most talented should be on *Drum*, where fine writing and integrity counted for everything, whereas any old hack could report *Golden City Post's* murder shockers, or count the number of goals at a football match or ghost the romances of nice-time girls. Cecil absolutely disagreed, just as naturally, and Bailey, to stop us tearing his publishing empire in two, had to play Solomon.

He'd recently given a verdict that appalled me, to split the working hours of sub-editor Chocho between our two papers. There was a rending in twain for you! I felt obliged to offer Solomon Bailey my resignation in protest and succeeded in overturning this. But when he later proposed to transfer to the *Post* my second-string feature writer, in compensation, I couldn't afford to invoke such strong-arm tactics a second time.

Consequently I lost the services of this man and was now looking around for a talented replacement. But where was one to find an experienced black journalist in a country where the average level of African education was graded as standard three, equivalent to what white kids tackled at age nine?

We'd virtually creamed the educated population to gather together our existing lot. Some had applied direct, some were friends of friends, some had attracted our notice by their entries in *Drum's* short story competitions. We never turned away genius – there's only so much of it in the world. So where to go next?

At this moment I had a letter from Rolf Sholto-Douglas, a man who'd been at school with me in Durban and gone on to teach Africans in the Natal countryside. He was extremely pleased with himself, he'd written to say he'd turned out a real prodigy, a black lad with brilliant exam marks in English, as good as Shakespeare's or Milton's it seemed. Better still this boy could boast on his *curriculum vitae* what even Shakespeare and Milton couldn't, practical experience as a reporter, having freelanced on *Ilanga Lase Natal*, the Zulu newspaper, during the early part of 1957.

I arranged to drive down to the coast near Durban to interview the candidate, a smiling and eager youngster named Nat Nakasa. 'Now,' I said, on meeting him, 'where can we find a nice, relaxed place to talk?' For there wouldn't be any cafe or public place where we could sit down together. I had the answer myself, we should slip down to a favourite picnic spot of my childhood, the beautiful and desolate river mouth at Amanzimtoti, or 'Sweet Waters', named so by Shaka a hundred or so years earlier on one of his long forced-marches of conquest.

We chatted generalities as we drove and as we sauntered down to the sea-shore past the bullrushes on the banks of the 'Toti. Small ducks paddled off up river, worried at our approach. A weaver bird sitting atop a swaying reed took fright even before it became aware of us – as the reed dipped down to the river surface it saw there in reflection what seemed to be another fierce little bird peering back up at it – and flew off on the instant. Nat and I chuckled. We were on easy terms by this time, the effect I wanted to create for him while he was on display.

The river, like so many in Natal, didn't debouch into the sea, it simply curled around and came to its end in a lagoon here against high sandbanks. Oceanside of the lagoon we had a little pebbly bay all to ourselves. It was all too good to be true, almost too good for a formal interview. Already he showed promise: personable, not overawed by authority and with the typical *Drum* way about him, able to exchange banter about 'The Situation', and not afraid to laugh at himself as a 'naytiff', or even as kaffir, munt, nig or Jimfish.

But there were unforeseen delays to starting our direct business. First I felt I deserved a swim to wash away the stains of my eight-hour road trip and I ran down the steep shore into the Indian Ocean, the half-circle of rocks that formed the bay keeping the big waves out, but it was too tepid to be refreshing. As I dressed, we discovered oysters in the rock pools! So on our haunches beside the pool we had to sit cracking open the oysters, as fat a little family, of them as you would ever come across, a distinction they were now paying for – before long a heap of plundered shells lay around, the plump owners having slipped down our throats.

Now there was another digression before we could yet get around to serious talk: we were startled by shouts and yells and yodellings coming closer and closer to us and suddenly we were surrounded by an army of men and boys and shrieking girls. We jumped to our feet, this was rather frightening, someone must have seen Nat and me fraternising and had called out the vigilantes.

But they simply swept past us down to the water, where we now noticed that the calm bay was fairly frothing under the surface. The men and boys of the crowd, brandishing buckets and cans, sacks, nets, baskets, were soon splashing into this turbulent sea, right up to their shoulders, quite forgetful of the villainous South Coast sidewash or the sharks.

Now I grasped it, this was the annual sardine run, a momentous occasion on the Natal coast. The sardines didn't arrive precisely to a calendar date, they came when they came, hordes of them, millions and millions of them, drifting along the coast in a shoal a square mile in extent, completely preoccupied with the business of spawning. You had to be ready when they were ready if you wanted to get your share of the catch. And there they were, they'd been signalled from further south and then spotted by watchers on a high cliff upon arriving here, these silvery fish now churning up the waters of the tiny bay.

In their frantic efforts to scoop up the fish the residents of Amanzimtoti were adding to the froth. The sardines hardly noticed them, having to concentrate all their attention at the moment on eluding the bigger fish that had first chased them into the shallows, and who were adding to the disturbance, these tyrants, a species of sawtoothed mackerel, in their attempt to get closer yet among the succulent bodies. While some mackerel knifed into the shoal, others shot up through the air, showing a twist of blue and white belly, to slap down again across the surface where they might get right on top of their prey. Seabirds were also taking advantage of the ferment, diving between one and all and making away with bitten-off halves of sardine, while stray dogs were barking wildly in the water's edge, eager to join in the party.

Nat and I were entranced at the scene and we waded in to snatch a few wriggling fish. In the ebbwater under our feet the sardines were teeming, several even flapping up on shore, preferring that unfishy place to the inside of a mackerel. The small children from 'Toti village galloped across the sands to pounce on these stranded fish too and sling them safely higher up the beach. They then dashed back into the waves after more, shovelling them out of the water with their bare hands and into the cans and baskets.

It was all mad and wonderful, and it went on and on until upon a moment the waters were absolutely still, the school of sardines having got the idea of slipping away to sea again – and the fishing was over. On the white sand there remained a spangly heap of fish, some still writhing, desperate in the end to return to the water ...

'Man, ou' Frikkie, there was more than all the fish I ever seen! Enough from here to hell-and-gone!' exclaimed a shiny-eyed boy strolling home to his wood-and-iron family quarters back of the beach.

'Oh, more than that!' said Frikkie, his older companion, witheringly, emboldened by his greater experience.

Even some of the local Indians had dared to join in for a portion of the haul. In that moment of plenty there was no need for envy and greed, and in the general euphoria the colour bar had lifted itself a degree to allow a jolly exchange of shouts between the races at their mutual triumph over the fish.

'More than I ever seen either,' smiled Nat. He and I felt closer to humanity, closer to each other, after that joint hunting rite.

Yes, Nat was a fine fellow, Nat was the man. He was friendly to the ANC, which put him in my best books, he had read the classics, and he knew *Drum*, its contents and its writers, quite as well as his school set books. His dislikes too put me on his side – especially his contempt for the *Ilanga* newspaper, white-owned and with a fawning editorial style. He was warmly welcomed by all when we arrived in Johannesburg, immediately taken up by Can, and taken in by him too as a lodger. Can spotted more in him than a double A in literature: under his genial and open manner were to be detected high qualities of character and grit as well as that lauded provincial genius.

It was only the authorities who weren't impressed with my prize recruit, insisting on putting him through the hoop of the pass laws. I had to attend at the Witwatersrand Native Labour Administration offices to show why he should be given a permit to live in this territory. 'No,' said the official, 'no, look here, Mr Stein, we can't have just anybody shoving in, there's thousands of unemployeds on the Rand, who must first be given the chance to apply for the job.'

'What, as journalists!' I gasped.

'No, come on, play the game, Mr Stein, do things in the right order, put in your application for this boy and we'll see.'

I made an elaborate production of it, advertising officially for 'an experienced court reporter able to take a "good note", and with 50 words a minute competency in typing. Must be able to tackle big descriptive specials when needed. Cuttings of past work should be produced.'

So Nat arrived as the clock was ticking away for us. He was last in and was to be one of the first out, though not of his own accord.

DON'T MISS
THE TIGER WRIGHT STORY

THE MOST EXCITING AND REVEALING STORY OF HORSE-RACING IN SOUTH-AFRICA AS TOLD AND WRITTEN BY HAROLD (TIGER) WRIGHT, HIMSELF

NOW RUNNING IN
GOLDEN CITY POST

OBTAIN A COLLEGE EDUCATION!

YOU QUALIFY FOR A BETTER JOB WITH MORE PAY WHEN YOU BECOME A TRAINED MAN!

An hour of study every day with a Union College Course can give you the education and training you need to get that better job.

WRITE TODAY FOR FREE INFORMATION TO:

UNION COLLEGE (Dept. 1/0)
P.O. Box 3541
JOHANNESBURG,
SOUTH AFRICA.

The Largest Home-study Institution in Africa

BUSINESS TRAINING
Bookkeeping.
Business Correspondence.
Office Clerk's Course.
Salesmanship.
Shorthand.
Typing.

TECHNICAL
Draughtmanship
(Engineering or Building).
Motor Engineering.
Practical Building.
Welding.
Woodwork.

EDUCATIONAL
Afrikaans and Taalbond.
Bilingualism Examination.
Junior Certificate.
Matriculation.
National Senior Certificate.
Stds. IV, V, VI, VII, VIII, X.
B.A., B.A. (Soc. Sc.), B.Sc.,
B.Com., B.Admin., LL.B.
Diplomas in Bantu Studies.

FARMING
Agriculture.
Gardening.
Poultry Farming.
Sheep and Wool Farming.
Vegetable Growing.

MISCELLANEOUS
Black and White Sketching.
Commercial Art.
Domestic Science
(Cookery, Laundry Work, Housewifery).
Dressmaking.
Freelance Journalism.
Handwriting.
Home Needlecraft.
Languages (English, Afrikaans, Bantu, Latin).
Native Law.
Photography.
Public Speaking.
Short Story Writing.
Window Dressing.

POST THIS COUPON FOR FREE INFORMATION

To: THE REGISTRAR, UNION COLLEGE, DEPT. AD 1/0
P.O. BOX 3541, JOHANNESBURG, SOUTH AFRICA
Write clearly in CAPITAL LETTERS

Please tell me about your Home Study Courses in —

COURSE ....

NAME ....

ADDRESS ....

.... AD.89.10

My age is .... Standard of Education ....

My man is strong

I give him Bull Brand Corned Meat

- Bull Brand is made from good, rich beef.
- Bull Brand gives you good health.
- Bull Brand is for energy and power.
- Bull Brand Corned Meat builds strong muscles.

- Bull Brand is already cooked.
- Open the tin — and Bull Brand ready to eat.
- All the family love Bull Brand rich flavour.
- Bull Brand is tightly packed, one tin feeds 6 people.

BULL BRAND
CORNED MEAT

15. AT THE TOP OF THE WORLD

While marking time on my own affairs and my own future – still making the final decision whether I really ought to go and if so whether *this* was the moment to go, now! now! now! – I needed to keep the magazine itself charging along at full momentum. It was the occasion once again for a big, rousing story, a controversial one even, for after all if I did leave I'd be glad to sail away across some nice choppy seas.

It happened that the story idea was waiting under my nose. I had a holiday trip planned with two close friends, chums from schooldays. These were Mervyn Susser, a doctor, who had married my sister Zena a few years back, and Douglas Saunderson, an engineer. We were to go pony-trekking in Basutoland (the Lesotho of today) and knew a man there who ran a country store from where he hired out horses with guides. He was a political contact, the heroic Ntsu Mohkehle, who at that time and for the next 35 years, was to be the main opponent of the traditionalists in power, eventually to become Premier.

Then, as so often, Lesotho was a sensitive area politically. It was nominally independent of South Africa, as a so-called British Protectorate, but being a land-locked island wholly within South Africa it could not deny the embraces of the ugly bear that enveloped it: this tyrant demanded an unrestrained flow of cheap black labour for its gold mines; furthermore it wouldn't tolerate any silly nonsense in the way of mocking the gospel of apartheid inside a territory right there adjacent to it.

The little country itself had not the resources to defend itself against the occasional punitive expedition of undercover assassins sent in from South Africa, and dared not step out of line. It needed to remain on diplomatic terms with its neighbour in any event since its main earnings were the wages remitted home by the labourers indentured to the Rand mines. It could just as well have been written up in big letters on the official notice at the border post that if Lesotho was too damn 'cheeky' the bear would gulp it down whole. Britain, the 'Protector', merely stood by and watched.

Ntsu and his democratic movement refused to accept such degrading feudalism, however, and had accordingly taken up a stand against the conniving leaders of the state – the Lesotho royal family and the head of government, Chief Jonathan Leabua.

I had my story right here I realised. While we roamed over this country within a country we could work up an exposé of the true state of affairs inside it, following up the hints of violence that were current and the suspicions of civil trouble beneath the surface. The holiday trip would be excellent cover, no one would find anything untoward in our presence. What we came back with would make good copy, for many of our readers were Sotho, and there would also be publicity value from any national and international reverberations that might be set off. Underneath it all, in any case, this was nothing more than a further exploration of our staple, fundamental apartheid theme. It was as much a South African as a Lesotho problem.

I thought I must co-opt Bloke Modisane on this trip, so that he could handle the research and the reporting – he would get more of an inside edge on it than I'd be able to manage myself.

Bloke was full of enthusiasm at first, but as the date for departure approached he took on a somewhat introspective look. 'Er, this ain't a Mr Drum story, I guess?' he asked, looking up at me anxiously, though trying to keep his widest smile switched on meanwhile. Of course not, said I, nothing too sensational, simply digging, digging; facts, facts – fundamental research. Nevertheless while packing ourselves into the car standing outside the office in Main Street on the morning we were to leave, he had an attack of cold feet once more. 'What if they get a fishy feeling about us?' he asked.

'Huh?' said I.

'This Lesotho government, what if they get suspicious of what we're up to there?' They'd be after us then, he went on, they'd hustle him straight into gaol, for sure. 'They're tough on "traitors", which is what they classify anybody making trouble against the "friendly" SA government, and those boys running the Maseru gaol are tough too, probably tougher if you ask me even than the warder guys at the Joburg Fort,' he argued plaintively, 'I'll never get out.' He sniffed. 'If I ever get *in* that is, and they don't first kind of accidentally shoot me dead or alive.'

'Well then you'll be a hero,' said the brusque Douglas, not one to humour the timid, 'a ruddy martyr'.

It wasn't the way to handle Bloke though. I had to coddle him along a bit. Yes true, he would make a big name for himself ... but we'd be protecting him unfearingly all the way ... and I'd take the blame ... it'd be fun as well ... a free holiday on the company ... he could let it out that he was just doing a drought story. Fast talk, and I had a further idea: 'Look, Bloke, there's even a better story we can genuinely do at the same time, which you'll love: Something lyrical, we'll have a four-page picture story of you returning to the land of your fathers, meeting the people, contemplating the beautiful views; we'll pose you on horseback against the moon and the mountains riding along in a troop of Basuto blanket-boys. And then pose you with some of the local beauties? Very dashing, very romantic, you can't miss it. Back home the pix of you will make all the girls' hair curl.'

'Man, I can't ride like my ancestors.'

'Go on, you even walk like a cowboy,' put in Douglas tartly, 'that bow-legged waddle of yours gives you away immediately.'

'I've never been on a horse, not ever.'

'But Bloke,' I wheedled, 'nor have any of us, this is designed for dudes this pony-trek and we'll all have to learn.'

He finally took it on – okey-doke then, dead or alive, he sighed – and we set off in my big old Chevrolet. As we motored down the length of Eloff Street I couldn't yet relax, I was still worrying about leaving Can in charge and what trouble might arise, could he handle the wretched white printers; could he handle Bailey breathing over his shoulder, itching to get his hands on the editorial as he tried often enough with me there, though not succeeding; could he handle all the work and still fit in his drinking hours?

Soon enough though we fell into holiday mood and drinks were passed around. As usual Bloke was seated at the back, disguised as our 'boy', not to let the police get the impression that we considered him our equal, so while we three in the front drank our beer straight from the Castle Beer bottles, he took the jokey precaution of disguising his beer too, sucking it from a ginger beer bottle. We were quite exuberant by now, singing and joking.

Once into the Orange Free State we passed through dusty Welkom and avoided Bloemfontein, instead swanning through Bethlehem and Kaallaagte (K double A double L double A, for short), before driving under that wonderful natural gateway shaped by huge rocks on either side of the road. Motoring on south and just a few miles short of Maseru we arrived at the border, but it was a border that was hardly a border at all, being quite unmanned, allowing us to drive without a halt straight through the faded official signs.

But before we'd gone 50 yards, Bloke shouted out 'Stop!' very suddenly. I pulled up hard, almost skidding on the dirt road in my fright. My singing died away and my heart stopped – what was this latest business of Bloke's? Oh, yes, I might have worked it out, blast him, I'd noticed that he'd gone quiet at the first glimpse of Lesotho. He was playing chicken after all! I tried to think of cunning ways to persuade him out of it if his mind was turning to flight, otherwise I feared we'd have to make do with the picturesque tribal story alone and dump the big one.

The back door of the Chev was pushed open by Bloke. He said nothing, but leapt out from where he sat behind the driver's seat, straightened up, surveyed the mountain prospect before us with great reverence, raising an arm in a ceremonial salute and calling out 'Bayete!', and walked right round the car with his bandy-legged swagger to arrive at the front door on the side opposite. He wrenched it wide open, bowing to Mervyn and Douglas inside: 'Now, Monsieurs, will you be so good as to take your seats in the back, *s'il voux le jolly plait*?'

Mervyn giggled in good-humoured style, clambered out and did as he was told. Bloke waited a while, then poked his head further into the car and appealed to Doug: 'Ja nou Oom, will Oom also give me the pleasure?'

'Damn you for a headless fowl,' Doug cursed him, not altogether ill-naturedly, and also climbed out of the front seat and into the servants quarters in the back.

Bloke took his place beside the driver, banged the door to, sat up importantly and gave me the order: 'Okay, fine! Lay on Macduff.'

We didn't quite know what was up.

'This is Basuto country,' he explained in a dignified tone, 'and here the laws are different. Here I'm a gentleman, too, and gentlemen may sit in front next to the driver.' We all laughed but he was really relishing it to the limit. 'My first time out of South Africa,' he added proudly, 'my first time for not having to let anyone push me around.'

As it happened it didn't make much difference to his apparent status even in Lesotho. Any difference was mainly theoretical. There was not much general fraternising there between white and black and the locals still understood him to be our servant toted along on the trip with the job of pitching the tents, laying the campfire and being the general fag on the white men's expedition.

We journeyed on to Butha Buthe, where we arrived at Ntsu's general store. We selected four of his best horses, all with tidily-plaited tails – and our guide, a handsome but taciturn man, took along his own little light bay, with smartly clipped hair. That strong, silent manner of his did give us a good deal of confidence, though; he'd be just the chap in an emergency.

Then we had three days winding in single file up frighteningly narrow mountain paths, the occasional stones clattering away down 300 metre cliffs from under our horses' hooves, and on up towards the Drakensberg peaks, the very top of the world. Lesotho is all mountain of course, two miles high for the most of it, which is why the British had in historical times graciously allowed it to King Moshoeshoe at the end of their series of inconclusive wars. He'd outwitted them for years with guerrilla skill – and at length sour grapes stepped in: who wanted to go to all that trouble for a piece of barely arable mountainside?

After the first hour we'd almost had enough. It wasn't only Bloke who was ready to give up – our townie thighs were aching, our soft skin was rubbed raw and our backs were cracking. Bloke threw us a reproachful look, 'I told you, man, I can't ride, nohow.' Douglas snorted back ungraciously: 'You're in luck, fellow, at least your face isn't being sunburnt to buggery.'

However, we couldn't show ourselves up as quitters in front of that strong-man guide of ours and we had to stick with it until the evening and time for setting up camp.

The next day was gruesome too but strangely by the third morning the muscles had got used to life aboard a pony and a good tough hide had developed on the inside of the legs where there had been but soft skin before.

We travelled as far as the high northern plateau of Lesotho, above Mont-aux-Sources. Here we pitched camp and spent the first days climbing a few simple peaks and taking a hard trot to the farther escarpment, to look down from the berg across South Africa herself, far distant and far, far below.

The area we had chosen was not a long stretch from where Chief Johnny le Jonathan, as the king's man was called by the populace, had his home kraal. We made arrangements to visit him. A formal and disappointingly tame affair it turned out. We drank a few calabashes of home-brew beer and exchanged views on the drought, which still had the whole of Southern Africa in its grip, but Bloke dared come up with no questions even faintly tinged with political colour. He had the ingredients in his hand but muffed it.

'It's just not something you can do in the tribal tradition,' he excused himself on the way back, 'first time, you can't ask a chief a lot of pointed questions, this ceremonial stuff has got to start with a good lot of prevarication.'

It wasn't any good nagging him about his own prevarication, he'd find other reasons to keep off contentious topics if we should be so lucky as to get ourselves invited again. So we set up the secondary story-feature, getting a dozen of the locals to gallop along in their blankets, with Bloke among them in a loaned blanket of the proper clan pattern pulled over his khaki shirt. He had to hold on breathlessly during the ride, uneasy in his seat and not able to indulge in any twirling of lassos or other gallantry.

Unfortunately that very morning the drought-breaking rains had finally arrived, with the consequence that there was no sun to favour my camera work. The rain pelted down all day, it continued the next day too and the next and then the next ... we became quite disconsolate. The one single holiday pleasure left was cooking the puff-balls that had sprung up with the rain. They sprouted out of the veld all around us, little white round fungi that gave the place the look of a golf driving-range. Otherwise we sat huddled in our tents, chewing over metaphysical gossip such as 'Who is the central actor in one's dreams, is it always the You - You *yourself* - who is under threat?' Other topics were the fallibility of teleology in explaining colour distinctions in man, the efficient distribution of milk supplies under socialism and the malign influences on today's world of Hitler, Dr Malan and God (in both his Christian and Jewish versions).

When we had talked ourselves out we decided there was nothing for it but to cut short the holiday by a day or two, pack our things and saddle up for the ride back to the car at Butha Buthe. A miserable mission, was our summing up. Yet at that moment we were on the verge of a good thriller of a story.

From where we were above the plateau we began a steady descent down a conical mountain from its peak, our route a winding spiral that would take us round and round the cone and down and down and round again. Before us shortly we came to a tiny stream, which we splashed across. It hadn't been apparent on our way up, then merely a disused watercourse, but it had now been called into life again to do its duty of draining the rainwater rivulets from higher up.

The next time we came up with it, as our spiralling bridle-path continued to cross the stream's winding course downhill, it had grown considerably larger, collecting small tributaries on the way and rushing down boisterously with them, now to reach up as far as the ponies' knees. This spot on the map and this little freshet, as it happened, represented the starting point of two of the great rivers whose job was to empty the whole of Lesotho, and much of highveld South Africa too, of the billions of gallons of rain materialising from above; in the act, answering the prayers of those fearing ruin from the drought. No wonder we were wet.

On our third spiral, dear heavens, it was a torrent that we met. This was no longer the proverbial South African river we'd passed on the way up, defined as one that when you fell in it, you had to dust yourself off upon getting up. This was a river in angry spate.

And at the fourth level it was no longer a mere torrent, but a white-water rapids, a cascade, a wild cataract. It had broadened itself out to the size of a main road and was carrying down along with it a mass of loose rocks and broken branches. We looked nervously at our guide for reassurance – nothing that could perturb us showed on the face of our splendid stalwart.

Now we had to cross. First Douglas, reckoned to be the most intrepid of us, was sent over. But his horse had hardly got going before it was whacked by a couple of the stones tumbling downriver, and it turned back to the bank shaking its leg in pain. The animal wasn't seriously hurt, but was trembling; it had quite lost its spirit for adventure. We stood there at the edge of the waters, five of us on five horses, wheeling around and jostling one another. What to do now?

Then before I could realise what he was up to and protest, the guide had given my mount a hefty slap on the rump and sent us off into the waters, with me holding on inexpertly. My steed and I slithered, we stumbled, we skittered sideways perilously close to where the river fell away steeply, we whinnied, we shrieked 'hey, what the hell!' – and we managed to clatter up the other side just as we were running out of road.

I hauled myself off the animal, breathing heavily, and looked back across the noisy river. Now I saw the guide steer Bloke's mount after me in the same way, straight into the turbulence. They slithered and stumbled, just as we had done, the horse skittered sideways, being forced down to the very edge of the narrow flat ford, the horse whinnied, Bloke bravely kept his mouth shut, the horse felt for its footing – and couldn't find it. Its right rear leg went under it, it toppled bodily over the edge and down into the torrent. It rolled over, over and over, Bloke under it; within seconds they had disappeared into the rushing waters and were being hurled down river.

From both banks we watched in terror. They were gone, man and horse! They could never make the safety of the bank against the downhill force of the river. Then came a final glimpse of the horse wheeling around on its back in a sudden whirlpool, its heels pointing up at the heavens, bobbing down river on its way to the ocean. But no sign at all of Bloke.

This was the ghastliest thing! He was surely dead already, drowned or head bashed against the rocks!

But now I caught a sight of him in his brown cape, his back to us, flung against a massive boulder about 30 metres lower down in midstream; he had clutched at it and was holding on, arms flung around its stony girth to stop himself being washed off again by the hungry current.

I waved crazily at the others: it was no good shouting, you couldn't hear anything above the rumble of the rolling rocks and the rush of the water. On each side of the river we scrambled along down the banks until we had drawn level with him. I could see I had no chance at all of getting a hand to the poor fellow. The other three, though, after a moment of indecision, made a chain of themselves, our African guide anchoring himself to a tree on their bank, then Douglas linking on to him and Mervyn at the end, well into the river but being thrust away from its centre and tossed back against the bank by the fierce spate. He tried to cast out his mackintosh, rolled up to extend its reach, but Bloke couldn't get near it. Each time he reached out for this lifeline it got yanked away.

Now there was a further sudden fear. Bloke's boulder began to rock on its footing; the weight of the water tumbling down, with his weight added, jolted it until it threatened to tilt right over. Any moment it would crash into the heart of the commotion and carry Bloke along after his dead horse. What hope for him?

At great risk of being struck by uprooted trees or tugged away beyond his strength by the current, Mervyn persisted. And at last Bloke's desperate, outstretched hand grabbed the tail of the mac. He let go his hold on the boulder and threw himself at the bank.

They had him out now, wrapped him up and sat him down on a rock next to the horses, to recover from the shock and the wetting. I could see Douglas seated beside him, with an encouraging arm about his shoulders, but from my side I couldn't communicate with them to find out if he was hurt and to ask what they thought we should do now – and I wondered what to do myself.

My position was difficult. They were marooned there in their sector and I in mine; if I went on and down I'd find the next point where the river crossed and it would surely be in still more of a tumult, gathering spill-off all the time. Eventually they made signs: camp down and wait. That was all very fine, but how? The tent was with them, strapped on Douglas's pony. Worse, the tools and cooking gear were in the guide's saddle bags, and worse still, the victuals in Mervyn's. In mine there was nothing but our clothing, most of it due for the laundry, well due.

There was nothing to do but to rig up a sort of bivouac, stretching my mac across two broken branches and packing down a heap of the clothing beneath to sop up the wet. When evening came I curled up on this damp and smelly pile. Across the way I saw a campfire had been started and cooking was going on, for they possessed the matches too! I had to be grateful for a couple of oranges they managed to sling over to me.

There was little chance of sleep with rain pelting down, trickles of it seeking me out on the ground. Through my mind raced thoughts of life back at home and affairs at the office. Can Themba as acting editor should by now have put to bed the last issue, and no cock-ups, I prayed. The cover picture we'd already selected. It was a winner; a close-up of two American women, the Wimbledon singles champion and her runner-up, kissing each other as the Queen handed over that famous silver shield! They were Althea Gibson, who was a black American, and her best friend Darlene Hard, who was white, exchanging congratulatory pecks on the cheek. The big point about it: Althea was the first black woman ever to win Wimbledon.

I hoped also that Can had worked up some good stuff for the following issue by now. I groaned, as I remembered that I was supposed to be bringing back the big lead story, but it simply didn't exist! All we had with us for filling a few pages was the moody picture-feature of Bloke playing cowboys with the Basutho, rather poorly shot by myself.

But oh, at that thought I suddenly sat up with a wild shriek, oh, oh, oh! They might almost have heard me on the other bank. Oh, catastrophe! Oh, ruination take it, even that story didn't exist now, for the camera and the spools of film had been stowed away for safety in *Bloke's* saddle bag and were now floating down the Caledon River, on their way to the Orange and the Atlantic Ocean. I lay there mortified,

I couldn't get this disaster out of my mind.

By morning the rain had backed off a bit and the river was much more under control. We could even make out each other's yells. The guide had decided the river was fordable, they told me, and was riding across himself to prove it. They then followed on his tail, and we got ready to continue downwards along the slippery bridle-path. The unhorsed Bloke was to ride behind Douglas on his roan mare, the sturdiest of our animals. As Bloke threw a nimble leg over to mount in the rear of him, Douglas observed admiringly: 'Too smart! You're not such a bad old Basutho after all.'

Bloke acknowledged this with an insouciant wink: 'Listen, man, Doug, I just put on a show, I didn't never have that sort of ancestor at all, I'm not from here, I'm *northern* Sotho, Sepedi really – no mountains like this. But I thought what the hell, I'd like to do the story.'

The slope soon flattened out and the river chose a smooth, gentler pace as its banks broadened out. Now we had a different problem. Although the river was wild no more, there was almost 100 metres width of it. How to get five men across on four horses, since even the roan would not be able to handle the double burden while swimming?

We solved this the way the canoeist of fable did when having to make a river-crossing with goat, fox and cabbage. He couldn't leave the goat alone with the fox or the goat would be eaten, he couldn't leave the cabbage alone with the goat or it would be eaten, and he could only take one item in the canoe with him at a time. If he took the fox first and left him the other side, that would leave trouble behind him, if he took the goat first and then the fox or the cabbage to deposit with him, either way there'd be trouble. Deadlock. And the solution? He took the goat, left him alone on the far side, then went back for the cabbage, leaving it now on the far side but taking the goat *back to side one again*, before picking up the fox and leaving him with the uneatable cabbage. Then he went back for a final trip to fetch the goat. So here, at the broad Caledon, the four of us had our horses swim us over, then the guide returned with my horse swimming empty beside him, picked up Bloke and the two of them borne on one horse each, then rejoined the party.

Even that wasn't the end of our problems. When we'd handed back the horses, settled with Ntsu for the lost animal and driven off in the Chev, we found the floods had bequeathed us more trouble. On the way in the dirt road had itself looked very much the proverbial dry river bed, but now on our return that too had become a muddy river. This meant many detours and delays, so in the end we arrived back in Johannesburg two days later than scheduled.

That in itself carried a further highly unfortunate consequence. It meant that Jim Bailey had left the country for abroad before he and I had found a chance to talk about the magazine and a new crisis that had arisen for it.

I could read immediately from Can's depressed face when I'd trudged upstairs to my desk that something had gone wrong and that there was much to discuss. He was grievously behind schedule with the next issue, but there was worse – quite disturbing news about the issue that had not long before gone to press, if rather late, and was now printed. He'd had to carry out a distasteful order from Bailey, which as associate editor he hadn't felt he possessed the authority to resist. On Bailey's instructions he'd killed the cover picture, lest the government take offence at seeing a white girl kissing a black – ja, on a magazine read by kaffirs – and we'd surely be banned. So a harmless last-minute replacement went on the front page instead.

'It was an utterly repugnant thing for me to do,' Can said, 'and a picture the punters would have loved! Sheer violence to my system and to the blessed mag's.'

'Sheer murder!' I exploded. I was terribly upset, infuriated at this flouting of editorial independence, no surer way to corrupt a magazine's integrity. But what was I to do about it now, the paper was printed and out and Bailey was away abroad?

This was a mighty important issue; ours being a political paper we couldn't have a proprietor taking this sort of decision. He had the right to argue and he had the final right of sacking, but he could not order up the editorial he wanted or didn't want, nor could he order around my second-in-command. I simply would not tolerate such a heavy insult. Who then was editor? I sent him a cable of resignation.

I meant this gesture very firmly and finally. There was no possibility of arguing the matter through because of his absence and no other way back. That was it. In my cable I gave him a reasonable term of notice so that he could find someone to take my place.

For my part I started to make immediate preliminary arrangements to take ship with the family to England.

There was a nice brouhaha in the press about this crisis at *Drum*, mostly supportive; Ruth First, the wife of Joe Slovo, in particular, in her journal, made a good old fuss of it. The Nationalist press got hold of the story too and as expected were very abusive and confrontational, but I had never, in a long professional and disputatious life, found any topic on which I could see eye-to-eye with them. The battle would continue.

Perhaps this was the right time to be off anyway.

for pictures you'll be proud of
you need a BROWNIE camera

*here's the way to get good snaps—
just point the camera and
press the button!*

BROWNIE
Cresta
CAMERA

Six-20 Brownie Camera Model I
Two large viewfinders—you can take your picture either upright or lengthwise. Takes eight 2¼" x 3¼" pictures on 620 Kodak film.

PRICE £2.0.0

Six-20 Brownie Flash II Camera
This camera has a built-in portrait lens, so that you can take close-up pictures of your friends and family, as well as ordinary snapshots from the usual distance. Gets eight 2¼" x 3¼" pictures on one roll of 620 Kodak film.

PRICE £2.7.0

Six-20 Brownie Flash IV Camera
You can do so many things with this camera! There is a built-in close-up lens for head and shoulders portraits, a yellow filter to make white clouds stand out against a blue sky, and with this camera you can also use a Kodak flashholder, so you can take flashlight photographs too.

PRICE £2.12.6

Simply fit the Kodak Flashholder and you can take snapshots indoors and after dark.
PRICE £1.6.6

This camera has a built-in close-up lens for taking close-up pictures. It also has a built-in filter to make clouds stand out in the sky. And you can take flash photographs indoors or at night because the "Cresta" camera is fitted with contacts for the Kodak flashholder (extra). The shape of this camera makes it easy to hold in your hand. To take pictures you just press a button. It is so easy, you will not shake the camera and spoil your pictures. Takes 12 2¼" x 2¼" pictures on a roll of Kodak 120 film.

PRICE £2.2

If you cannot get supplies in your area please write to your nearest Kodak branch:

always use KODAK
Verichrome Pan Film
for better pictures in any light

Brownie Cameras & Verichrome Pan film are made by Kodak. "Kodak," "Brownie" and "Verichrome" are Registered Trade Marks.

Kodak (SOUTH AFRICA) (PTY) LTD.,
P.O. BOX 735, CAPE TOWN
P.O. BOX 763, JOHANNESBURG
P.O. BOX 1645, DURBAN

BLOOD TROUBLES *GO!*

ACTION 1

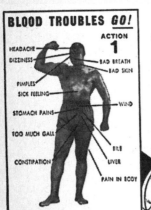

HEADACHE
DIZZINESS
BAD BREATH
BAD SKIN
PIMPLES
SICK FEELING
WIND
STOMACH PAINS
TOO MUCH GALL
BILE
LIVER
CONSTIPATION
PAIN IN BODY

Lewis's "TWO-ACTION"
MASTER PILLS
bring health and strength to men and women

Lewis's two-action Master Pills correct both kidney and blood disorders and relieve all the troubles shown on these two figures.
Just take two pills at night. Next morning you'll feel well and strong—ready to enjoy a healthy, happy life again.

ONLY 2/6 for 24 pills

"TWO ACTION" MASTER PILLS

IN THE RED & YELLOW TIN

KIDNEY TROUBLES GO

ACTION 2

RINGS UNDER THE EYES
WEAK AND TIRED FEELING
BACKA...
LUMBA...
KIDNE...
RHEUMATISM
STIFF AND SWOLLEN...
BLADDER TROUBLES
BURNING URINE WATER

NOW WITH SUPER POWER

Two-action Master Pills now have new SUPER POWER to make your bowels work EXTRA well the very next morning and your water will change colour as the poisons are washed out of your kidneys.

Lewis's "TWO-ACTION"
MASTER PILLS
EXTRA STRONG BLOOD PURIFYING AND KIDNEY PILLS

Ask for them at any chemist or store.
You'll be glad you did.

DISTRIBUTORS:
South Africa: Westdene Products (Pty) Ltd., Dept. No. 591, P.O. Box 7710, Johannesburg.
Central African Federation: Geddes Ltd., Dept. No. 591, P.O. Box 877, Bulawayo, S.R. Price: 3/- per tin.
East Africa: A. H. Wardle & Co. (Uganda) Ltd., Dept. No. 591, (next to Service Stores Ltd.,) P.O. Box 1671, Kampala, Uganda. Price: Shs. 3.00 per tin.

FREE PROOF

Prove for yourself the health properties of these new two-action Pills with Super Power. For a SAMPLE just write to your Distributor.

16. THE SHERLOCK OF TEMBULAND

In the weeks before leaving South Africa I determined to have one last hard search for the person who'd struck down Henry. Had we really paid enough attention to Mpedi's airy auguries and the soothsayings of his *tokoloshe* from Tembuland with their tales of some mystery middle-man?

I would nag Can to go with me to find the person at whom the delphic finger had pointed. If that wasn't the actual perpetrator of the deed, at least he might know who was responsible.

After work one Friday I put it to Can. 'Oh,' he said, waving away this request of mine rather lightly, 'forget it, just forget it, Sylverstar, man, I already unearthed him.'

'What!' I said with excitement and some annoyance at his holding it back like this and some admiration too for his insouciance. Nevertheless why hadn't he done anything about it!

'Well, nothing to tell. The same stale old trail again, Syl my friend, I fear. It led right back to Pinocchio, where it started. The dear old *tokoloshe* of Tembuland had merely re-broadcast the old original rumours, which he'd picked up long after anyone else, still echoing around the airwaves; and Mpedi, thinking he was onto something new, re-circulated them once more, but they were nothing more than the very whispers we'd heard at the wake.

'Nevertheless, although he got the message late, he brought to bear on it his native divining skill, and that of course is of real value, being in the final construction the application of intuition harnessed to good, sound common sense, exactly the technique used by the pipe-smoking *sangoma* of 222b Baker Street. Medicine man and detective: they look and listen for clues and rumours, fasten on titbits of hearsay picked up here and there, some dropped unconsciously by the very suppliant or 'client' himself when telling his story, or jolted out of the suspect by a bit of mumbo-jumbo that gives it extra authority. They then work up their theory, considering motive, opportunity and so on in the classic way, and solve the whodunit, coming up with a startling revelation or accusation. At which point they pounce, and manipulate a confession out of a scared, passive and superstitious suspect, enough to hang him.'

Can pronounced his own verdict in peroration: 'However, in this case, m'lud, our African Sherlock had simply smelled out a very stale old scent indeed.'

I was deflated. Then I was elevated again, for Can got up, put on the rakish hat he was affecting at the moment, chucked away the match used to pick his teeth, and called to me, imperiously, 'Come on, in any case, let's be off, where's your Chevvy?'

I was stumbling along beside him. 'What for, what for, where are we going?'

He grunted. It turned out that in spite of the stated scepticism he'd been affecting, it was indeed Pinocchio we were going to visit. Perhaps he really did know something, Can said from where he was sitting, for discretion's sake, in the back seat of the Chev. 'Perhaps there might be something,' he admitted grudgingly.

We swanned around the remnants of Sophiatown all evening, from shebeen to shebeen, but Pinocchio hadn't been seen anywhere. We determined to stay on the job the whole weekend, trying out the moonshine in every hideout and speakeasy in the place and all those in neighbouring Fordsburg and Vrededorp as well. 'Aha,' Can came out with at last on the Sunday night, 'how silly of us ... I know, I know, I know where the little creature must be hanging out, aha, stupid!' Can, bright to the last, on top of his form in spite of all the drink, while I was at the bottom of mine, said confidently: 'We'll find him in Madame's.' He laughed: 'Of course, I should have realised, Western Native, scene of the crime.'

So we set off again. 'Pinocch's a complex little fellow,' said Can as we drove along the tramlined road to Western Native Township, which was neither Johannesburg proper nor yet Soweto but somewhere between the two, 'he's very complicated and abnormal ... for a start he doesn't act anything like what he looks like.' He was right. Here was this very tiny jazz-groupie, so small he made even Casey look as if he was on stilts. When my wife Jenny first saw him, she couldn't help muttering in a motherly way, 'Shame!', that South African phrase that can be translated as 'Sweet!' in an Englishwoman's mouth.

It was his size taken with a wrong decision early in his musical life that had got him where he was. As a lad he was very musical and had embarked on a promising jazz career, but took up - what a mistake – the trombone. You can imagine the picture, the dwarfish fellow with a long, long brass instrument – being the bass trombone at that – and his short arms propelling out further than they could reach, needing help from a push-stick. The audience couldn't help sniggering, if in the nicest way, but he took it personally and simply could not perform adequately. Instead he drifted into the unrewarding profession of groupie.

Yes, Shame!, or Sweet! ... but sweet he wasn't, which is what Can was implying in the scornful tone of his voice. He had a jolly and impish look, certainly, hence his name, with a mouth that turned up at the corners in the cheeriest way, and cheeks that bulged over his eyes, giving a wrinkly, smiling look. But in fact he was no wag, not at all a cheerful personality, always gloomy and downbeat. Here was a paradoxical guy – upturned looks and downcast character.

'He's such a pessimist,' said Can, as the car lurched this way and that with the tramline ruts, 'that if he was rich as rich, he'd be exactly as defeatist as ever, you can hear him saying I may be rich but I still have to face the worst thing in life, waking up in the morning, and you can't alas hire anyone to do that for you. Another thing: for all his connection with the rough and tough and the Spoilers, he's a funk. I hereupon name him a tiny turd from a tall ox.'

Certainly Pinocchio showed some symptoms of fear when we tracked him down to Madame's, and sat beside him with our fifth Pin-Ups of the day swilling round in the tin mugs in our hands – and one supplied to him too.

'Gesondheid,' Can toasted him. He said nothing.

'Would you say the man who murdered Henry did it through his girl friend?' asked Can.

He sat frozen and didn't reply. 'Through Henry's girl friend if you like,' Can repeated.

'Well, I can't say,' said Pinocchio, 'I can't say whatever, Mr Themba.'

The madame bustled past, giving the oilcloth on the table a swish with her vadoek (cloth).

'Gesondheid,' repeated Can, ignoring this intrusion and deciding to sit and wait for something to come out of the Pinocchio guy. Can sat and sat and filled the time by picking at his teeth with the end of a match.

First nothing at all from Pinocchio, but once his tin-openered can had been emptied and filled a second time, a very slow and nervous apology emerged, 'No, well ...' But finally he had to talk. 'All right, I'll tell you this dream, Mr Stein, Mr Themba.'

Can replied for us, with a sneer. 'No, come on, Pinocch, I don't want to hear any of your tripey dreams. I'm of the belief that the dreams of a genius are of greater value than the dreams of men of lesser IQ. If so, by corollary the dreams of a mere Pinocchio will be of very little interest at all to anyone.'

'No,' Pinocchio said again, in timid, self-deprecating vein, 'not me, not my dreams, Mr Can Themba, this one what I'm going to tell you is the dreams of Mtetwa.'

That was one of the Spoiler gunmen. But Can dismissed this just as lightly. 'Sound and fury signifying nothing. The dreams of a tribal soothsayer would be more likely than Mtetwa's to enlighten us on what life had in store for us – and death.'

'It's his, it's his, it's Mtetwa's dream, he tole me to tell it to you.'

'Bah!'

Pinocchio said slyly: 'It's about you, his dreams, hey, Can.'

Now we were interested. 'Oh, so? Mmm, okay, go on then,' nodded Can, shouting for more hooch for himself. His can was filled.

'Ja, well I'm sorry, man, boss, but okay I'll tell it.' He addressed this to me now, as if he was scared to tell Can direct. 'All right, in this dream there's this line of round things like footballs hanging down together next to each other from strings, all in a line, twisting and swinging a bit and sometimes they bang into each other. When you come closer you see they're heads what's hanging on the pieces of string. Hollow heads.' Pinocchio pauses, and looks even more apolo-

getic and has to make an effort to overcome his fear before he contin-
ues. 'No,' he says, 'it's all right, they're not bleeding or anything'.
Quite nice. Then you look harder and you see who they are, the heads.

"The main one is Mr Themba's, then next to him is Mr Todd
Matshikiza's, then Mr Bloke Modisane, then Mr Casey Motsisi, then
Mr David Sibeko – a big, heavy face like he's got – then Mr Nat
Nakasa, then Mr G R Naidoo, then Mr Gwigwi Mwerbi, then a lady's
head, Miss Hassim, then Mr Fatman.'

This seemed an extremely curious and horrid thing to us, causing
me anyway to shudder.

'So now,' Pinocchio went on, 'you see Mr Stein, Mr Themba,
someone who you can't see who it is comes along with a big baseball
bat and he swings it and swings it with all his muscles and hits out at
the head of Mr Themba and splits it into a couple of pieces full of
blood and knocks it off until it rolls on the ground. Then he does Mr
Todd's head, hits out at it with a heavy *knobkerrie* (knobbed stick) he
picks up when the baseball bat has got broken to splinterers, then Mr
Bloke's, then the others until there's nothing left on the strings, and
they all roll in a crooked way along into the gutter where all the time
there was already lying three other heads that's now got themself covered with all the blood that's splashed down. These ones are Bob
Gosani and Johnny Mau Mau and Bob's uncle Henry Nxumalo.'

He has finished the dream. 'I'm sorry, hey,' he adds awkwardly,
squirming around like a spider.

We say nothing. Can sits there, still picking away very slowly at
his teeth, with a pin this time, then parks the pin in the lapel of his
jacket, gets up, says 'Jeez!' in a shattered tone and walks out, with me
hurrying to follow.

'No, sorry, sorry, sorry,' Pinocchio shouts after us, 'sorry, hey, but
I just want to tell you that one of the heads gets smashed is my own
one, Pinocchio's.'

FREE!

New United Catalogue illustrating
OVER 100
Swiss Watches including Invicta, Lanco, Roamer, Rotary, Buren, Benrüci, Bentley and Elgin
OVER 110 DESIGNS
in Wedding and Engagement Rings, and other jewellery
Write TODAY for this great FREE catalogue

All these watches have unbreakable lifelong mainsprings and written guarantees.

MONEY-BACK GUARANTEE

We are so sure you will be satisfied with your purchases, that if goods are returned to us within 7 days, we will refund the price in full.

15/- Monthly. Men's Swiss watch, 15 Jewels. Beautiful design. Written guarantee. £6.10.0. Deposit £2.10.0.

20/- Monthly. Men's Attractive Swiss watch. Shock, water and dust-proof. Long second hand. Written guarantee. £8.10.0. Deposit £3.5.0.

10/- Monthly. Swiss watch, sturdy and handsome. Shock, water and dustproof. £4.10.0. Deposit £2.5.0.

Ladies' Watches: Same makes available at same prices.

UNITED WATCH & DIAMOND CO.
(PTY.) LIMITED
P.O. BOX 3978 — CAPE TOWN
VISIT OUR TWO SHOPS WHEN IN CAPE TOWN

Dazzling-Bright
WASH FOR LESS WORK
AND LESS MONEY
WITH
JAVEL

A little Javel in the washing water makes all your white things dazzling-bright, sweet-smelling and free from germs. Stains and dirt come out without hard rubbing. Javel is strong—you use less, so you save money.

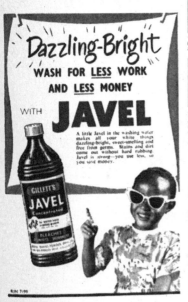

GILLETT'S JAVEL Concentrated

F 2058

Get HEALTH and POWER

This was me a short time ago. Troubled with backache, tired and weak. Not enjoying work or sport.

My friend Ben said "You want De Witt's Pills. They clear bad poisons out of your body and make you fit."

So I got this

Kidney & Bladder Pills
ONLY 1/9
New Trial Size

RESULTS IN A FEW HOURS

With my own eyes, I got proof. De Witt's Pills worked fast on my kidneys and my urine changed colour.

All my pains gone now. I feel so well, full of POWER for work or sport—thanks to De Witt's Pills, the wonderful tonic medicine that makes you fit and keeps you well.

Stop BACKACHE JOINT PAINS ACHING MUSCLES KIDNEY & BLADDER TROUBLES
with
DeWitt's
Kidney & Bladder PILLS
for POWER

ASK FOR
BOXER
TOBACCO

BOXER 'N' BRAND PIET RETIEF TOBACCO

For SMASHING STRENGTH and GLOWING HEALTH
GET DR PAGELS PILLS

Women Love and Respect a Strong Man

If you are weak and run down, and would like to be as strong as a lion,— then you must get DR PAGELS PILLS to-day.

Gilbert Nhasito of Johannesburg says: "I was weak and thin and very worried about losing my job; until one day a good friend of mine told me to try DR PAGELS PILLS—to-day I am HEALTHY and STRONG—thanks to PAGELS PILLS"

Dr. Pagels Pills have given thousands both men and women instant relief from ... Overweight, Rheumatism, Stiff and Swollen Joints, Backache, Lumbago, Burning Urine, Rings under the eyes, Frequent getting up at nights, Sciatica, Blood impurities, and Weakness.

Dr. Pagels Pills act directly on the kidneys, and after using them only a few times you will feel full of power and your blood will pump with refreshing strength.

Remember there is nothing else just like them. Show this advertisement to your chemist or dealer to make sure you get the right thing.

Write for FREE Sample

2 6 PKT.

Trade enquiries: P.O. BOX 4603, JOHANNESBURG

Small 25 Tablets 2/6 · Medium 60 Tablets 5/- · Large 140 Tablets

17. THE DIASPORA

The Rule of Law

Moses!

The Voice had called him back. It was the Voice of ' '.

MOSES!

In its tone he sensed concern. I'm still here, ' ', Moses replied. Don't worry!

Don't worry, it echoed? I am worried. With you nearly dropping the parcel of Tablets! So, this is what I want to say: here's some of them I altogether forgot to hand over.

No problem, ' ', I'm still here near you.

Yes, a nice little extra set of tablets I forgot to give you, said the Voice. You can understand I was worried a moment.

Quite so, ' ', said Moses, I'm here to help.

It's the tablets for Roman-Dutch Law, Mo. They're especially for South Africa! A perfect set of laws, my boy, very ancient and all the same very modern. And I nearly forgot!

' ', I can handle that still, Moses reassured him, taking it from ' ', He piled them on top of the rest. As he staggered down the mountain with his load of laws, the Voice called after him, to explain in detail the great value the Roman-Dutch statutes could be to a shotgun government:

*Readily divisible into one law for the poor and one for the rich.

*Doesn't make too much of the Ten Commandments.

*Quite adaptable to the Christianity of the Dutch Reformed Church.

*Provides in the small print for conviction without trial.

*No need for sticking to conventions of international law.

*And if necessary ...? If necessary the whole collection can be thrown into the garbage can – and with strict adherence to the rule of law!

We hurried away from *Drum* and South Africa ... we sneaked away, we scampered over the border, we sailed away by sea. One after the other we gave up the impossible struggle against the implacable churchmen in jackboots, to seek our luck in a freer world.

The editor was first to leave. Should it rightfully have been me who was the one to lead the diaspora; was that the correct protocol when abandoning ship? Perhaps not, and it was not intended that way, but in the end I'd been pitchforked into action unexpectedly by the quarrel with Bailey, which also ruled out my earlier agreement with him to go in the first instance to Nigeria for a year to put the West African offshoot of *Drum* on its feet.

This precipitated a very packed final few weeks of crisis for me and my family, at a time when the crisis in South Africa itself was coming to a head. It was late 1957, the Treason Trial was trailing on and now the big bus boycott had started. For weeks Johannesburg's African workers, tens of thousands of them, men and women, were walking to work each day the eight or nine miles in and out of town from Alexandra Township rather than pay increased bus fares. The government was infuriated by these independent-minded ("cheeky") commuters and threw its full support behind the bus company, Putco, which had the effect of turning a merely commercial boycott into a major political matter, and provoked bloody skirmishings between the blacks and the police and army. Sympathetic liberal-minded whites had been using their cars to ferry women and the disabled home in the evenings – the police attacked them too. Driving the family car, Jenny, always defiant in the face of authority, tried to crash through a police check barrier with her contraband passengers. The police cursed her, she bravely heckled them back and they locked her in the cells.

This rather put my nose out of joint, *I* was supposed to be the family hero as well as the bread-earner, though in the end of course I was proud of her. All I could boast of in the way of brave deeds myself was to have my camera smashed once more by the Special Branch and be threatened with arrest for a satirical 'situationer' despatch to the *London Evening News*, whose local stringer I was.

We threw a series of crazy, farewell parties in those last days ... and

there was more police intimidation. Most of our friends were
detained at the Treason Trial or were under house arrest or on 'Ninety
Days' imprisonment. My youngest child Alex was admitted to hos
pital for an emergency operation at that very moment, I was scrambling in the early mornings to finish the manuscript of my next book,
to be smuggled out of danger of seizure together with the manuscript
of Bloke's book and have them placed with a publisher in England.
Finally there was a love affair to be tied up, a car-parking offence that
had become very confrontational and was now set down for a high
court hearing ... there was the putting down of our aged ridgeback dog
who couldn't come abroad with us ... the sale of the thatched *rondavel* cottage, unfinalised as yet two days before our departure ... and the
farewells to our dear retainers. A mad and merry crescendo.

We drove down to Durban, singing all the way, in a truck piled with
life's belongings, our papers, our memories, not to mention one or two
matters still to be sorted out, the unravelling of the big, unsolved problem of the Mr Drum murders, the grand plans to overthrow the regime.

Now we were beside the mailboat quay at the port of Durban,
alongside E Shed, from which I'd set sail during the war, on that occasion steaming slowly out past the 'Lady in White' (Perla Gibson), a
large white patriotic lady dressed in a long, flowing outfit and singing
Land of Hope and Glory to the troops through a speaking trumpet.

E Shed was a well-known landmark, the departure docks for the
Union Castle liners – at 3 pm every Thursday since the start of the
century. Now we were at the close of that comfortable era, almost the
last to leave by the weekly mailboat sailing. It was the end of an age
of romantic travel, of no hurry and no stress and no airport babble, of
shipping off 'home' in the mauve and white-painted liner that slowly
eased away from the dock as her brass band played Gilbert and
Sullivan. Paper streamers linked to friends ashore were tugged from
their fingers to flutter down into the churning water of the harbour.

The port doctors had already cleared us for the voyage, the Harland
and Wolf engines were throbbing, our twin screws were throwing
gouts of discoloured water against the concrete of the dock wall and
the ship's siren was hooting our farewells. And suddenly there was
stress after all. Up the last remaining companion ladder, already

roped to a huge hook dangling from a quayside crane, came charging, two steps at a time, a pair of police officers. They were met at the top by the bearded first mate, and from our position peering down over the bulwarks two decks above, we could see him after some palaver escort them inboard.

The passengers were enjoying the drama. Aha! it must be to do with illicit diamond buying, South Africa's most romantic crime. Or they were on the track of the men who'd stabbed Rosie Dry, the brothel-keeper, last week, or was it no more than a passenger discovered without a ticket? Rumour buzzed, the children nagged for information, then we saw the ship's bosun in faded navy-blue Union Castle jersey and sailor hat with ribbon threading his way along the crowded deck and heard him calling out where only minutes before he had been crying 'All ashore wot's goin' ashore, all for the shore, ladies and genl'mun!', now singing out my name in the same monotone: 'Mr Stein, passenger to Southampton, Mr S R Stein.'

Oh!, we shuddered. This was a fearful thing to have happened, when we thought we'd made a safe getaway. The Special Branch ... at last they were after me then, I'd be a hero after all, I'd be added to the Treason Trial accused, I'd get a dose of Ninety Days, I'd be arrested and electric wires applied to my toes to frighten the names of co-conspirators out of me? What to do, what to do!

I was led, Jenny hastening after me, into the purser's office where the policemen were waiting. We were shut in, away from the public gaze. I stood there, wondering what it could be, worrying how to handle it, would they take us all off the ship, what would befall the family?

The police played an exceptionally courteous game for once, no doubt due to our being in front of the British ship's officers. 'Mr Stein? Mr Sylvester Stein?' – Yes, oh god, yes, oh guilty – 'It's my duty to serve papers on you on behalf of police headquarters, Transvaal...' – Tr-Tr-Tr-Transvaal? – 'regarding an offence under the General Laws Amendment Act.' – W-w-what, wh-which section? – 'Section G, sub-section bis ii, motor car parking laws enforcement.'

I was astounded and relieved, and indignant – and now extremely courageous. 'Car parking?' I snorted, 'Oh, no, damn it, I can't believe it!'

'Mr Stein! No sir, Mr Stein, it's not that offence you are charged with, but contempt of court, refusing to return the warrant issued against you by the Witwatersrand Supreme Court and to subsequently attend for the hearing of your parking offence.'

This was still quite worrying, it was not such a trivial matter, failing to turn up on the orders of a judge in the high court. That was something else I'd been rather pleased at, cleverly sneaking away without attending to this little bother nor shelling out on a fine.

'Come now, Mr Stein, I am Lieutenant Stevenson, S.A. Police, Natal, and I am serving you with the warrant in person, and I ask you to sign for its receipt.'

I signed, what could I do, though the doughty Jenny of course was at my elbow, scolding away at them and ordering me not to sign without a lawyer.

'Well, thank you, sir,' said the lieutenant, taking the paper gently from me and packing it away with others in his wallet, 'that will be all. I expect you will hear from the Witwatersrand court officers in due course.' He and his number two saluted me, if you please, saluted Jenny, turned around, saluted the captain and the first mate too and clattered off at the double down the gangplank, which was soon enough skied high up in the air and swung clear of the ship's side, allowing her to sail out over the bar and past the Point into the open ocean roadway, where half a dozen vessels were already riding at anchor waiting to enter harbour early next morning.

Last touch!

The Editor was first to leave. Correct practice or not, it was the signal that all was over, the others hurried after.

Some called it the chicken run. In all the years of oppression to follow, there were friends and political allies who never quite forgave us for going. Even Oliver Tambo, president of the ANC, who was stranded outside the country when the final crackdown came and was ordered to remain outside as his organisation's emissary and carry on the struggle from abroad, came in for some back-biting from men who had to spend years in jail, though these did not include Nelson Mandela and responsible leaders.

After my departure Zeke would be next to go, then Arthur, then Bloke, who'd left Sophiatown just in time before it left him, when it was given the full and final Hiroshima chop by the Nationalists in pursuit of their government's commitment to the Group Areas Act, apartheid's legislative jewel. Bloke Debonair Modisane left the country by the backdoor dressed as an uncouth 'naytiff', ready to behave very bravely – no longer a timid man – and if nothing else was left for it, to hitchhike north up Africa, with the police on his trail.

Soon *Drum's* Todd, Gwigwi, Lewis, David Telephone of the PAC, Peter Magubane, Nat and others were to follow, some before the Sharpeville shootings, some after, some hoping to settle in other regions of Africa, others making for England or the US. And with them were going the stars we'd written about, the singers, jazzmen, sportsmen, politicos: Miriam, Peggy, Dambuza and the Manhattans, Dollar Brand, the Isaac Stein soccer family, D'Oliviera, Resha, Joseph, Nokwe, almost the whole of our dramatis personae. And Jean, the English backroom sweetheart, who remained an influence in the years to come, though not always with the happiest outcome in spite of her love and sympathy for the crowd.

The most notable of the steadfast ones choosing to remain were Can and Casey and of course Jim Bailey, though he had easy access in and out to Britain, and Jurgen. Would all be forced to leave in the long run? On the other hand would any who did leave later change their minds and make the return journey before the eventual great metamorphosing moment of Mandela's release and the freeing of South Africa?

In those first years Can would be remaining on as ruler of a roost that hardly existed any longer, he and Casey holding court over its ruins and over the ruins of *Drum* in the special world they'd helped to create, though no longer so original and so true to its period, and no longer in Sophiatown.

The rest of us would be trying out a new world.

PART THREE

TOP LEFT:
Arthur Maimane.

TOP RIGHT:
Todd Matshikiza.

LEFT:
Casey Motsisi.

18. HOME BOY

Very early in the morning a large, heavily-patched army great-coat wriggled and wormed itself along the inside of a wide concrete pipe until it was sticking quarter-way out into the frosted Transvaal air. Any military tailor present would immediately have set the coat down as dating from the Boer War. Even the patches on it had served an honourable lifetime, and had been pensioned off or patched in their turn. The coat lay still for a moment; than, having satisfied itself that no one – not even a military tailor – was present, it cautiously owned up to a head.

The head made further researches into the surroundings on its own account and confirmed its satisfaction. It was a small head, covered with black wiry curls (known as peppercorns), and connected internally in some way to two skinny, black hands, which now emerged from the sleeves of the large coat for the purpose of being blown upon and warmed up.

Then the coat shuffled right out of the piping and stood itself up on two cracked sandshoes, while the hands retired inside the sleeves again. The whole object began to jump up and down inside the shoes for a minute, to generate more warmth, until it was encouraged to take the next step.

The head, in charge of operations now, arranged for the concrete pipe to be slid back into the mound of assorted rubble from which it had been projecting like a gun-barrel from a pillbox. The patchwork greatcoat thereupon marched off in a military sort of way to Johannesburg.

The tattered khaki coat was the sole personal property of Staffnurse (commonly pronounced Stuffness) Phofolo, an African youth, and the dugout at the end of the pipe was his sole personal residence. As the coat was four or five sizes too large for its inhabitant it gave the appearance on the march of

*moving along on its own, a trace of black peppercorn visible
above the collar.*

*Staffnurse was a vagrant, we are sorry to say. In terms of the
law he was idle and undesirable and had no pass. He wished to
work but as soon as he found a job the law picked him up and
ordered him out of the urban area – because he had no pass to
seek work. He would then find himself out of work once more,
and was then picked up for being idle. Somehow he thought the
system was not running smoothly.*

from *Second Class Taxi*
by Sylvester Stein

One by one we received them in London, the *Drum*
refugees following in our steps. Landing on our feet in a splendid house at Primrose Hill, myself a newly-published author, knowing
everyone that mattered and a lot more who didn't, we were able to
help our old friends meet new friends and make useful contacts, find
them somewhere to live and join us in creating again in London the
Sophiatown social whirl. The parties, the songs, the laughs, the *kwela*
dances, the drink! British guests at the parties stood in clusters at the
doorway of the big living room, watching entranced.

One of these noisy affairs was to launch my novel about Staffnurse,
the Non-European from Non-Europe, who gave free rides in his taxi
to the bus boycotters. The book went down well with the literati and
my English friends and with most South Africans, but not as easily
with my black colleagues, who found it a bit condescending, *liberal*
even, which was just about the worst calumny you could work up. I
understood more clearly over the years what it was that grated on
them, and this understanding helped me in the end to a deeper intuitive feeling on the racism question. No Uncle Tom-ism, no patronising, no treating of the blacks as objects of charity and kindness! No
part acceptance or half-hearted compromise, but full equality, all of
us members of a single family.

They were correct, of course, and equally correct in their censorious attitude to the political liberals, who would never fully accept the
principle of sharing out their democracy equally – one man, one vote

– until it was wished on them right at the finish, brought in by De Klerk if you please, sitting supposedly on their right.

Despite that one reservation, our old friends and colleagues were pleased enough to have me publish the first apartheid satire, satire always having ranked as one of the strong cards of *Drum*. And they were as affronted as I when within a week of publication it was banned in South Africa; the satire, gentle enough really, nevertheless jabbing the government censors too sharply in the ribs. When my friends' books came to be published, they were banned in turn, every one of them. One couldn't have blacks meddling in culture.

Among the first of an avalanche of these books from *Drum* was that by Bloke, stowed away in my swag on the voyage to England. British publishers were eager to take this on, and to accept many more. It was part of the honour shown to our exiled men once they'd arrived: they became in their early years in London the toast of the literary world, meeting famous writers, being invited to speak to literary institutions and being dined by academia and the aristocracy.

From over the ocean came offerings from those who'd stayed behind. Can and Casey sent me tales of irony to be included in an anthology, and submitted articles for a proposed book, 'Illegal Living'. There was a diminishing flow of this work, though, and a slowing down of letters from them about *Drum* and telling of their own life at the margin.

Those, along with Modisane who took the exile path to Britain, bringing their manuscripts and their families, included Mphahlele and Maimane (after a stay in Ghana); Malcolm and Jean (after a stay in Kenya); some such as Matshikiza on the wave of fame and money that accompanied his musical *King Kong*; others nervous and not at ease, and at least one in police charge, and he the very first to follow me into Britain, and a hanger-on at that, and a quite unexpected one to be turning up there.

Announcing the arrival of this man was an unusual herald, John Dankworth, the leader of a jazz band. He telephoned me one day at the *News Chronicle*, where I was the science reporter, to introduce himself and to say that there was a black South African musician who'd just arrived by sea who was hoping to work with him and his band. But first he needed Dankworth to stand bail for him following a little drama on the voyage over, and he'd given JD my name as a reference. A year or two back the Dankworth Seven had done a tour of South Africa taking in the black townships, and it seemed this man had been at all his concerts. Now he fancied a job as an instrumentalist and arranger in the new Dankworth big band.

'Oh, yes, is it Gwigwi?' I prompted, quite ready to be helpful. Gwigwi, musician as well as *Drum* worker, had been planning to get away abroad and bring with him his township arrangements plus a wild, waltzy triple-saxophone composition based on that genteel number, *Tales from the Vienna Woods*. 'Benjamin Mrwebi?', I added, seeing that the name Gwigwi didn't strike any recognition.

'Mrwebi?' repeated Dankworth, making a poor go at pronouncing the guttural (Mghwerbi it should be), 'no, I don't think so ... a trombonist,' he added. 'Don't know his official name.' He had a good laugh at himself for his oversight: 'Didn't think to ask.'

'Oh, you don't know,' said I surprised. 'H'm, the trombone, eh, the trombone?' This definitely didn't fit Gwigwi and his sax and wasn't much of a clue to placing anyone else.

'Yes, trombonist, could double as singer.'

'Tromboning, singing, arranging ... ?' I mused, running over the music pros I knew.

'Anyway, calls himself Pinocchio.'

'Aha, aha!' That was my initial, surprised – frightened – response, putting me directly on my guard. So little Pinocch was aiming to pursue the profession of jazzman and jazz groupie in Britain, was he – that was the assumption I made – or was that just as a cover for something else?

Pinocchio, it turned out, had arrived via his own style of cut-price travel package, stowing away in the Union Castle mailboat. Discovered when she was two days out, he was put in irons and after making Southampton was given up to the police. The only thing he knew about Britain was Johnny Dankworth and he'd waved that name about as a talisman when questioned. JD appeared at the court hearing to stand recognizance for him and when freed drove him back to London. Two evenings later the three of them, Pinocchio with John and Cleo Laine, John's lead singer and new wife, turned up on my invitation at that launch party of *Second Class Taxi*.

Little Pinocchio hastened to scramble out of the taxi on Cleo's heels and show his readiness to be allies. 'Mr Stein,' he said, shaking my hand the ANC way with an outstretched finger over the palm, and looking up at our five-storeyed Victorian house: 'Man you got a nice little *pondokkie* here.' That, however, was the only joke he made. Although on his squitty face there was still that upturned grin and twinkle, it soon became apparent that in his heart as ever reigned a mournful darkness, even blacker than of old, for I think he had already begun to understand what a cold, cold world he had let himself in for, in spite of the hot doings at the party. It seemed to him that the cold in the streets was caused by some never-fading cold in the hearts of the British, rather than the other way around. 'England,' he said with a grimace, 'it's same as Africa, man, only exactly worse. Things is all downside up when you get over the Equator. It's cold here when it's hot in Africa but then man it's still cold here when its cold in Africa.' He'd discovered the British summer.

When you think of it, he'd voluntarily exposed himself to enough hardship to make anyone depressed and murderous. At home on the Rand, judging the hopelessness of ever being allowed a passport or if given one of ever being able to pay the fare, he'd tucked himself, a small black almost invisible bundle of a chap, under the rods of a train to travel the 1600 kilometres to Cape Town. To sustain him he had used what was left of his life's savings on a packet of dried raisins stuffed into his one pocket and a handful of monkeynuts in the other. Finding his way from the smoky marshalling yards where the train was shunted after arrival at the Cape Town terminus to the harbour area, he had got the help of a black stevedore to sneak him aboard a docked liner – due to sail for a UK port, by very good luck – slipped under the tarpaulin lashed over a lifeboat swinging in its davits and huddled himself up in the stern sheets, prepared to spend the next 17 days living on the remnants of his tickeyworth (3p worth in old money) of nuts and raisins and the smell of tar.

As Can had often said, Pinocch was a dim though complex character, downside up himself in all ways to what one expected, and always anticipating the worst outcome. 'If he'd been a weather forecaster,' Can used to jest, 'he might have announced one day on the best advice that the weather would be bad and then be most unconsolingly upset – the worst has happened! – when it turned out bright and sunny against his prediction. No happy enjoyment of the good turn of luck.'

His pitching up in London was certainly worrying at first. Was he here with some fell purpose? Was this the long arm of the Spoiler Gang still out to get at us? Or had he helpfully brought over some mystical newsflash from his home-town witchman, some clue or rumour about the Henry Nxumalo case? But, no, poor Pinocchio, no messenger of evil or of good was he and no danger to anyone but himself. All the sinister side of his power had been knocked out of him fetching up in this strange and drizzly land – 'The Queen of England, long to rain over us!' he sniffed. In spite of bringing along a small bottle filled with river water from near his home to keep him in touch with his supporting spirits, it seemed that they too couldn't do the business while standing on their heads and didn't manage to save him from his fate: he endured a few sad, uprooted years loitering around the jazz clubs before eventually succumbing. In the end it wasn't to be any weather prediction that turned out to have hit the nail on the head too precisely for him, but a prophecy of grimmer consequence – yes, his own skull did roll in the gutter.

I don't suppose there was one of us from that uninhibited land of Africa and those uninhibited circumstances that did not find the English way of life punishing, penalising and oppressing. As much as anything, of course, it was due to having one's roots yanked out of the home soil and then without the help of roots being required to settle to a new way of life and forge a new success in an environment suited to the needs of other makes of humans, races who'd been adapted to it over centuries. Music-making was an instance; we needed it and we didn't get it in Europe. This was because, for Africans, even us whites brought up in Africa, music and dance was not just music, it was a huge dollop of life itself, it was a whole, meaty chunk of one's existence; not merely something academic and intellectual, it was what helped to pump the blood around the heart. As was dancing. Something about the way African bodies worked demanded music and dance from the earliest years. I have a picture in my head still of a group of half-clad black five- and six-year-olds on the verandah of a house in Sophiatown aimlessly playing around, then of one of them dressed in nothing but a vest that didn't quite reach down to his navel, beginning in an absent-minded way to wag his naked brown backside in time with a song he sang and to kick his pudgy legs from side to side. Others joined in, until all were quite effortlessly and naturally launched into a jive routine, chubby legs crossing over from left to right, the lot of them swaying together in perfect time, left and right and right and left and left over right again and right over left in a twinkling chorus-line, wobbling in rhythm like one single plump, shivering brown blancmange.

Perhaps that's one explanation of why the professional musicians and dancers were hardest hit in this transplantation. I saw them stream in to set up life in Britain, the great stars of South Africa, yet hardly any of them found their feet. I'd followed the career of the greatest, the Manhattan Brothers, a team of singers, from 1955. At that date they were already celebrating their 21st anniversary as a four-man group. That this should be so seemed utter fantasy to a white man – who the hell were these people one had never heard of even, one thought patronisingly? Their 21st anniversary indeed! Yet to the black community they had long been famed stars, and on the first occasion that I came across them myself, appearing top of the bill at the farewell Johannesburg concert for Father Trevor Huddleston, they instantly scored a tremendous win with me. I shook my head – here they were in my own country, as great a jazz team as any of those I'd admired in the US, yet I'd been quite unaware of their existence and of their very records, which sold to the South African blacks by the lorry-load! Blacks to us as ever were the invisible men.

Dambuza Mdledle, their giant leader who was chosen to play the title role of King Kong in the smash musical, first in Africa and then in London's West End, went on to work the clubs and cabarets of Britain over the years that followed, together with Joe, Ronnie and Rufus, his partners, but they achieved no further big hits, no fame, no real public acclaim in all that time. I was one of a sad last handful who went to Dambuza's burial in Hackney, an out-of-place cockney-style funeral, with a black nag pulling a coach decorated in flowers that spelled out his name Dam-Dam. He died a disappointed man, a sunny man in an icy land.

In America it was different for musicians. You could see how very different, from the story of Miriam Makeba, she of the glorious voice. She arrived in London, with the Cape pop-singer Sonny Pillay as her partner. I brought her to meet JD and he did his best, throwing a party for this great jazz lady so that she could meet all the chiefs of entertainment in Britain. The only notice taken of her was to be offered a 10 minute slot on Television West and Wales. TWW – why, I could have auditioned for that myself, belting out varsity songs in my own rusty rugby voice.

The truth is the British do not assimilate strangers easily, they are slow to warm to someone new, slow to invite new neighbours in to tea – suspicious is it, grudging, unenterprising, sceptical? Well, Miriam wasn't going to spend a lifetime working her way to the top in that jazz-cold climate and turned to the States instead. Within weeks she was auditioned, taken up and promoted by Harry Belafonte, then splashed on national TV networks; her *Click Song* became a hit, a world hit – a hit even in Britain – and she embarked on a quarter century of fame. As for Sonny, that lean, dark and handsome Coloured man, I never heard of him again. On the other hand Hugh Masekela, a young trumpeter, protegé of Father Huddleston, went directly to New York to take off on his long and celebrated career.

The rest of us all had our times out of water. Not educated to the sophisticated standards of the British, not able to read their subtly-coded messages, disappointingly out of our depth, we couldn't properly adjust to life here. Nor could any of us cope with the sheer numbers, life in the antheap, one among so many impersonal millions. In Johannesburg or Cape Town one would meet everyone in one's circle every so often walking down the main street, or at public functions, or friends' parties. In London you might go 10 years without cannoning into your acquaintances. If you did not cultivate the orderly art of networking you would soon fall out of touch, endure a sorry and unfulfilled time and finally disappear, your ashes more than happy to settle for an early scattering.

Many of our exiles felt the draught and trekked on, only to become wanderers over the face of the earth. For some *Drum* men this would already have been their second move – they'd touched down first in Nigeria or Ghana, looking to be clasped to the bosom of Mother Africa, granted a hero's welcome, since *Drum*'s reputation as daredevil challenger of the obnoxious white man had spread across the continent. Thousands of readers in West Africa had written to our Henry Nxumalos, our Can Thembas, our Arthur Maimanes, hailing them as martyrs and allies in the common struggle.

Not a triumph though but a shock was awaiting them, there was no really happy landfall even in their own continent. Stepping ashore they found no arms open wide to receive them as heroes of the black race, they were treated as if aliens, as if ethnic others – heaven help us, as if they were whites! That was a most hurtful, chilling response, to be branded expatriate, no closer kin than the European conquerors and settlers.

Before long they moved on to join the others of us in the UK, and some still not finding a footing there, moved again to the next square – US, France, Italy, Germany, Ireland.

All kept on hoping, kept on searching, though inside most there would begin to burn as the years dragged by a desire and an ambition to go back to their own country and there solve their problems as well as hers.

A Message for "DRUM" readers

from America's newest star discovery— your own

MIRIAM MAKEBA

Yes, fellers, it's me
Miriam ... the girl f
Mofolo. I'm writing
from 8,000 miles a
... from New York
where the people
couldn't be kinder. T
tell me my singing is g
over big ... that I'm r
But though it seer
dream, it's all real enoug
me to stop for a mor
and remember the pe
who helped me to get s
Like the people who r
President Giant Cigare
They've always be
the background helpin
and of course, they c
forward when money
needed to put "King Kong
the stage. I need hardi
you that "King Kong"
my big chance! Yes, we all h
lot to thank President Giants fo
quite apart from their wond
cigar
So, if you chaps want to do M
a favour ... smoke President G
... and you'll be alright b

19. RETURN OF THE NATIVE

They wait for those who never return
for those who come to die;
they wait for those who flee
the arch tormentor
to wander under alien skies.
They know each time
the sweat-fire fear despair
of birth
and cry 'Who will atone who will atone?' –
each time
the ogre thunders down the thoroughfares
of freedom lovers:
who like Naledi
stand and wait and give and pray –
I offer up my tale
for you to sanctify.
from *The Wanderers* by Ezekiel Mphahlele (Macmillan)

All night through a gusty wind had been gathering up litter from the roads only to send it bowling away down the pavements. The paper cups tumbled and bobbed along as if they quite enjoyed being out on the town, while the empty shopping bags let themselves be ballooned high up the fronts of the buildings, an exhilarating experience for them. But for those of us on the streets it was not pleasant at all, a wet and windy, grey and grimy morning.

The litter, the weather, the broken pavements ... it could only have been London. It was North London, Camden Town in fact, close to our home at Primrose Hill. We were meant to be waiting back at the house to receive a dawn taxi from the airport. But instead we were out on the chilly town, searching for a neighbour's missing dog, roaming around shouting 'Scottie! Scottie!' into the wild wet wind. That was the moment when the taxi did arrive, carrying Zeke, who was to become Es'kia, and Rebecca his wife, and with them Theresa and the rest of the family – all the way from West Africa but no one at the house to greet them and give them breakfast.

They found it somewhat uncaring of us, and Zeke was to record it in his writings, a rankling little paragraph. It seemed to him not very different from the South Africa he'd left behind, where dogs took precedence over blacks.

The chill didn't last long, however. We soon flew back to greet them, with our mission accomplished, then the men carted in the bags while the womenfolk sauntered arm in arm into the house, the children lingering behind to chatter together eagerly under the huge untidy buddleia at the front steps and to laugh at their previous meetings in such different circumstances. The children matched one another in age, Zeke and I having ourselves been born only a month or so apart.

Zeke before entering had blinked through his glasses up at the house with great admiration, head tilted right back to take it all in, and had hit on the same joke again as Pinocchio's: 'You know, man Syl,' he said, frowning and smoothing his palm slowly over his closely cropped hair in his characteristic absent-minded manner, 'you've got a fine little *pondokkie* here.' He giggled politely: 'Heh, heh, heh, a fine *pondokkie*.' He shook his head in a measured way, in admiring disbelief. 'Ja, man, I tell you, a great *pondok*, Syl.' He giggled again and slapped me on the back. 'I shall call it Schloss Stein.'

He and his family now joined ours in the vast breakfast room, a massive cube of a room, as high as it was long as it was wide, and big enough to have swallowed in one bite their own little *pondokkie* in Soweto. To remind them more cheerily of home there hung in the air as we seated ourselves at the refectory table the lovely and familiar whiff of slightly burnt mealie-meal porridge, which we had cooked in their honour as an African treat – and there safe and sound again was Scottie the next-door dog, leaning his jaw on the children's knees, his dewy eyes looking upwards at them to beseech his share of this nice-smelling foreign stuff. We were friends again, all of us, South African blacks and South African whites – and curly black Scottish dogs.

We sat down to gossip about times past and to wonder about those

to come. First, sitting on two high-backed wooden breakfast chairs
pulled round to face one another, Jenny and Zeke talked together, their
heads bent intently forward. He had always found her a fine source of
advice on his writings and his career, for they had an excellent understanding between each other and he appreciated Jenny's judgments
about people and valued her powers of intuition, which helped her to
read the dramas in her friends' lives with uncanny accuracy and spot
any mischief lying in wait behind the arras. She came out with it all
in very a matter-of-fact manner while she poured herself cups of tea
from a big brown teapot. This faculty of hers of second sight evoked
amazement among people, being put down by some to bewitchery, but
in fact it was no more than the outcome of simple, speedy reasoning
processes in the conscious and unconscious, starting with guesswork
of a high order and continuing with shrewd analysis and the pressing
into service of a memory that could call up matching items stored
away inside circuits of the brain quite remote from one another (in the
manner of a well-trained data processor of today). Common sense
would then follow to provide the bottom-line answer, through the
identification of meaningful links and suspicious pressures, and to
conclude with the throwing up of original strategies for moving forward.

There was her characterfulness too, which attracted those like Zeke
who thought and felt deeply – she herself had feelings that reigned at
high intensity over long periods, feelings of abiding loyalty for those
she favoured and of unforgiving enmity for those who blundered off
the path of true virtue. Nor was there an easy way to avoid knowing
which lot you fell into. No sabre-toothed tigress and not malicious
ever, she yet could be censorious and would not suffer fools gladly,
with the exception perhaps, one should add while yet pooh-poohing
what might be implied in such a benighted thought, of her own
husband.

Then Jenny and Rebecca talked together. Rebecca, known by
friends as Ribs, was a big, handsome woman, dressed for the occasion in a double-breasted suit of stiff white material with a black
buckle to the belt and a large black bow-tie flopping out of the top of
it, but she was nervous about whether this was right for London, and

with Jenny being something of an authority on dress, she didn't wish to show herself up as too much the country bumpkin. Jenny, despite her familiarity with form and fashion, rejected their dictates for her own purposes and was dressed that day as always in absolutely her own style, in warm browns and golds. Zeke could have competed with the two of them, being robed from throat to ankles in a gorgeous Kente cloth brought with him from West Africa. Only I was in bland European livery of coat and trousers, shirt and tie.

The women then engaged in a dress-memory contest, not too concerned about the uproar reaching us through the house from the front garden where the children were playing a highly competitive skipping game on a square of paving, with Scottie the dog clamouring in a non-stop fit of yapping for a chance to get a jump in too. Jenny simply walked through to fling up the high front-room window and through it sing out to the kids: 'Listen, you lot, keep the street gate closed. Don't let that stupid Mr McBarker get out!' This was lest the over-excited Scottie dash into the road to hurl himself against the passing cars. She called out also to the dog, ordering him to shut up instantly. He gave her a sidelong look, held his peace for a second or two, then went on barking but without allowing any noise to come out of his jaws – an eerie sight.

In the grown-up's contest Rebecca scored first: 'Hey, man, Jenny you remember that purple thing you came along in that day for Ezeke's BA?' She laughed at the thought. '*Purple!*' she joked, '*purple!*' She was referring to the unsuitable ensemble, in great-aunt style, that Jenny had appeared in at Soweto township for Zeke's graduation ceremony some years back. Thereupon Jenny countered with a photographic description of the dowdy frock – small white spots on blue, the unfortunate missionary pattern – that Rebecca wore the day they had first met, a year or so prior to that.

They were a pair of remarkable observers who not only made critical inspections of the outer trappings of a person but also of the character of the one residing within, and of the thoughts floating around inside that person's mind. Rebecca could be seen at her study of personality attentively scrutinising one's face. Whether she divined as much as or more than Jenny did in these examinations, is uncertain.

Anyhow on this day, her hand resting on the warm giant teapot ready to supply herself with further cups, or leaning over to grip Rebecca's wrist tightly in a gesture of affection, Jenny went on with her virtuoso act, recalling exactly what *I* was wearing when she had first met me in London just as the war ended, all of 15 years before. This was not a very taxing feat of remembrance, to be truthful, for she had gone with Arthur Gavshon, a friend in his own right of each of us, a South African – Jenny herself was English – to get a first view of me without my knowing it, and I was in quite eye-catching gear. They'd come to the Old Vic theatre to see Laurence Olivier in that historic post-war production of *Oedipus Rex*, and there I too was on display, in a walk-on part, having taken up the stage a bare month or so earlier, after coming out of the Navy. Gavshon had hopes of making a match between us and pointed me out to her when the curtain went up, an aged Greek beggar. She was there to give me the once-over before committing herself and it seems she must have approved of what she saw, though this could only have been through an outstanding effort of clairvoyance, as I was hidden behind a grey, extremely bushy false beard and inside an all-embracing ragged black toga, altogether not the smartest of outfits though memorable enough, for she did let herself be persuaded to come round to the stage door afterwards for that first meeting and must have judged the omens favourable enough to agree very shortly to a more permanent arrangement.

To keep an eye on the excitable dog and the smaller children who might also be tempted to rush blindly out into the street, the talk between Jenny and Ribs had adjourned to the floor-to-ceiling window at one end of the front living-room, as true a cube as the breakfast room and even larger and more grandly set off with golden Georgian mouldings, a bronze chandelier and a massive fireplace, while Zeke and I came to sit in the corner, discussing *the* problem, of course – the eternal South African problem, a subject never left undebated in any gathering from our country. I was much more anxious to hear of any news he may have brought about our old companions, being somewhat fearful of Can's fate in particular, but no, we started straight in on the main course, politics.

Zeke normally took a more nationalistic stance than I did. This was not merely because he was an African and I wasn't, for there were whites with a strong feeling for the PAC and for black national-ism, such as Benjamin Pogrund, author of the standard life of the PAC chief, Robert Sobukwe, who with Mandela and Steve Biko was one of the three most noble leaders of their people but also because he, Zeke, was inclined in the direction of Africanism through instinct. For my part, I, a rationalist in all things, would consider dispassionately all points of view in a case and would thus inevitably end up, after being pulled in every direction by every possible faction or force, landing plump in the safe middle ground.

'No, that's very undermining, my boy, you undermine your own strength if you're going to be so darned considerate all the time,' Zeke criticised me gently.   Then he scowled, not so gently: 'Remember they're mostly *skelms* and *skebengas* on the other side, anyway, with bad, bad ideas.   Don't let them get away with it! Don't, Syl!' I had to admit that it really was a weakness in a person's nature to be like this, ready to accommodate all viewpoints, to give house-room to any half-way and superficially sensible contention, being ready therefore to temporise, negotiate, stumble around in No-mans-land and in the end completely overdo the reasonableness, right to the point of grovelling for mercy – instead of staying strong and adamant, right to the very edge of ferocity. Who will win who cannot show teeth drawn back fiercely?

I turned over this home truth in my mind, slowly and deliberately, not caring much for the conclusion arrived at, which sapped my self-confidence. Zeke, waiting patiently for this thinking process to work itself through, scratched his own head meanwhile to dig out more points for levelling at me.

I was accustomed, in establishing my personal principles (after all not so overwhelmingly meek and mild and toothless in spite of this admitted characteristic, I defended myself at that moment), to pay close attention to what Zeke had to say. He was one of three people arguing from three different points of view that I would at all times listen to with care. Another of the three was, as it happened, that same Arthur Gavshon, our go-between of years gone by. Since my acting days Gavshon and I had met and re-met again over many years,

both in London and Cape Town, where he was sent as diplomatic correspondent of the Associated Press of America to cover the periodic
crises in the SA Parliament, and where I was working as a Press
Gallery reporter – this was before I joined *Drum* – so we were able,
in a great long *tête-à-tête* of a debate, continually adjourned, to challenge each other's ideas and keep mulling over our own, and eventually firm-up our individual opinions about the way to set things right
in South Africa.

Gavshon was a quiet, serious man, and rather shy in his manner,
though that was not to say he couldn't heartily appreciate a joke and
even now and again crack one of his own, just a bit apologetic for the
daring. He wore a military moustache, small and a bit crumpled-up,
his face seeming too narrow to accommodate anything of greater
breadth. To be frank this moustache did little to give him a fearsome
look; a more effective piece of male equipment was a pipe shoved
between his teeth though never actually alight, for the reason that he
would be sitting there, a preoccupied frown on his forehead rehearsing his next thought with care lest it come out too precipitately ... and
concentrating, concentrating, concentrating, by which time the match
held between his fingers an inch or so above the tobacco in the bowl
slowly burnt to an end, until – ouch! – it needed to be waved out very
suddenly.

Gavshon's great quality as a journalist, apart from the penetration
of his thinking, was complete discretion; he never whispered a word
of what was told him in confidence, and though always chasing
rumours he never started one. He became in later years a greatly valued confidante and adviser to the leaders of the ANC and of other
groups fighting the regime. Few people knew of this work of his
behind the scenes.

Zeke's contribution to the debate came from the heart, he felt the
way to move forward, with true instinct as well as intellectual application. Gavshon, though, would sweep his arguments away when I
trotted them out, to state very categorically what he held to be a proper unemotional appraisement, a cool world view.

The third viewpoint that in later years I would always give serious
credit to was that of Joe Slovo, who became one of President

Mandela's closest and weightiest comrades and one of South Africa's greatest men. He would sweep away both their sets of arguments, for being artificial, unstudied, having only ad hoc authority, lacking true grounding in the texts of the classic European philosophers and showing little understanding of what they had studied. His scorn for other views was clothed in a kindly manner, though it wasn't hard to divine his view that if they weren't built on Marxist dialectic they were built on sand.

When Joe, a bulkily-built man, always worrying about his waistline, which was plainly indebted to his habit of eating too much and left him agonising continually about whether he might get away with just one little bite more – when Joe talked, hunched up in deep thought in his armchair in the small terrace house backing on to a canal that he and his family occupied (with the grandparents squeezed in too), often his wife, Ruth First, would join in. Her point of view over the years began very slowly to deviate from his, and in the end quite sharply, as the course of events in the Soviet world unrolled and started to hammer a wedge between the various elements of the left. For Joe right into the 1990s the Communist countries remained a great and necessary source of aid for the outlawed ANC, whose Communist wing he led and for which appropriately he acted as unofficial ambassador to those Stalinist countries; perhaps this need to draw on their generosity was what kept him cleaved to the party line.

In the earlier decades of his exile, the mid-1960s and into the 1970s, things were very quiet for the ANC movement, both in South Africa where the membership had been emasculated by bannings – every leader jailed or rendered absolutely invisible and made voiceless by decree – and in the democratic world outside, which had not yet come round to a full and proper support and sympathy for the African cause.

By its bannings and other wieldings of the force of law the regime had seen to it that there was purely one-way argument or debate between itself and the resistance movement. While official gazettes proclaimed that it was illegal for Joe's words to be quoted or even so much as hinted at in the press of South Africa, it was on the other hand quite in order for the President of the Republic, C.R. Swart, to slander him at will, talking of the 'Snake that is threatening South Africa – and that is the Snake of Communism, whose head stretches across the seas to hide in England, and I want to tell you that the head of that Snake of Communism is Slovo and that head must be crushed.' In spite of such continual and vicious attacks on him, Joe on his occasional trips abroad and in his daily life in Camden Town took no security measures at all; he went where he liked, fearless and relaxed.

In those earlier years in London, Joe had time on his hands, more than he could use. It happened that I was in the same state of idleness at this period, travelling through one of life's little depressions, so Joe and I often kept ourselves busy with those substitutes for war, football and poker. Surprisingly, in the poker game Joe Slovo, acknowledged genius of tough negotiation, brilliant lawyer, subtle mover in diplomatic circles, was out of his depth. For all his straight face and tight-shut, thin-lipped mouth and his heavy deliberating, he convinced no one at the table. If he bluffed they called him out, if he 'had the goods' they immediately folded and left him with a minimal win, peanuts as the phrase had it. In the end he and Bloke Modisane, another member of the poker school, found themselves losing consistently, losing money that they barely owned. That was enough to make them judge it a dull game really – a pollyana affair Bloke named it, with an attempt at a derisive chuckle to cover up his hurt – and drop out of the school.

The Slovos had known Bloke, Henry and all of us in the old days and been regulars at our social affairs. So here they were again in London, family friends, the children in each family pairing off one by one. Their children were all girls, taking after their beautiful, steely-strong and highly intelligent mother. Joe's political activities did continue spasmodically in this period, though I never commented about them, keeping my mouth shut and my ears too. It didn't seem right to put questions to him about his clandestine trips, presumably to Eastern Europe and Cuba, or about the underground ANC guerrilla troops that he directed from afar – only later did he return to live in Africa, nearer the front line.

Meantime, Joe had to comfort himself with a very small audience

for his philosophical speeches, having to level at such as me his theoretical arguments on capital and labour and political cause and effect
and to quote Lenin on the class war and the national question. He
would quite floor me with those dialectics of his. It was all profound
stuff, and just because it was so profound I found it hard to digest, it
spilt off down my back without soaking in. Once out of my depth I
didn't try to follow conscientiously and so understood even less. 'No
come on, man,' he might grunt irritably, for he could see from the
glassy look in my eyes that I wasn't being the bright boy of the class.
Still, a little of this philosophy of his did in the end permeate beyond
my frontal bone to help me with defining my own position.

For the rest my thoughts were coloured mostly by my personal attitudes and interests – after all I was primarily a journalist not a politician. I thought of things in terms of stories and 'exclusives' and personal dramas. And nothing affected me personally more deeply,
nothing was more symbolic than Henry's death and the fate of my
other comrades. How he died, why he died, were the focal points for
me. A distorting and subjective standpoint, but it had a right to be
considered. As had the present dilemma, currently reported to me
from home, of Can and Casey. For Can had needed to absorb a number of very hard knocks – the girl he had loved was gone and he could
not follow her, all his colleagues had run off, the life was leaking out
of the magazine and he'd been banished from his milieu, his House
of Truth and all Sophiatown. Casey too, as his side-kick, suffered
from the side-effects of Can's depressions.

So when all the debating had been done, there we were, Zeke,
Arthur Gavshon and Joe, and I had to choose between our four very
varying points of view, and I needed to make up my mind precisely
what policy I should adopt, finally and firmly, so as not to be left
dumped helpless on my backside by this pull in diametrically opposing directions.

At least we four were united in one thing: whatever the ethnic,
genetic, Marxist or emotional arguments, the regime had to go.

On the day he arrived in England at the *pondokkie* in Primrose Hill,
Zeke and I had been again able to trade conflicting views while con-
firming this one certain area of agreement. I boasted of the commit-

tee we first few exiles had set up in the past years, later to become the Anti Apartheid Movement, but I think he found this too moderate a body to throw himself into. He was circumspect about attacking it, of course, in deference to our friendship, but you could read his intrinsic attitude in the very lack of enthusiasm he demonstrated for this body, 'a bit namby-pamby, Syl'. We were always having to read each other's thoughts like this because it was too hard to say certain things outright to one another over the barricades of the separate cultures we had grown up in.

Personal relationships between black and white in those days were still difficult and delicate. And it wasn't easy to fool one another, even by leaning over backwards – all that achieved was to make it obvious that one *was* trying to hide something. We dared not dig too deep into the unstated truths floating about in our minds, we still had half-strangled and distorting racial doubts and suspicions about one another, despite all the years working together to combat racism. *They* thought that we thought a black wasn't as good as a white, and we thought guiltily that maybe they were right and we did think so. I believed I read in Zeke's eyes what he thought he read in mine.

So now after that first hour or two of renewed political debate at Primrose Hill, our need for argument was satisfied for the time being and we could come to matters I regarded as being quite as important as politics, perhaps more so; I'd been itching to get down to them and I cleared my throat as a signal. Zeke cleared his too, a courteous response, it was the way the Zulu or Sesotho would show respect as a listener, by echoing the last words or even sounds of the one addressing him, thus agreeing with him, even if not actually being so very much in agreement, as the next words might immediately demonstrate.

In any case I now had the floor and broached the subject of the colleagues we'd left behind. Especially, because of my anxieties about Can, how was he, could he survive, and how were Casey and the others, was there any news arising from our pokings about in the matter of the death of Henry, and was the old magazine itself managing to get on without all the rest of us?

Zeke shook his head doubtfully. 'That Tom Hopkinson they say is being a bit of a blighter, Syl. A real bit of a blighter.' That sounded ominous. He read out to me from a letter that had come to him on his last days before leaving West Africa, a rare letter since one hardly ever heard from those people a continent away, taken up with their own local affairs. Tom Hopkinson, editor of *Picture Post* in its famous wartime days, later Sir Tom, had been imported by Bailey to succeed me as editor of *Drum*. 'Yes,' went on Zeke, 'he's got a problem with Can, has Tom, and he's being a bit of a blighter about it. Just a bit. It's the old problem, yes, the good old damn problem, it seems Can has taken to the bottle lately' – we both laughed at this euphemism – 'and Tom feels things are getting out of hand and he can't control him, and believes an editor must be an editor and act like an editor ...!'

'And he's reading the riot act to Can?' I asked. 'Yes, ja, no, that's just about it, reading him the riots,' he answered, in a worried voice. 'And he means it?' I went on. Zeke nodded his head bleakly: 'He means it for a definite fact.' It was foreboding, it was a sinister development, as if Tom were preparing the ground for something terminal. Zeke repeated slowly and anxiously, 'That's about it, man, ja ... no, that's about it ...'

'Nothing about Casey?'

'Nope, safe enough I guess, our Casey.'

The letter-writer had given this general interpretation of what was happening. Tom, truly great editor though he was, seemed more interested in cleaning up the paper – its typography and its staff behaviour – than in preserving its raw strength and bite and its cheekiness and power, and the efforts of its old warriors.

Jurgen too had found this clinical policy of Tom's a bit of a trial, and, by nature impatient of outside interference, he'd beaten a retreat, transferring to the news-picture department of the local big white Sunday paper. We laughed at this, Zeke and I, thinking how Jurgen's rebellious ways would surely soon make for a far bigger explosion when working with an authority many times more conventional than Tom's. Anyway, with him also departed from *Drum* there was hardly a single one of our old stars left to give the paper backbone. What remained was a crown without the jewels. Can, tottering in his seat, and Casey, always likely to totter wherever Can tottered, were about the only ones left to constitute the genius of the place.

Even Todd the musician, prize giant ruby in the centre of the crown, the witty, lyrical little fellow, whose broad shining grin, teeth parted in a huge smile, head thrown back, as this poet of jazz was always pictured, had gone. Even he; he'd been obliged to give up work as musician and journalist and take a job as razor-blade sales- man on the rough streets of Soweto. A poet and jazzer driven to razor-blading door to door! That's Nemesis for you, that's jazz!

A horrible twist it was, and Nemesis was already brewing up events that would lead Todd elsewhere and further.

Congratulations KING KONG

...we're proud PRESIDENT GIANTS played a leading part in your show!

The success of King Kong is now well known. After an amazing run in South Africa it is now going overseas, to the U.K., U.S.A. and who knows where next? But President Giant Cigarettes were in at the beginning. When King Kong was just an idea in someone's head, an idea that would cost a lot of money to present to the public, President Giants quickly came forward with money to make it possible for the show to go on. President Giants are proud to have been able to help launch this fine show, and still more proud of the wonderful success it has achieved. May its popularity grow even greater.

Where your pleasure and enjoyment are concerned, you can always rely on President Giant Cigarettes.

Photos: (top)
Courtesy "Zonk"
(Centre and lower)
Courtesy "Drum"

10 for 10d
20 for 1/8

PRESIDENT GIANTS

20. KING KONG, BRAVE AS A LION

King Kong - mountain gorilla,
King Kong - lord of the ring,
King Kong - heavyweight killer,
That's me, I'm him.' King Kong.
The greatest guy! The greatest guy!
King Kong! King Kong!
No other guy so wide and high,
King Kong! King Kong!

Now events in Todd's life were to take a different and better twist ... so it looked. As Nemesis riffled through his little diary of things to come he'd tipped Todd a cheery wink, pointing to where he was ordering up a happier future for him than razor-blading. Ah, the old deceiver!

There was, in particular, one wonderful event in the air that seemed bound to guide Todd, and with him all our party, up a far jollier road. It would surely influence the future in our favour and numb our personal pain at the loss of our colleagues as well as soothe our hurt at the searing public tragedy of Sharpeville in 1960.

It would take us forward in a very gay and positive way, this event, for it would make its entry to the accompaniment of African gusto and irrepressibility – and it was, in fact, immediately foreshadowed by the arrival in Britain of Todd himself, that most jovial, glittering and irrepressible of Africans, released at last from his grubby career in doorstep sales. He had decided to take the refugee route, encouraged by old Nemesis, and was bringing with him a mighty band of his comrades to put song and fun into the chilly hearts of us strays and exiles.

This happening was something real and something splendid. It was the *King Kong* show arriving in London in 1961, and with it the whole team, its 99 strong cast and orchestra straight from Soweto. This was not 'King Kong' the story of the gorilla and Fay Wray; this was the township jazz musical that Todd had composed, with Harry Bloom and Pat Williams as librettists. In Johannesburg its enormous success had finally knocked into all South Africa's heads the fact that inside their own country, on both sides of the colour bar, wondrous theatrical and musical genius existed. Now after a houses-full tour of all Southern Africa it was transferring to the West End, looking to go on to Broadway later. A triumphal way out of the apartheid prison for Todd.

King Kong, story of a heavyweight township boxer, was nothing less than *Drum* set up on stage. Music, dance, sport, politics, crime, *shebeens*, sex, township life ... the complete *Drum* cocktail. What's more not only Todd but many other ex-*Drum* men were in the company, even Gwigwi Mwerbi, the circulation manager finding a slot as saxophonist in the orchestra. All were taking the chance of freedom and cherishing hopes of fortune and lifelong fame.

So now, with the ANC also having set up a presence in London, almost the whole of our former wonderful circle was there. It was the high point of the diaspora. Invitations to meet the rich and famous rained down on our heads, and the rich and famous in their turn fished for invitations from us.

There was an open party one night at my house, a 'function' you'd call it, that turned out too popular for its own good. Organised by the anti-apartheid people, under the grand patronage of Lord Lugard, Gwen Ffrangcon-Davies, the actress, Lady Caroline Wedgwood-Benn and a pair or so of Cabinet ministers, it drew an unexpectedly huge mob of curious English socialites, as well as unrestrained numbers of our exiles who'd worked themselves up into a democratic fervour at the chance to shake the hands of the aristocracy they usually found so beneath contempt. Early on our three great living rooms were stuffed beyond capacity, with not a square inch of space for the drawing of breath let alone for dancing – and a queue of clamourous ticket-holders still arriving, to be turned back down the garden path again in another queue that bulged out through the iron gates and along the pavement towards the Underground at Camden Town. An enterprise smothered by its own success.

Aside from that flop, however, *King Kong's* fame and promise were bringing cheer, bathing us all in the spotlight and brightening our lives. Now that the show had opened in Shaftesbury Avenue, thought the optimists in the company, money and fame for each performer was surely guaranteed for ever. Let us celebrate immediately – and forever!

Todd himself threw a party of the township kind, high-voltage and non-stop.

The Matshikiza family was by now living in a basement flat up the road from me beside the green slopes of Primrose Hill, where two or three other old friends had already come to roost, each new family snuggling in beside the one who'd turned up just ahead of them so you soon had a nice little community squashed up together and continuing to grow around the nucleus of the first who'd been sent out to take shelter, as in the game of Sardines.

It chanced in that period that not one but two different sets of people had settled in the road. There were these South Africans of ours, and there was a second clique made up of Britain's bright new satire generation of entertainers and writers. They too had piled up very close on top of each other, another clump of sociable barnacles.

The two sets mixed happily together, soon making cross-colony connections. Eleanor Bron moved into a flat in my house; next door to us on the one side was Jonathan Miller, and semi-detached to us on the other was Sylvia Plath with Ted Hughes on the middle floors of a tall, elegant Georgian residence with a rather superior rocking horse in the front window (more than 30 years later it's still there, rocking away with that same supercilious look on its face, though of course Ted and Sylvia aren't); around the corner lived Bill Oddie; regular visitors were John Fortune, John Bird, Marty Feldman, the pop-eyed comic, Eric Idle of *Monty Python,* also something of a pop-eyed comic, Desmond Morris the *Naked Ape* man, cartoonist Mel Calman, the Dankworths, themselves *ex officio* members of that same jazzy scene, and Dudley Moore, then known only as Dankworth's pianist and not yet sanctified by Hollywood. This crowd of neighbours was invited to our festivities, that was the South African way.

There was a quiet start to the Matshikiza party, a good omen surely, for how many quiet beginnings didn't we all remember that ended in wild and wonderful dancing and singing? On arrival I was offered a first drink by Todd, whom I found in ruminating mood, working up his impressions of the great city. Being sensitive to race matters, he had already smoked out aspects of apartheid that had followed us here. Laughing expansively, to show it didn't *matter*, he told me how he'd gone to a barber shop in Camden Town but been turned away. 'I'm afraid, sir,' the barber had said to him coldly, refusing to pin his clean, white sheet around this black man's neck, 'we don't handle your sort of hair.'

Todd sniggered bitingly: 'He's *afraid*! Still I'm sir to him, anyway mind you, my dear sir, yes man, yes sir, I'm known as sir, one of the untouchables or not!' He guided a pint of beer past his moustache. 'And, hey, Sylverstar, what do you think of this, it's ghettos again here too, we're back living in a ghetto of our own again, all us blacks fenced in together.'

'It's only sardines,' I grunted. I had to admit to myself, though, that it truly was a ghetto, building up apace in the wake of the Sharpeville massacre as more and more of our colleagues tumbled into London. But I played it down, now the patriotic Londoner. 'Just only the sardines game,' I said again.

'Huh?' came from Todd, eyebrows rising up slowly, though his eyes twinkled beneath. He shortly got my point, however, while maintaining his own, even extending the metaphor further. He saw the effect as part of the bigger waves of blacks and other immigrants from over the world moving into north London, each ethnic group segregated into its own territory. 'First impressions from a traveller making notes of local customs,' Todd said to me, laughing in his hearty way, head flung back, with another drink preparing to find its way through the moustache, that bristly moustache that seemed so much a part of his laugh as well as his drinking. 'Look at the map of London here, Sylvestapol my boy, these English natives have got it all worked out very nice and pat to keep the interlopers off; there's all these separate little boxes, with tell-tale names pinned on each of them: they've packed the Caribbeans away together over in British West Hampstead as you might say, then there's the Jews up in Golders Greenstein, yes very nice and pat, specially designed for them, it could be Golders Greenberg either, and finally behold ... there's Belsize Parkistan and there's Muslim Hill!'

Now there arrived the soignee Pat Williams, who'd written the lyrics for *King Kong*, introducing her friend Desmond Morris to Todd. Morris, a large solid man, stood next to Todd, towering above him, while they looked out of the window across the enclosed yard at the 'view', an unlovely wall of faded russet-coloured old brick, only a few feet away and bulging inwards a bit, trying to come still closer. 'It makes me uneasy,' Todd observed of this rather claustrophobic London phenomenon, 'so near, it stops the air coming in.'

'Certainly a *bijou* little place you have here,' agreed Desmond giving it the kindliest construction.

'Bijou!' Todd liked that. 'And, hey, there's a bijou little cat strolling on it above us.' The cat now stopped and crouched there, camouflaged against the rusty background of the wall, a marmalade cat with just two legs dangling down, each foot and the tail showing white at the tips. 'At a distance you read it as a patch of small white roses dotted across a reddish creeper,' Todd commented.

Desmond was charmed by the lyrical statement. 'Absolutely,' he said, pulling a lock of lank black hair up across his brow and screwing up his eyes to see if he could call up that vision for himself.

'To be perfectly frank with you though,' – in some moods Todd was certainly frank, even confrontational – 'what we really need here, man, is not a cat but a dog. It would remind us of home, as we weren't allowed to keep one out there. A nice bijou little doggie.'

'You'd be much better advised,' Desmond laid down in a booming lecture-room tone, 'to have a very large, easygoing dog, such as a labrador; if you're going to keep your family pet in a very limited space, don't get a small, snappy dog like a corgi.'

'Done!' ... Todd replied, 'and we'll have just one very large bijou tree in the middle of the yard for its convenience.'

'Convenience!' smiled Desmond, seeing here a joke Todd hadn't intended. Todd moved away now to greet others, the place was filling fast. What Todd didn't know was that Desmond Morris at that time was curator of mammals at London Zoo just down the road, and that he had just learnt from Desmond one of life's great truths, – that a big dog is more restful than a small one.

One of Todd's kids came up, to tug at his father's coat, eyes shining, 'I just seen Paul Robeson,' he whispered admiringly. 'Everybody's here.'

'Everybody only not the Pope,' said Todd. He turned to me with a wink, 'it was *Robertson*, the TV man.'

'And only not the Queen either,' added the kid, one of his own expectations dashed.

'Just keep a watch out for her,' Todd said, packing him off. Then turning to me he said, 'This drinking gives me a thirst, what about another?' Before we could look round his wife Esme was there, pouring us each a beefy one; a good-looking and very self-possessed person she had been circulating through the party with a vast jorum of wine, donated by the Matshikiza's landlord, another of our South African 'sardine' neighbours, Ivan Stoller, an idle young millionaire and as it happened owner of the dog Scottie. The wine, cheap and cheerful, had a speedy affect in turning up the volume of the general chatter.

Suddenly, a shrill cry. From the corner where my wife Jenny was, arose something of a strident scene. Sylvia Plath, with whom she'd lately struck up a close friendship and who'd been talking to her and Bloke, had jumped up with a small scream in the middle of their conversation and dashed across the room and straight out between the crowd through the front door, to set off other little frightened shrieks from a woman she'd brushed past at speed.

'Sylvia – my God!' yelped Bloke too, his eyes popping out, 'what's she got the huff for, what have I said, what have I done? I never pinched her bottom or nothing nice like that.'

Jenny ticked him off. 'Don't always think it's on your account.'

'What's it then?'

'She's pregnant.'

'Pregnant! How can you tell?' Bloke was even more pop-eyed. 'And did she just suddenly find out? Who's it by, anyway, so quick? Not me!'

'Bloke, there you go again, don't always think it's you.' She pinched his ear in a teasing way: 'Get it? Get it Bloke?'

It appeared to have been another of Jenny's great inspired guesses. 'I simply said to her two of our kids couldn't come to the party tonight because they were kept home with german measles. She looked as if she'd been shot, jumped up suddenly and rushed off without a word.'

'Well, whyfore? What's she got against germans' measles?' asked Bloke, astonished. 'And how could that make her pregnant?'

'Because when you're pregnant – so you see she *knew* she was - it can harm your unborn baby to catch it.' Jenny spoke severely to him, as if he should have known better: 'So there you are, two plus two, it's simple. She's being silly though, how could she catch it from me when the kids're at home? H'm, so she's pregnant is she!'

Bloke rather muddled about all this, apologised for his stupid questions and played for a laugh, 'Hey, I better clear off as well, otherwise I'll get you girls pregnant too.'

We gratified him with a good round of laughter. By this time a crowd had come over to hear from Bloke and Jenny what it all was about. The Matshikiza kid, circulating through the party at his own lower level, had also quickly darted over between the knees of the adults to where the action was. To distract him, so that he wouldn't over-excite himself, Ivan Stoller, who'd appointed himself uncle to the family, put a friendly arm around him and said: 'Nice pink pyjamas you got there, sunshine!'

This had the effect of recalling Todd to his duties. 'Hey, you ... you should be in bed!'

'I can't sleep.' He was quite right, it had got very noisy. The flat was packed and everyone had something to say, or rather to yell. Things were still in a reasonably genteel state though, but now a second small sensation came up – a good thing really, a successful party is very much elevated in mood by such fruity and emotional real-life episodes, items worthy of gossip hatching out before one's eyes being of especial benefit.

This next business that raised the tempo was a noisy falling out between two of us, normally warm friends. Thus ...

On a battered green and red-striped sofa near the window there was sitting a party within a party, all squashed together across each others' laps, giving the sofa the look of an overcrowded life-raft in stormy seas. They were discussing contentious though highly intellectual matters. There was Arthur Maimane, Gwigwi, Dam-Dam, Robert Resha, the ANC man, Barney Desai, the Africanist, and Rose his wife, James Phillips, the vocalist who always led the singing of *Nkosi Sikelel'i Afrika*, Malcolm and Jean, Monty Berman, our latest refugee friend – and now Bloke joining them, squeezing down beside Jean and manoeuvring her up and over so that she sat on his knee. So then, he was still on the long chase to get closer and closer to her, was he – one day, his attitude seemed to show, who knows, who knows ...?

Arthur, one of those whom alcohol might befuddle but never destroy, consistent drinker though he was, was knocking it back busily and had put to these castaway mariners the proposition that Sol Plaatje, who in 1912 had been one of the founders of the ANC as well as the author of a number of books of high literary value, both fiction and polemic, could confidently be described as South Africa's greatest African writer. Arthur was maybe out to start an argument, though for a moment it didn't catch fire. 'Yes well, who else?' concurred most of the voices on the sofa. 'Plaatje!' Resha hailed him, lifting a glass.

'Yes,' said I, supporting the motion, 'agreed, agreed ... but you know what' – as a daring thought came to me – 'maybe you should group equally with him our own great Zeke.' Zeke, author of a series of fine and true stories of African life, his autobiography recently published and more books in the pipeline, wasn't to be embarrassed by this, he was abroad. It did the trick, though: my intervention brought trouble. It caused Bloke, poking his head out from behind Jean, to frown severely. 'No, no, no, you can't say that. Ridiculous – Zeke!'

'Oh, yes, it's certainly a bit ridiculous of you, Sylvervest,' Todd backed him. 'Our nice old Zeke, surely not, come, come, come.'

'No-no, *wag -'n-bietjie* (wait a little), don't object too quick. Look here,' I argued,' just judge the literary quality of the man. And though Zeke is still only at the start of his career, he already matches Plaatje: he has depth, humour, humanity, a wonderful line, a style of his own, and, most important of all, he has a theme. And he's no lightweight.'

That caused Bloke to wrench himself right out from under his pretty burden, brush her off him virtually – 'excuse me honey, excuse me'

– to stand up and expostulate very loudly. He actually exploded. This normally smiling, accommodating man let a wave of sheer, sneering laughter rip out of him – it was laughter not meant to be funny but derisive ... cutting. It was a great fortissimo outburst; I half expected the children to pop back out from the bedroom again. On Jean's face there appeared a sardonic and quizzical look.

What could have turned him so emotional and harsh, I asked, as Bloke went on making a fuss about it? I realised what it was: the great green god of envy hovering in the background. Behind the sour laughter, you could imagine Bloke asking the world, 'Am I not weighty too? Haven't I too a big theme?' It made him bristle, this praise for Zeke. The worst of it, I surmised, is that he must have felt that it was part true – that's what would have rankled the most. It's not to say that Bloke was not also a writer of quality, but he never achieved the poetry and philosophy and depth of feeling of those other two, Plaatje and Mphahlele. And Todd too, backing him up here as another overlooked writer, had wit and charm, but could not achieve the depth, the gravitas.

Bloke was sorely betrayed by this bitterness that showed under his usually engaging and congenial surface expression. And while he revealed personal bitterness, interestingly enough *Plaatje* had displayed none – was there ever more gentle and forgiving a man, although he'd had to labour under even greater obloquy in his life than had the Africans of post-Second World War?

I said nothing more, though, just packing away in my head the thought that what one had seen here was plain jealousy. 'How could you class Zeke so high and not me?' was what must have been passing through Bloke's mind. It brings particular heartache to feel one is being overshadowed by a peer and contemporary. Not to say that I didn't suffer a little soreness myself, I felt rather sadly that I would have liked to be classed as an African too, and thus eligible for the competition, with three or four novels to my credit, not to mention a textbook on running!

I switched to another subject, sitting down next to Dam-Dam – Nathan Dambuza Mdledle the singer who played *King Kong* in the show, that human gorilla – to talk to him about the big gumboot dance he did on stage and its origins at the Durban docks, where the whaling station workers would meet in the vast flensing shed and despite the turgid smell of whale blood and blubber, dance in wonderful unison on the greasy floor, doing their gumboot adaptation of the traditional barefoot Zulu war-dance. It produced a still greater slapping, stamping noise than did the original, it was very stirring and strangely flamenco in feeling, from Spain rather than Africa. Or perhaps where Spain first got it from was Africa?

In the years since that contentious conversation, I've often returned to the proposition, who's the greater and in fact the greatest African writer from South Africa, Plaatje or Mphahlele? Amazingly enough, to make it a fairer contest, it is not only Mphahlele whose publishing output has had a chance to grow and burgeon since that night, but Plaatje's too, in spite of his death having taken place long before, in 1931. For his early novel *Mhudi*, which had been issued in a private edition only originally, was given general publication in later years; his *Native Life in South Africa* became ever more widely known; and miraculously, his beautiful diaries of the 1899 Siege of Mafeking, where he had served as an interpreter, were brought to light for the first time, unearthed from an old family hut as long as 80 years after they were written and 50 years after his death, to be published finally amid great acclaim. What intrigued me was the style and tone of the text of that amazing diary, which, save for the fact that it was hidden from view all this time, might well have been the model for the characteristic sound and style of the *Drum* writers. Presumably there is something particular and intrinsic in the way that African writers express themselves in English.

Esme, now anxious about the drink running out, came over to ask Todd what she should do. 'We need more, where's the nearest shebeen?'

'Shebeen, shebeen!' Todd cried, facing this drought crisis, 'where do they keep their shebeens, these natives?'

'Simply send to the off-licence,' suggested one of the natives, the well-informed and imperturbable Desmond Morris.

'So late at night!'

'They stay open precisely as long as the pubs.'

Amazed at the liberality of the law, Esme, shaking her head in disapproval of such lax public morality, went out with a large basket, and myself as company. Our return did the life of the party a great deal of good. The walls of the small flat no longer pressed in on us, but seemed to expand as Esme's reserves of liquor carried out their happy work of bolstering our confidence, our spirits and our wit. Mind, there was still some disappointment in certain corners because of obstacles in getting at the drink. The crush meant that glasses had to be passed along overhead, and did not always arrive, being appropriated on the way – which had the curious effect of diminishing the level of intoxication and noise in proportion to the distance from the kitchen. This led to a polite pushing and jockeying for positions nearer the kitchen and to some vociferous repeat orders from the outfield.

From the rocky sofa near the window a low chorus of song now drifted across, turning before long into a general sing-song. How could we have spent so long neglecting our customary party joys! The hearty singing drove up the voice level needed for normal speech. *Inyani*! (in truth) - it could have been Sophiatown. Home sweet home reborn!

Todd was now playing his piano, hammering out numbers from *King Kong*. But there were whispers behind his back when he started on the tune of *It's a Wedding*. 'A bit tumpty,' groused an English musician with a pasty face, a noisy and obstreperous fellow. We did have to admit though that this was partially true. There had certainly been lukewarm comments about the production from several London critics and we had to agree that the show hadn't quite come off the way it had in Africa. Though a major event for us, it wasn't yet sure of being a long-run hit among the British. It was a precarious moment for it.

'It lost some of its raw vitality on the way in,' granted Ivan Stoller, 'it got cleaned up a bit for the West End, what a mistake, what a mistake.'

'Eheh, raw vitality,' Dambuza acknowledged the shortcoming a bit glumly.

'No, it lost Miriam Makeba, she was the star of the show,' corrected Jenny sharply, not sparing sensibilities. She spoke the truth, the management hadn't been able to keep Miriam in the star part she played in Johannesburg, they couldn't settle terms with her. Miriam! You can still hear that golden voice of Miriam's on the old LP, it stands witness to the difference between the South African cast and the one that had been brought over, for Miriam was much more than merely an actress singing.

'Miriam! Give me a cherry every time!' a raucous admirer of hers now sang out, a quote from the show.

A momentary dampener was put on things. To beat it off, Esme kept circulating faster than ever with her life-preserving liquids. Todd in particular was drinking more and more and now did one of his popular turns, very exuberantly, standing up before us, a small proud man, and rattling through in his best elocutionary manner the speaking of the Xhosa phrase ...

> *I-qaqa liqikaqikeka e qaqaqwni,*
> *laqhau'k uqhoqhoqho laqhothaq-hothek' umnqunho'*

In translation this had something to do with a skunk tumbling over on its side and down green slopes and snapping its spine. No matter, there was a great deal of phonetic richness about it, a virtuoso display of Xhosa clicks, clacks, sploshes and pops, which went down famously with the company.

There were more cheers and laughs and downings of drink and frolicsome attempts by the locals at these click sounds until the house supplies again looked in threat. 'Now it's really after pubtime, we really need a shebeen,' Esme appealed.

'Don't panic,' said a knowing fellow, one of the early arrivals from abroad, 'now we simply go to the back door of the pub instead of the front. I know the guv'nor.'

'So they *have* got shebeens!' exclaimed Esme. 'And not a madame but a guv'nor.' Off we trotted again.

Bloke and Malcolm and Gwigwi, with Todd joining in over his shoulder from the piano, were continuing with a very high decibel conversation, nostalgic stuff about how brilliantly the musical had gone down on tour in Rhodesia, which then recalled to the musicians their experiences in bands in earlier days humping their instruments around on their way to a gig in the townships, only to be stopped and searched by police believing they'd surely find stolen property tucked into those double-bass and cello cases. 'And the buggers expected a *gun* inside mine, instead of my tenor sax. For sure!' called out Gwigwi, laughing loudly. 'And when they saw only my nice silvery sax inside, "Where did you pinch that thing, kaffir, come quick, hand over, hand over", they'd shout'. A practised raconteur with a rubbery visage, he believed that the louder one laughed and the wider one pulled one's face the more likely it was others would see the point. At this stage in the party nobody was going to be too critical and all laughed as noisily as Gwigwi himself, while the piano, trying its hardest to get a word in above the row, kept banging away at the top of its *fortissimos* and a reckless clanking came from the kitchen from the washing up of more and yet more mugs and glasses.

Generally one had here one of the finer pandemoniums. Then suddenly KO! KO! KO! A really frightening rap at the door. Rap-a-rap-rap! Our minds asked immediately: Is this the knocking of an unearthly Nemesis? Instantly the party hushed, all one could hear was the clink of Esme softly bustling about, guiltily concealing any evidence that there had been drink taken.

KO! KO! KO! KO! again.

Still for another moment or two nobody moved. Finally, Hello, Hello, Hello was shouted impatiently through from the other side of the doorway, anyone there?

At this the brave host called himself to attention, marched over to the door, having to squeeze through the crowd of his guests to get there – *eksuus mense, eksuus, eksuus*! – flung it back and retreated a step ...

21. THE REAL WORLD

As Todd opened the door we saw there at the threshold a tall, tall policeman, who saluted him, then removed his helmet and stooped down to squeeze himself under the doorjamb to enter – yes, very necessary, those were the days when police were big and burly, nearly two metres in height at least.

The much smaller Todd looked up at him with an engaging smile beaming out from beneath the moustache, staying very chipper and cheerful, although not knowing if this was to be a criminal, political or diplomatic matter.

It soon enough became clear, the whole business was done with in a minute. 'Excuse me, sir, there have been one or two complaints from neighbours about the noise from here, might I ask you folks to keep it down a bit?' The policeman accompanied his request with a smile more affable than Todd's even – but then those were the days too when the police were fatherly and kind.

'Oh, right away, officer,' returned Todd quickly, bowing most agreeably, 'we were about to close off with a last hymn.'

'Some children along there are having a problem sleeping, you know,' added the policeman. With a wink he added: 'To tell the truth, sir, it's disturbing some of the day staff down at the station too.'

'Children! Ach, *shame!*' tut-tutted Todd. 'Why don't you come in and enjoy a little nightcap with us, officer?' But he was turned down politely and the policeman went on his way.

At the moment the door shut behind the cop, I burst out laughing, which was responsible for as loud a noise as there had ever been before, but I couldn't help it, recalling the contrast in treatment here with the last party we'd had at Todd's, in his Soweto home, and the serious trouble we'd expected then but for the cop being bought off with a drink.

'Sir!' quoted Todd a second time that evening with relish, laughing away to accompany me. And laugher echoed from every corner where there was a South African, all of them instantly enjoyed the 'home' joke.

Our laughing though was as nothing to the howls coming from Malcolm, Jean and Bloke down the room. For them there had been evoked a different echo from the old days, a particularly sweet memory, but they were incapable of sharing it with us as yet, quite blubbing with laughter. They were obliged to spend a minute or two recovering before they could get it out properly.

'That party at Bloke's place in Soph ... in Sophia ... in S ... S ... ' sobbed Malcolm. He couldn't go on. We all waited, laughing encouragingly, though truly we couldn't see much to laugh at so far.

'That huge bully of a cop in khaki uniform that horned in ...' Jean tried to amplify.

'And good old Pinocchio!' came from Bloke.

Quite hopelessly, all three seized on this. 'PInocchio!' cried Jean. 'Pinocchio,' spluttered Malcolm. ' Oh, oh, Pinocchio,' yelped Bloke again.

They straightened themselves out to give us the remembered story from early days. Bloke, vastly impressed by Malcolm and Jean, the enchanting pair then newly arrived from Britain, almost the first whites ever to disregard the colour bar and identify themselves with the black community, and wanting to impress them in turn, invited the pair of them to a quiet threesome at his room at Sophiatown, in one crumbling wing of the yard it occupied and where were installed the shiny fridge and the radiogram in its polished cabinet.

He had left work early that afternoon to get in some dainty snacks, spilt them out on plates dressed up with genteel little lace doilies, and put down a pair of bottles of real wine with real labels to them and three unchipped glasses. He adjusted the table-setting in a lady-like manner a few times, standing back hands on hips, head on one side, to check the effect, then when satisfied that all was right went round and warned off his neighbours and friends: they were not to turn up, they were not invited, this was strictly private for his two 'European' guests. At work was Bloke the social climber (and also Bloke putting in a pitch for a beautiful girl, if he could chance to get rid of her   partner).

A knock at last as he waited there, listening in studied pose to his 12-inch record of the Artur Schnabel version of the Emperor. He gave a few refresher turns to the winding handle of the fat gramophone, then let them in, his new friends. They shook hands formally, then the three of them sat themselves down, rather self-consciously, before helping each other to little cheese-bits and smoked almonds while the uplifting music played away in the background.

Ha! Almost immediately, though, there was another knock. Bloke shambled swiftly to the door in his bandy-legged gait, allowed it to open an inch, and called through in a hoarse whisper: 'No, who's that, no, no, Pinocchio, no I can't see you now.'

But the little fellow had an urgent foot in by now. 'No, Bloke, it's all right, man, it's just because I see a car outside here, I was thinking, man, you gotta be having visitors.' He bellowed: 'Come on, Bloke, come on. Let's get social!'

'Pinocchio, I can't see you, *boetie*, it's a confidential meeting on some business.'

'It's just ...' went on Pinocchio, pushing hard the other side, 'just that I could do with a quick little can.'

Bloke pushes back and yells now: 'Get the hell out of here, Pinocch.' But he has no chance, he's betrayed by the fifth column inside. Its Jean wheedling at him in her generous way: 'Oh, come on, let him in, Bloke, it'll be fun, go on let him in.'

In a moment Pinocchio was in, and pouring a large kitchen mug of the vintage stuff for himself. The snacks didn't interest him at all.

Another knock came on the tail of Pinocchio's, and then another. Within five minutes there was a rollicking party going on, Beethoven had been levered off the turntable by someone and a hot bit of jazz had replaced it, there was lively song and dance, and Bloke had been required to send out for more drink, strong drink this time, with or without labels. Luckily by this time everyone, especially Malcom and Jean, were enjoying themselves greatly.

But now it was when another sort of knocking came, this time the dread KO! KO! KO!

It was a cop, of course, a black one and in khaki uniform, with a fat knobkerrie strapped to his side. Bloke's heart thumped, he was committing a double crime, wrongfully consuming alcoholic drink, as the statutes put it, and far, far more sinful, consorting with a white girl, but the cop kept his kerrie peacefully in its place, and did nothing at all except stand there at first. He was in fact utterly bemused at Bloke's fancy guests and was positively honoured to accept the invitation to come in when it was offered. To maybe dance with a white girl! He could certainly overlook the drinking then. There was one minor snag, however, or rather a major one: on the side of him opposite to the *knobkerrie* he was carrying another large burden. Handcuffed to him, tethered to him, was his first haul of the night, a man he'd picked up at a local burglary job, now due for the police cells. What could one do? The burglar had to be brought in too, he had to have a drink too and when the cop joined in the dancing, boldy stepping in to grab Jean as partner, the felon had to follow him, unwillingly but inevitably, being twirled around the floor the length of his arm away from the pair of them, his large bare feet banging against the sides of the fridge.

At the end of the story, there was much laughter, which slowly died away as we remembered the need for hush. The rowdy talk and the singing died away too, people began to drift home and gradually all became soft and quiet.

Over on the striped sofa sat Todd and Desmond Morris talking about life and science, for Todd had by now found out about his distinguished guest. Todd always kept a store of little oddments of general interest in pockets of his mind for shelling out to appropriate persons: 'Of all the long line of my direct ancestors, do you know not one of them died in childhood?' He offered one of his genealogical gems to Morris the biologist.

'Really! Really, is that really so?' Morris didn't quite know how to take this – one sensed the question turning over in his mind: 'Could this be a note about some ancient and peculiar custom in Todd's tribe?'

In another part of the room Arthur Gavshon and I were in a sombre, even maudlin mood. I had shoved thoughts of Henry and memories of injustice at home to the rear of my mind during these past few months. I had been occupied busily with settling in to a successful career, exploring new social circles as well as holding on to old ones and had become half-hearted, I had to confess, about reinstating the fading contacts with my correspondents at home. But Gavshon was just back from one of his sorties to Cape Town and Johannesburg to report to the world on the state of things there. He had met Can and Casey and to be honest was not very heartened by what he found. Cautious fellow that he was, he didn't try to panic me, but I was worried. This made me think again of the affair of Henry.

Gavshon said he was going back again soon, which prompted me to ask him if on this trip he would try for any information about Henry from official quarters. There might be records about this mystery that had never been shown to us – station reports, post-mortems, etc. Being a foreign correspondent he had the ear of ministers and their departments to a greater degree than did the reporters of local newspapers. I gave him another commission, to ask Tom, now the *Drum* editor, to keep an eye on Can.

We were talking very quietly by now, almost whispering. There were just the three of us left, Todd sitting on his own over at the piano searching out a few dark, plangent chords. 'Scriabin', he announced, looking round at us, while tugging with one hand at the few scrappy strands of beard on his chin.

The party was over. Those soulful notes of Scriabin heightened the mood of foreboding about what might come next. What plans had Nemesis still in store for us?

Get this STRAIGHT!

It's the gals with the glamorous
straight hair look that catch
the eye of the guy in the public
eye

And that goes for the
ladies too! It's the men
with the slick straight hair
look I fall for,

Permanent straight hair can easily be
yours NOW, when you use

Pandora
PERMANENT HAIR-STRATE

Pandora Beauty Cream

This is the cream you
know so well for DAY use.
Famous PANDORA Beauty
Cream.

Standard size 1 6
Queen size 2 6

AND NOW—

Pandora Black Magic

The skin-lightening, night
cream you've asked for. Black
Magic BLEACHES while you
sleep. Black Magic BRIGHTENS
while you rest. Black Magic
makes your skin LIGHTER,
BRIGHTER, MORE BEAUTIFUL AT
THE PRICE YOU CAN AFFORD,
ABSOLUTELY SAFE, IT IS NOT
POISONOUS.

Standard Size 2 6   Royal (Large Size) 5/-

From stores and chemists everywhere

TRADE ENQUIRIES: P.O. BOX 5772, JOHANNESBURG

SOLD AS A
COMPLETE KIT
OF 4 UNITS

From stockists of Pandora, Products or if un...
to obtain send MONEY OR POSTAL ORDER
coupon below. If you require "BLACK MAGIC"
5/- extra for large size.

TO: PANDORA PRODUCTS (1938) (PTY) LTD. BOX 2914, JOHANNESBUR...
Rush to me, my kit of Pandora Hair-strate

Name ....

Address ....

UNION OF SOUTH AFRICA 23/. POSTAGE 1/6 TOTAL 26/6	S & N RHODESIA 25/-: POSTAGE 3/- TOTAL 28/-	KENYA, TANGANYIKA & UGANDA 25/-: POSTAGE 8/- TOTAL 31/-

22. ZEKE WANDERING

In the early 1960s still, as the Mphahleles migrated onwards, I caught up with Zeke again in Paris. He'd tried West Africa and London, now he was on the Continent, and he was yet during his travels to find temporary landings in New York, Philadelphia, Denver in Colorado, then London again several times, before finally moving on ... to where?

Firstly though this move in the '60s was to the heart of Paris, the family's chance for settling down. Among the French they found a welcome rather warmer and more sustaining than in Britain. Here, working for the magazine *Encounter*, they occupied a generous company flat on the Left Bank, large enough to fit all my family of six too, on a continental holiday.

The whole dozen of us would go off for staid family walks in the Luxembourg Gardens, a street or so away. I felt obliged at this juncture to edify everyone with my reminiscences of a stay in that very same *arrondisement* when a boy of six (visiting Europe so that my father might put his name to a new mathematics theorem and reap the reward of a PhD), and of a fortnight playing every day in that self-same park of sumptuous flower beds, joined together by paths of smoothed gravel that wound between low, immaculately clipped hedges.

In the style of the 1920s, every promenader was as done up as the park itself, the women so very chic, the men buttoned up in suits and wearing brushed felt hats, nowhere a bare head. Even the well-mannered little Parisian lads sported grey cloth caps and, in the fashion of the day, plus-fours and silky blouses, and played at nothing more hearty than the newly-invented game of yo-yo; or they read the brightly coloured comic pages pulled out of newspapers and bought – these young adults, with their own pocket-money – 'Eskimo pies' from a choc ice-cream handcart, decorated all over with tiny French flags and arty posters. In all things the note was elegant orderliness. And consequently there was nowhere for a small boy accustomed to open spaces to run off to misbehave.

Meantime our English nursemaid Mabel was being whistled up by the ice-cream man, until she learnt to chase him off. The people at the little hotel advised her: 'Shout at him, *allez tout-de-suite*, M'mselle.' And she did, 'Alley tootsweet, alley tootsweet.' And it worked, it was a kind of less robust version of our own South African *voetsak*, so useful in this sort of situation having been designed in the first place for hurling at dogs and Africans.

It was almost as formal and unrelaxed still in the 1960s when Zeke and I, both as it chanced devoted to running, dared jog round that park, though being a bit circumspect, deciding to go out in the early mornings when none was there to spot us. Whereas a quarter century later, in the cool and couldn't-care-less 1980s and 1990s, when the raked gravel paths, still in existence, were once again crunched underfoot by myself, it was done quite openly, and in the company of hundreds of local joggers, who seemed if anything to be eager to show off how relaxed and vulgar they could be.

There are laid out for study seven decades of nostalgia, that disease of pain from memory. At that time in Paris Zeke was also devoting himself to nostalgia from the same period, the 1920s onwards, having already published the first in his series of volumes of autobiography, *Down Second Avenue*, memoirs starting with his childhood outside Pretoria, while *The Wanderers*, an autobiographical novel, was imminent. It was those together with other novels and short stories, later to be brought out in book form, as well as his books of poetry and yet more autobiography that confirmed the soundness of my judgment of his eminence among African writers.

I decided to ask him who his nominations were for this literary list we had compiled, though modesty forbade him from including his own work in it. He thought most highly of Sol Plaatje of course, then Can, Peter Abrahams, and Alfred Hutchinson, and he was impressed too with the younger ones coming up, Alex La Guma, Nat Nakasa, Lewis Nkosi and so on.

'Bloke or Todd ...?' I prompted.

He shook his head slowly from side to side. 'Not enough bulk,' he disagreed gently, 'not enough bulk, Syl, they've got to come out with a good bit more work before they qualify as writers, real dedicated writers, rather than majoring as actors or musicians.'

Mention of Can brought me back to that permanent concern about our friend. And yes, Zeke had heard further uncomfortable news about him. 'Can, he's written his epitaph, many times. Written his own epitaph, I'm afraid.'

'That's one of his pieces we don't want to receive on time,' I grimaced. We sat there, the two of us, shaking our heads sternly at one another.

Zeke had also lately heard other news. It was to do with his own affairs, which he'd brooded on for a day or two. It added veracity to recent rumours and suspicions that *Encounter*, the French/English magazine he worked on, seemed to be subsidised by funds from America – from the notorious CIA. That revelation gave him the itch before long to move on again. Eventually he was offered a post teaching English and African literature in Pennsylvania.

A remarkable and dedicated soul, dear Zeke, this completed for him in his lifetime a journey of a thousand years, from tribal herd-boy through lower and higher schools and lower and higher degrees earned in correspondence courses right to the top, to an important professorship. Nor was he to end there. Dedicated, determined to a fault, and a fount of literature and philosophy, he went on learning and mastering the art of writing forever, while forever he soldiered away at teaching. He and Ribs also needed to wrestle with the problems of rearing children who had been jolted in speedy succession from one set of cultures to another and then another and another, never quite able to run their roots down through the stony topsoil to reach for sustenance, understanding and a sense of belonging.

A wanderer, a rambler, a nomad, Zeke the philosopher eventually transcribed his thoughts into permanence in that great number of stories, essays and biographical facts and fictions of his. He became a literary success, yet complete fulfilment still eluded him. As his experience expanded, his character developed more solidity and depth, but it wasn't enough to stop him growing gloomier too, gloomy at being away from his environment. We talked of another one who suffered like that, the painter Gerard Sekoto, whom we had visited in Paris. There after 35 years away from South Africa he still had enormous renown in his home country, but little in France. He was still painting his dear Africans, but painting memories only, fading year by year, being copies of copies. Visiting him in Paris, we saw the danger: his emotions were becoming memories of memories.

Was this the fate that Zeke feared for himself? He was being offered university posts in South Africa. Should he then return and bury his roots again in the warm soil of his fathers?

How could he accept? In his home country there would once again be onerous restrictions on his movements, there would be the loss of his rights as a citizen and, as a further agony, most of his children, grown up by now, would rather accept the milder penalties of staying in America as black Americans than return to what they could only label as serfdom. Yet how could he but accept? 'Am I being a bit of a duffer, Syl?' he asked me – not really for advice, he'd make up his own mind.

How could I turn him against it? For I knew that his inner strength would be enough to guard him, now under a new name, Es'kia, from the worst that might befall, from personal violence and insult and from ANC criticism that he would be violating the sanctions they had imposed against the regime.

23. SUNSHINE AT NIGHT

A rthur Gavshon and I were lunching at a spot that had been our favourite since post-war days, Bertorelli's, one of the very first of those ten thousand Italian restaurants that were later to penetrate every village and high street of Britain and bestow on the British at last a cuisine almost their own. The chatty young waitresses, all related to the old padrone and with a close family likeness to him, save for his alarming black handlebar moustache, were dressed in the Bertorelli uniform, a short frock of black bombasine with the smallest of lacy white pinafores stuck across its front. They now marched in with our ravioli: Napoli for me, Bolognese for Gavshon. By the time the parmesan and the pepperpot had been shaken over everything, Arthur had already twice taken up his pipe from the sideplate and put it down again to feel in his pockets for tobacco, not quite remembering where he'd got to with the filling process. Either way, full of tobacco or empty, he was going to puff on it – in those days it wasn't all that outrageous to smoke through a meal in company.

Gavshon was back in town without having persuaded the SA Justice Department to shell out a great deal of fresh information in the case of Henry's murder, the summary of the police report being rather skimpy, as one would have expected. In the autopsy it was stated quite bluntly that a heavy concentration of alcohol had been found in the blood. One could hardly doubt it. He had been a steady enough drinker, Henry, and wasn't likely to have been abroad at such a time and such a place simply to attend a temperance meeting. But this fact didn't get us much farther with motive, opportunity and so forth. All it did was offer Gavshon the platform for some statistics on the perils of alcohol. Drink was at the bottom of most murders, most family rows and divorces, most road fatalities and most other unnatural causes of death. And as an added topical instance it was believed by people he'd met in Johannesburg that it was behind the endemic illness that had lately carried Casey Motsisi to his sickbed.

Topping up our glasses from a bottle of red wine – yes, alcohol in moderation – taking up his gnarled old pipe and immediately resting it back on the table again, now to search for matches, Gavshon also reported to me on Can, and here was another case for moralising on the damned devil drink. This was something more definite, though, if all the less pleasing for that.

'It's Hopkinson, I'm afraid,' he said as an introduction, a phrase I'd heard before.

I pulled a wry face – as if I didn't know what was coming. And yes, I was right: a little while back Tom Hopkinson after warning Can about his timekeeping, his unexplained and lengthy absences, his lack of discipline - as his other editors had - after warning him and warning him, had warned him yet again, as his other editors had, and finally he'd given him 'one last, finalwarning' and after that the sack. As none of us had.

Yes, the very worst had happened, and it was no more comforting for having been long foreseen and longer in coming. A great man of Africa thrown down!

Tom had felt there was nothing else for it. Perhaps he thought this would teach the fellow, he'd take it to heart and come back again ready to play the game. And perhaps Tom took pleasure too at getting one in against the evils of drink. But of course not, it didn't work with Can, a man of too much character to be tamed, he swanned around the old regular haunts a bit, was late again in doing whatever he was doing, stayed drunk for days again - and had too much pride to ask to be allowed to work his passage back. And of course this 'firm hand' of Tom's didn't work for *Drum*, either. The decencies were now strictly kept, it's true, you had the snaffle and the curb all right, but where was the bloody horse, as Roy Campbell once asked of South Africa's writers?

Can essayed some freelance writing, which could provide no real living despite its being of a quality that has kept it in print until this day, and at that moment he was still undecided about his future life. One could reckon that it was likely to be precarious.

At Bertorelli's I drank a sad silent farewell toast to *Drum*. With Can Themba gone finally, what was left, its soul and its crew spilt out all over the world?

At a lunch at Bertorelli's again some time later, Gavshon was to relay to me further devastating news, of another *Drum* tragedy. Nat Nakasa, who had been one of the youngest to depart the land of *Drum*, had lately become one of its youngest to depart the land of the living. Sad, sad news indeed.

Why was he snuffed out, who and what had caused his death? Was he pushed or did he jump? That remains the seminal question at the heart of the entire story of *Drum* and its people, both before the diaspora and after.

In a very short time since coming up from Durban the young Nat had made his name on Drum, and before long enhanced it in another contribution to the struggle in South Africa, the building of the long road to freedom, with his editorship of The Classic, a 'little' magazine, to use the politico-literary idiom of the day. It was established later than Drum or Africa South, Ronald Segal's trenchant intellectual quarterly, and was one of the last to hold the fort when others had folded weakly or decided to meet police oppression with deferential little smiles.

Nat had been initiated into the rough, tough Johannesburg life by Can. Can had decided to take this 'country boy with the puckish, boyish face' and drop him in at the deep end, explaining: 'Not that we planned to persecute him, we only sought to divest him of the naiveties and extraneous moralities with which we knew he would be encumbered.' He showed him his room, a one-minute look around, then for the rest of the day he showed him the *shebeens*. In the evening, having to rush off on the track of one of his girl friends, Can dumped him in strange, hostile parts for a while, to cope on his own with the *tsotsis*. A rough initiation, but he came through it; scared though Nat was of the *tsotsi* world, he did not show his fear and he earned respect.

Nat speedily learnt from Can his way about the neighbourhoods of the big twin-city and its various ethnic and political manors. He also learned, as Can wrote, 'about the genuine values in those people who were not trying to prove or protest anything: God knows, South Africa begs any stranger to prove or protest something. Nat sought for something inside himself that would make language with the confused environment in which he now existed. He sought, fought, argued, struggled, posed – but I doubt if he found it. The South African stubbornacy was too much for him and he had to go into exile.'

He went. By now Nat and his magazine had won support from well-meaning circles in America, and he was invited to take up a scholarship at Harvard. The regime at home, however, would allow him no passport for this purpose, no leather-covered booklet, only a one-page one-way exit permit, another manner of saying 'Voetsak, kaffir! – we hope we never see you again'. A chilling choice for Nat, to study, travel and accept hospitality abroad or to stay at home ... to choose freedom, but without the freedom to return home. Well, he bethought himself optimistically, when the time came he'd surely find a way back? So he took up the permit.

He had a very good innings in the US at the start, swanning around on the literary circuit and the jazz circuit, but eventually he believed he was getting nowhere and his feelings of love for his country and his duty to his own people prevailed. To go back! To see *Egoli* (Johannesburg) again! Homesickness made it more and more pressing. Permission to return being refused to him on a renewed application, he languished in a terrible loneliness and misery. In 1965, aged only 28, he threw himself out of a seventh-floor window in New York.

A chilling message for the exiles in London and elsewhere.

Was he pushed, in the same way as so many who 'threw themselves' from high-up windows in police buildings in Johannesburg? Perhaps not, yet surely apartheid's long arm had managed to reach out to him there and send him flying?

'At the time of his death,' as Can reported, 'he was planning interesting things, journalistically speaking, interesting things ...'

24. THE YEARS OF THE SPIDER

So by the middle of the 1960s another man from *Drum* was gone, and *Drum* itself was in a kind of half death, lying there prostrate, its sting drawn. Although it went on being published thereafter and for the rest of time, step by step it lost its style and lost its vision and degencrated in the end into a genteel women's tabloid.

Viewed from Britain at that time, it didn't seem that there was much sting left in the whole blessed South African liberation movement either. Within a couple of years, in the middle of the 1960s, Mandela and Kotane and others were in jail, Tambo and Slovo and others in exile, the official opposition rather relieved to be tied up in legal knots and safe from the need for positive action, and the Nationalists boasting, in imitation of their hero Hitler, that they'd be in power for a thousand years. In London we kept up a desultory defiance. For me this took the form of joining the committee of Fenner Brockway's Movement for Colonial Freedom and attending at the lobby of the House of Commons for its weekly meetings. This body did help develop a number of strong young people for the fight, not least among them Frene Ginwala, who became Speaker of the House in Cape Town 25 years later. For the rest my resistance was expressed by the singing of anti-apartheid songs at noisy parties.

At least I could offer some useful help socially for my mates. Bloke for instance – at one of the literary dinners at my house I was able to introduce him to Jean Genet. They hit it off right away in spite of some awkwardness in that Genet would speak no English and Bloke could speak no French. Bloke stretched a hand across the table: *'Parlez vous monsieur'*, he chuckled heartily, trotting out his best attempt at the language, 'yes, apologies, hey, but I'm a bit *lassy-fair* in your lingo.' Genet responded with the help of a neighbour to the effect that he should speak Zulu, it was much more euphonious than English and anyway had something of the same 'song' about it as French. That meeting resulted in an important career change for

Bloke, for Genet wanted him in the cast of his play *The Blacks*, soon
to start rehearsing at the Royal Court Theatre. After that Bloke per-
formed regularly on the BBC and on German television, and wrote
plays for those media also.

'Why don't you dramatise your own story? Your story, our story,
starting with the unsolved Henry murder,' I put to Bloke when he was
chatting to me one day about new plots for television drama. 'The
days on *Drum*. Your book ... ' – I was talking about *Blame Me on
History*, his autobiography – 'gave the general background, now build
it into drama, there's a genuine whodunit there.'

He didn't react very positively. 'Blame Henry on History?' he
sniffed.

'Plenty of thrills, plenty of comedy to bring in – and an exploration
of some important themes, no?'

'Ja, man, ja, nice idea man, but ja, h'm ... ' he said, still in doubt-
ing tones, shaking an unconvinced head.

But I wasn't going to drop it so easily, because I could suddenly see
that here was a plan that could at last bring the Henry mystery out into
the light. 'Henry deserves a monument,' I went on. He still hummed
and hawed and butted and iffed – it might have worked better I thought
if I'd said Bloke himself deserved one. Do you know, yes, that was it,
that had hit on the head. 'No, man, Syl,' Bloke argued, 'me write
about Henry? That would be sort of silly, sort of backwards to front-
wards, it would be sort of the Life of Boswell by Johnson.' He seemed
to be saying, *me*, Bloke Modisane, writer, actor, playwright, who has
hob-nobbed with Genet, John Osborne, Menuhin, Sybil Thorndike
and with various middling marquises and milords and who's played
stud poker at what might be termed the highest level, with famous film
writers and painters and layabouts of distinction – it's *me*, the great
Modisane surely, who is the Dr Johnson figure.

'The royal me,' I sniffed to myself. But I pressed harder. 'There's
terrific musical material!' said I, 'Jozi, Jozi!' - quoting one of his
favourite Sophiatown songs, '*Jozi, Jozi, salalapo.*' He showed a bit
more interest. 'And super love interest,' I tempted him.

'True, true, man.'

'Yes, and what about good old Jean,' I particularised, 'what about we get her to act her sweetheart part in person? She's into the stage now.'

'Good old Jeannie!' He was now suddenly won over. The thought of having her acting opposite him sent him into a frenzy.

'Ho, ho,' he cheered, slapping his thigh jovially, 'now you're talking. Cherchez la *femme fatale*!' He guffawed: 'The Germans would just love it, first there's the airing of a nice bit of anti-apartheid politics, that eases their own race conscience very nicely, then the exotic setting, then a bit of bang-bang and yes, buddy you've got it, ho, ho, the tasty blonde among the blacks, very nice, Sylvest, very nice, you've hit it.'

I was quietly pleased, this was a story he could do justice to, he could get the attention of the media, it would revive public interest in the matter and maybe even help to dig some of the truth out. It struck me that when he did get on to this project he might have to make a clandestine trip into South Africa again for his research, but I wouldn't mention that frightening thought to him until he was well warmed up and on the way. 'Keep me in touch, then, Bloke, I'll help all I can.'

Bloke was generally on a high at this stage, but for Todd and the *King Kong* company on the other hand it was no longer parties all the way. Jollity had long since been overtaken by anxiety and hope by closure, with unemployment to follow.

King Kong seemed to have proven an uncanny literary litmus test for success and happiness. Those who were members of the company and who had originally thought themselves so lucky to be part of it, turned the litmus paper blue, an extremely chilly blue – which meant they were to suffer in their future careers. Whereas for those outside it a rosier hue came up, and for them the path to prosperity was unobstructed.

You could attribute the especial depression of the KK people in the following few years to the dashing of expectations - they were one moment the favoured ones seemingly bound for the top, and the next sprawled at the bottom. This was worse than if good fortune had never beckoned at all. Harry Bloom for instance allowed himself to be knocked right off his chosen route by this, his very personality fractured. One night he was at the show, sitting in the royal box with

George Merrick, the renowned US producer, talking over a six-figure deal for Broadway; yet a few months later, the show closed down, the cast dispersed, Merrick on to the next sensational discovery, he was a complete down and out, he'd crumbled. When he did pick himself off the floor after two or three years of hopelessness it was to go for a less-bruising challenge, a career as law lecturer in the provinces.

Dambuza, too, began to run out of success, so did Gwigwi, Peggy Phango and the other singers. They'd never been so high, now were they never so low. It was Nemesis, bringing his prophesies and paradoxes up to date.

As for the greatest of them, Todd, he toiled away in a small house in the suburbs, persisting with his compositions, economising with his outgoings, but not quite summoning up another big hit. After two or three years he quietly slipped anchor in London and made for Zambia with his family, for an administrative job in the music world. At least it was closer to home, though still no more than halfway back to his artistic roots – rather better at any rate than selling razor blades door-to-door.

Even I, who'd enjoyed no more than a groupie's involvement with the musical, found myself going into a sort of vicarious free fall upon KK's demise, though also on account of my own musical written in tandem with Dankworth, which in a similar way was heading one moment for Broadway, and the next for the back of the drawer.

In contrast Miriam and others who'd stayed out of the ambit of the musical were enjoying their hits, enjoying the world and surviving. Jurgen arrived from South Africa and set himself up as an international photographer, sailing from country to country – and from wife to wife – on the living he made from his work. Arthur Maimane had come on to the UK from Ghana and now was in a prime slot for a journalist, editing television news programmes. He also sported two families, one of Africa and one of England.

Barely a year later Gavshon was off south and back again. He had been untouched personally by our despondencies, whether in his career as war correspondent and author or in his life as energetic owner of a fine mansion and garden in London. Nevertheless at his next report-back meeting to me he had a grey look about him when we sat down to talk. He started in cryptic fashion. It was in his nature to keep one in suspense this way, though he couldn't help but telegraph that here there would be no happy ending: 'Syl, it's like a Shakespearean tragedy,' he started off, choosing as always the literary allusion.

'What?' I asked, anxiously and rather grousily, 'what is?'

'And with a Shakespearean villain if you like.'

I looked properly irritable at this, impatient to be brought to the point.

'Shakespeare's bottled spider!' He spoke it out gruffly, with venom.

I wished he'd give up the quotes, though it wasn't hard to know who he meant: 'Richard the Third?' I checked, 'so then who's the villain playing Richard, who's your bottled spider in this story, who's the foul bunch-backed toad, who's the one that did for Henry?'

Gavshon tucked his inscrutable pipe into his jaw. 'Not who, but *what.*'

'So who's what?' I asked, 'or am I supposed to say what's what?'

'I'm working on that. More later. Meanwhile I can tell you that Can has got himself exiled to Mbabane in Swaziland. And there he is a schoolteacher, and married they say, and can he cope with that way of life, they ask? And Casey's still back home, but drinking ominously hard.'

That was all there was for me to go on.

Left on my own for a while to digest the distasteful impressions he had communicated to me and to imagine the rest, and after that to get on with my own depression, it appeared to me that our investigation would have to rest for a while.

But no, not for long, it turned out: as the 1960s careered onwards, other actions were impending that were somehow to hurry things ahead. I had to try to explain away to myself exactly how this could be, by packaging everything together into one mystical experience relating to the nature of time. Of course this didn't amount to much more than what we all find as we get to middle-age, that time accelerates, that it gathers itself up and hurls itself at you faster and faster, so that you come to each successive year sooner than you did to the one before, according to some unfair rule of perspective. When I was a young lad a wished-for day had seemed to me to take a year to arrive, but as I clocked up the decades I found that on the contrary a year now took but a day to arrive – yes verily, it is there in a moment and in another moment the whole 12-month collection has flashed by.

Thus, although I myself stood still, having no wish at all to be hurried, time, like relativity, was scudding along with me on board, and now was treating my particular world to one of its more dreadful whirligigs, to borrow again from Shakespeare. Swiftly, swiftly, ever so much more swiftly than it would once have been possible to imagine, situations developed, people failed, lives rotted.

Events streamed past before my eyes as if I sat in a high-velocity train. The platforms swept by with such rapidity that I could barely read the nameboards on them, swept by so close to one another I was minded of the chain of narrowly-spaced stations along the line travelling north up Africa out of Cape Town ... Woltemade Number One, Woltemade Number Two, Woltemade Number Three, Woltemade Number Four ... so called after Meinheer Wolraad Woltemade, who in the old days rode into stormy Table Bay to save the lives of shipwrecked sailors. Those stations were erected to honour death, being the four entrances to the Cape Peninsula's sprawling cemetery, which was located right there along the wild, windswept strand upon which the old sailing ships had smashed themselves.

The names I fancied I read, as time sped me along, were on newly-built stations of death: here was Can Themba's, there Gwigwi Mwerbi's, there Todd Matshikiza's, there Dolly Hassim's, there the brave G.R. Naidoo's, there that dear sweet lad Casey Motsisi's ...

25. IN THE RANKS OF DEATH

No hero on horseback was there to dash through the surf and rescue our men of *Drum*. Within a year Can, Todd and Gwigwi had become victims of the wrecking of the land and its peoples that has to be laid at the door of South Africa's ruling race during its long regime of plunder. These three died so very young, as had the others, and still almost within the same 10-year span that opened with the death of Henry.

At the time the impact of their deaths was not felt as one sudden, connected effect. We members of that original *Drum* community had spread across the world, lost touch, lost the connection. Those next three died in different countries. Our information of each tragedy was scanty. It was slow to arrive. Although by the end of that first decade as many as five or six of our little group had been swallowed by the storm, the shock of the separate tragedies was dispersed and diffused, leaving little room for suspicion that a single agency might be to blame for all.

Gwigwi's was the first unexpected death. Some time after *King Kong* had been taken off after its disappointingly modest run, he was lucky to skip over to another active scene, being awarded a scholarship to the Juillard music school in New York. A family man well into his thirties, he let on to friends that he found it daunting to be thrown, a rough and ready fellow, in among a group of bright, highly-educated young virtuosos, though he did boast that he gave these sophisticates a chance to see how life could be lived to the full, the raw African way.

But not for long. Whatever the cause – pneumonia, stated the official bulletin; drink, said gossip – Gwigwi's ebullience and noisy rumbustiousness and his blastings on the saxophone were silenced, soon and forever.

Can too died in a foreign land in 1968, though one closer to home, the British Protectorate of Swaziland, and in pallid obscurity, enduring a last few years of life quite unlike the old one. Here again an official and respectable cause of mortality is pinned up on the bulletin board, coronary thrombosis; yet gossip had it that he tumbled off a lorry on a drunken spree, breaking his head and bringing on a heart attack. Yes, no, well – yes, perhaps the official verdict was right, strictly right, for whatever the actual mode of his going, he surely died of a broken heart.

Todd had not long been in central Africa when he fell ill, and he died in a hospital in Lusaka, soon after Can, in 1968. The official bulletin? Cirrhosis of the liver. Gossip knows well enough the usual cause of that disease: alcohol, alcohol that he'd employed to give him solace during his frustrated and unfulfilled years.

Then Casey, Dolly Hassim, Fatman were gone in the following few years, the mystical time-lapse effect again making it seem even closer in actuality. And after them one feared others were doomed to join them, not to live out their prime.

PART FOUR

TOP LEFT:
Bloke Modisane.

TOP RIGHT:
Jurgen Schadeberg.

MIDDLE LEFT:
Jim Bailey.

MIDDLE RIGHT:
Zeke Mphahlele.

BOTTOM LEFT:
Bob Gosani.

26. A SLOW FLOWERING OF TRUTH

If all be true that I do think,
There are Five Reasons we should drink;
Good Wine, a Friend, or being Dry,
Or lest we should be by and by;
Or any other Reason why.

Henry Aldrich (1647-1710)

I was on to Bloke again, in the early 1970s, needling him to get on with the drama-investigation of Henry Nxumalo's death and, I threw in tentatively, why not bring the other later deaths into the scenario too, Nat's, and even Mau-Mau's, and certainly the devastating recent passings of Can, Todd and Gwigwi? For no one could now deny, surely, that there was a connection between them all, which is what I'd begun to conclude after some slow, halting workings through of the possibilities in my head. 'Anyway now's the time to get on with it, Bloke. And by the way what about your German TV people, are they being helpful?'

'No, ain't so keen,' said Bloke. 'But look, wait a minute, wait a minute, why bring in those other guys' deaths too if we're on about Henry's?'

'No, not so keen? I'm surprised,' I said, 'they should be, why aren't they keen?'

'Well ja, in actual point of fact, they did say yes, but only if I go out myself with the camera team and play the lead. Out of the question. But look man, why mess around with the other guys' dyings, what's the percentage in that?'

'So?' I greeted the German TV channel's reaction, putting warmth and enthusiasm into my voice, maybe being a touch patronising too, 'that'd be good, that'd make an important film, Bloke, setting it up out there gives it authenticity!' Perhaps I pushed too hard, forgetting that the idea of him travelling home to the old country might frighten him back under the bedclothes. 'So then, are you on for the trip?'

Suddenly he boiled over: 'You think I'm mad, Syl, you think I'm mad!' He let it out in a roar, furious with me for expecting him to put his head back in the noose.

'Monty Berman went back in disguise,' I tried persuasively.

'You think I'm mad!' he shouted again. 'You think I'm damn-fool mad? Monty's white – it's all right if you're white. But if you're black, stay back, stay back!' He quoted the old folk song triumphantly as justification for his own attitude and to prove that I was asking the impossible.

Nor could I argue really. Few would be intrepid enough, the brave Monty apart, and I doubt whether I would have been, white or not, and well no, I *didn't* think him mad.

'You've gone mad yourself ... acting like you're bloody editor still. Anyway,' he said flatly, 'the story don't work, Mr Editor. It just don't work. And I ask you again, why bring in all those others too?'

'Thematic,' I said, rather too laconically for his liking. 'We're looking for a theme now, a general connection, rather than individual spine-chiller episodes.' He waited for me to react in more detail, moving round the kitchen of his basement flat off Primrose Hill, very nimble with that shambly gait of his, reaching for this and that, making us tea and throwing crumbled biscuit to Scottie the dog, who I'd borrowed to bring along for a walk.

I said nothing, but notwithstanding, he came out with what he had in mind. 'Look, here's for why your story don't work, particularly not your new plot, particularly when you shove in this new twist you got in your head, dragging in all those other guys too. That really shows it up as gunning up the wrong tree. Look at what the grisly list adds up to, I'll count it up for you if you're looking for a theme: first, Henry was three-quarters drunk at the time or he'd never have let a useless son-of-a-bitch *tsotsi* put one over him; second, Bob was weakened to death by chronic drink; third, Nat was in a drunken depression, all alone in New York, couldn't get anything published – you knew that, hey, I suppose you knew that, which wasn't given out in the official story?; fourth, with Can it was drink, pure drink; Gwigwi drink; Todd drink. If you lay all the verdicts together head-to-head in one line it'll stretch right round the block in one long chain: alcohol, alcohol, alcohol, alcohol, alcohol, alcohol.' He threw his arms wide and shrugged. 'So there's no story, all what you've got for a plot is *cherchez la vin*. What they were all victims of was alc-o-hol. Under the influence, short-term or long.' He went rollicking on: 'The African disease, the whole African tragedy – you can even sing it, "there's always a reason for drinking, always a reason to drink."'

I looked mournful. 'No, no,' I responded unconvincingly, I could not take that terrible verdict as being in any way a reflection of the truth. It did put the finger on a single agency, as Gavshon had hinted, but surely not the one he meant. It wasn't an acceptable theme.

'Ja, ja, yes, yes, we've got the full answer there, my boy,' he said with one of his knowing grins, rather pleased with himself now for his perspicacity, 'and what's the answer? – I repeat, no story! They were done in by the demon drink, each and every guy of them. "One cause fit all!" as they might say in the *lingerie* shops. It don't need any dead-of-night research to prove it, it don't need me trying to sneak in past the *Ossewa Brandwag* (Oxwagon Sentinel)to prove it, ja, and then they grab me and kill me within an inch of my life, hey?'

'No, Bloke,' I said again. 'that's not it, you've got hold of the wrong end of the rope.' I shook my head as I slowly climbed his basement steps, 'No, Bloke ... No, Bloke ... No, that's all wrong, Bloke. One cause fit all, maybe. But that one's not the true cause. There's a more profound explanation. There must be. Who did he get his orders from anyway, your demon drink?'

I tried out to myself as I walked the dog Scottie home:

> *If all be true that I do think,*
> *There are Five Reasons we should drink;*
> *Frustration, Being trampled underfoot;*
> *Race discrimination, Getting no bloody chance at all in life,*
> *Or any other Misery why.*

My thoughts drifted on, the list added up to more than those five, the list had no end ... no incentive to succeed, no opportunity, degraded education, break-up of family life, no decent housing, no jobs, doors closed in your face, hundred percent unemployment. That's it, if you're born black there's no cure for it – and reform is not possible! And no vote to give you the chance to put things right. And to fight for a vote is itself illegal.

The blacks were driven to drink to ease the pain. And here was an extra anomaly: the law, by banning liquor for blacks, effectively encouraged it the more, glamorising it as forbidden fruit.

Any and every one of those reasons and pressures for falling victim to the demon drink applied to all blacks. Even to Bloke, and here was a new sharp, worrying point I could feel sticking into me, to do with him. Wasn't all that talk of his a revealing cry from him, wasn't he perhaps, underneath, really worried about a possible drink problem of his own? Until lately he had been able to keep himself well enough in control, being cocky and confident from his year or two of success and his acceptance in English society. But society's interest had long since shifted away. His book *Blame Me on History* had been lost sight of beneath a pile of new wonders coming along, leaving literary society too busy to stay on his case. He naturally felt it hard. 'They just throw you away when you're squeezed,' I'd heard him say with a bit of a laugh in the pub the previous night. 'They chuck you under the chin the first few times they meet you, like a charming little black boy-slave in the eighteenth century, dressed in velvet, very sweet, very cuddly, very cutesey tootsey, but then it's over, it's the end of a five-day wonder ... *c'est finito.*' He came out with it as if he meant it to be a joke, but one could sense a flinty reality eating deep into him. 'Have another one!' he said, raising his whisky glass.

The paradox was that living in freedom he expected more, much more, than when living behind the pale, and this brought a new kind of bitterness to him. Earning a precarious living as freelance writer and actor, losing his heart to that blonde girl again and by now quite losing hope with her, thinking himself already a back number who'd done his best work, he was beginning to drink recklessly, relentlessly.

It took me a time to get home; people kept stopping us in the road so they could give Scottie a pat on his curly black back; he had a quaint, stiff little walk, high-stepping like a stormtrooper, very cutesey-tootsey, as Bloke said. 'Yes, I know, you see he's trained as a military animal, very charming,' I would reply with a rather evil grin.

'Please watch out, though,' I angled a warning finger at them, so's I
could get them to sheer off and leave me in peace, 'when he remem-
bers his rank he can turn nasty and bite.' Scottie immediately spoilt
the impression by turning round and giving them what I think was a
smile. So it still annoyingly held me up while I was trying to concentrate on those provoking opinions of Bloke. Was it really a natural weakness for drink, a *genetic* susceptibility to it, that was the basis
of the African problem, or if not, what?

The best way to find the true answer, I determined, was to call a
council meeting of my three wise friends, if I had to summon them
from the ends of the earth. And that was the awkward thing, it's just
where they were at the time. Joe was in Cuba on a visit, Zeke was
teaching in the United States and Arthur Gavshon was being diplomatic correspondent to the world.

Instead I had to set up my forum of four purely in my imagination
to inquire into the true reason for the extinction of my brilliant colleagues. I sat the other three counsellors down before me in effigy
and put arguments and answers in their mouths that I reckoned they
in their wisdom would have provided.

A SLOW FLOWERING OF TRUTH

Question: Why did those men and women die!

*Because they were stabbed in brawls? No, some were
stabbed, but was that the reason for their being killed, was that
really why Henry died?*

*Or because they poisoned themselves with concentrated
drink? Gwigwi and Todd did become alcoholics, but that was-
n't originally why they were doomed, surely?*

*Or threw themselves from high windows? Nat threw himself
– but where must we look for the root cause?*

*Or tumbled off a truck, like Can, or succumbed to unnatu-
rally early disease, or had their throats cut by the Spoiler
Gang? Or pined away in foreign lands? Or over-indulged in
tobacco? Yes, yes, yes, that's what overtook Bob, Si, Henry
Telephone, Dan, Fatman, Sam, Teaspoon, Benjamin, Benson,
George, the woman Hassim and many others. But was that the*

*common thread?   National suicide?   National martyrdom?
National allergy?*

    Should one put it down to coincidence or was there a common cause, and was that common cause alcohol, and must that be accounted an indigenous disease of Africa?

The forum answers:

    1) It's nothing but the way with journalists everywhere, they're all alcoholics, said the sceptical ghost of Gavshon, emerging from a puff of smoke, they like to believe that drinking with one's contacts is the only way to pump stories out of them.

    2) Put it down to our wounded psyche from being bottom dogs, said a tokoloshe *from Philadelphia, an insubstantial version of Mphahlele. What the English did to the Boers drove the blighters to take it out on us blacks and in turn squash us to the bottom of the pile.*

    3) See Stalin's analysis of Communism and the National Question, said a red spectre in the likeness of Slovo.

    4) In reality it was the fallout from the clash when nation meets nation in the scramble for land and wealth, said Stein, the only one present in reality. Blame Darwin.

I tabled a joint judgment from the four of us. We were obliged to record a common cause for the deaths of so many in one small group. Dare we claim otherwise, dare we maintain that it would have been natural for so many friends and associates to have died so closely together, so young, for totally different reasons?

No, statistics maintains that nothing is by chance and thus it is straightforwardly provable that some one single agency killed our dear chums and heroes. There could be but the one murder suspect. But who or what was that? Was it then a lone *tsotsi*, a single jealous husband, an isolated creditor – or government provocateur, or gambling boss?

Or was it in fact the demon drink? The forum said No.

So was it something more cardinal than any of those? Yes, surely it was.

Something Lost in Translation

This is the thought that God put into the head of Skilpad (tortoise), the great Afrikaner translator: Skilpad, ou jong (old chap), why don't you do something good for the kaffirs (the blacks)? Teach them culture.

Skilpad went straight to the Ministry of Bantu (Kaffir) Affairs and asked for a grant to carry out this instruction, telling them that what he planned to do to please God was translate all Shakespeare's sonnets into the language of the black (non-white) people.

The board looked at him uncomfortably for a moment or two and finally said that though they themselves stood for the good of the Bantu (bloody kaffirs) they did not see how this would help these people at all. What about doing the Bible instead, considering that the suggestion came from God himself in the first place? That would be of benefit to these people.

It's been done, it's been done, cried Skilpad ... several times! And, as they knew, he himself had already translated the sonnets into Afrikaans and for the sake of state security would undertake to do native (naturelle) translations direct from the original Afrikaans (Christian) version.

No what, man! – so the board protested – God would want something useful for the Bantu (munts), not this abstract intellectual stuff, far above their heads.

Well then what, asked Skilpad?

Teach them something about the history of their own country, said the board, of how it was discovered by the white people and became the upholder of Western Christian civilisation.

But I'm a translator not a historian, objected Skilpad.

Well translate for them the great historical work, The History of the Voortrekkers, ordered the Board; then the God-

verdomde nie-blanke (Goddam non-whites) will be able to understand more clearly why God has placed them here.

It was the great watershed year, 1976. It was in that year that the arrogance of the Afrikaner Nationalists finally brought tumbling down upon themselves the full wrath of revolution, triggered by their own benighted decree that black children should be taught through the medium of Afrikaans.

Children in the classrooms of Soweto took that ruling as wilful incitement. They rose in outrage against being forced to make use of the oppressors' language, and indeed against bantu education in general and against the state itself.

Thus was roused the first effectual opposition to the regime for many years. The adults followed where their children had led; and the ANC rushed to place itself at the head of the smouldering rebellion. In the end, after vicious police suppression of the children, tens of thousands took the road to exile in neighbouring black-governed countries and there became the nucleus of the army that would be built up over the years by the ANC. The ANC, through this raising of black awareness, was able to develop as a national force wielding mighty international influence, and eventually under the great Madiba, Nelson Mandela, lead the people to victory.

The irony here was that the Afrikaner zealots had themselves come to power on the back of a holy war against an alien language forced on their children. In 1902, at the end of the second Anglo-Boer conflict, Britain, in order to eliminate the troublesome Afrikaans language, which had given comfort to the Boer rebels, in a move exactly paralleled by what was to happen in 1976, compelled Afrikaner schoolchildren to be taught through the English medium. This created bitter resentment, offering the Afrikaners a heady grievance to exploit in a patriotic fight to usurp power and the control of South Africa's riches that went with it. That fight continued for the run of the twentieth century, during which they never ceased to wrap themselves in the language banner; it was the ideal emotive issue to rally their people when in the wilderness of official opposition during the Thirties and the Forties and then on seizing command of the state machinery in 1948. Once in government they rubbed the nose of the English-speaking whites in the language of the state, and then in 1976 thought to ram it down the throats of the blacks.

Yet there was no real need for continuing this crusade into the 1970s – therein lay a further irony – since the language theme had served its practical purpose in the Boers' campaign for power, and they were now enjoying the tangible fruits of that power: the land they had grasped and the wealth it created.

They were well aware of course that this great wealth could not be tapped without the cheap labour of the African. They had recognised this from the beginning, even before the first and second Boer Wars (which they called the 'Freedom Wars' – freedom for the Boers, the loss of it for the blacks). From their earliest Voortrekker days they had had an insatiable desire for land and, once settled on the choicer bits of veld, they had been every bit as greedy for a reservoir of low-paid tribespeople to work the vast morgen for them.

Though they'd lost those two wars, they won the peace hands down, within a few short years. From as early as 1910, granted full franchise by a generous Britain within the newly-independent Union of South Africa, they could undertake a remorseless campaign to have the black man turned off his land and from there directly into their farm enclosures – there was no other place left for him to go.

That is what Sol Plaatje understood clearly and crisply long before any other commentator, as early as Union in 1910 and the founding of the ANC in 1912. Plaatje so long ago had cut through the mists of emotional and racial spoutings that obscured the fundamental issue and stated categorically: the Boer nationalists coveted the labour of the 'Native' and it was precisely for that reason they needed to bundle him off his own land. This unjust and unlawful act of theirs – this act of robbery, in short – had then to be squared in the eyes of their religion, and for this purpose they came up with a sophisticated deception, the pretence that Africans were non-people. Dehumanised, dubbed kaffirs and handily picked out in a different colour by God, the Africans, and all other blacks, could then be treated as belonging to a lower order and barred from claiming human rights - all accomplished without offending the Boers' spiritual delicacy and their compact with God.

So, in the very way that the Boer nationalists had hoisted language as the flag in their war for power, they used colour as the slogan for their campaign to entrench serfdom in the constitution.

Plaatje protested against the policies of these extremists, who even from their unfavourable outpost on the opposition benches were powerful enough to force the moderate Boer premier, General Louis Botha, to repudiate his three-year-old promise to Britain that the land rights of the blacks would be respected forever, and their scant voting rights too.

Plaatje devoted his life to try to win back these rights for his people. He stumped South Africa with his admonitions, with dignified deportment and with compassion and good humour, and later embodied his case and his pleadings in the enthralling book Native Life in South Africa. He sailed to Britain with it and stumped the corridors of power there too, trying to influence the mother country to honour its undertaking to oblige its former colony to honour the treaty it had entered into for keeping black privileges sacrosanct. No notice was paid – without any delays for decency, the new Union of South Africa, with Britain looking on benignly, had passed its draconian dispossession law, the Native Land Act of 1913, and in the coming years continued to whittle away at African and Coloured rights, the pace forced the whole way by the nationalists, in or out of office.

History will not forget, however, that the British, the English-speaking colonials and the moderate Afrikaners have all to accept a share of dishonour for their collusion with the hardliners.

Plaatje failed to move the white masters, as he was doomed to, and for the next 70 years the ANC, first in peaceful, then in forceful, opposition, continued so to be doomed and so to fail.

Finally though the tide began to turn. Starting from that 1976 children's uprising against Afrikaans, it began to flow against the regime. The long, long campaigns of the people – military, political and social – gradually began to bite.

And now a ghostly and wonderful phenomenon materialised: a spectral army arrived to join battle on the side of the African people...

28. CASEY AND CO

If Bugs were Men

Two bugs were sitting and chatting in a nook of a wall in the House of Discussion. One bug scratched its head and said: 'I was just thinking. Last night I bugged that chap who calls himself president. His blood is flowing in my veins, so I'm his blood relation in a way. Maybe in some centuries to come I might evolve into a human being, and who knows I might be elected president too!'

'What will you do when you're president?'

'I will make laws. Humane and human laws. Nothing but laws.'

'That means you will forget your bug brothers, even me?'

'Nix, chum. I will appoint a Minister of Squalor, whose sole business would be to see to it that every human being stays dirty. I will ban all disinfectants; encourage bug immigration; and tighten up on emigration. Anybody who disagrees with me will be named a bugomist and banished to a concentration camp.

'By bugs, I'll make such laws bugs will build me a monument after I'm dead.'

The other bug yawned and said: 'Stop talking like a human being and let's sleep. Wake me at midnight.'

The two bugs fell asleep and dreamed of human beings.

From *Casey & Co*, by Casey 'Kid' Motsisi

Cometh the hour cometh the men! Summoned to duty from beyond the grave, at the precise and valuable moment of need the murdered *Drum* writers returned to the land of the living to strike their blow in the war for freedom.

Not in the flesh, but in their images and their powerful works they returned, called in as recruits in the battle against apartheid, ghostly victims of it themselves.

Their past writings were given the kiss of life, and they themselves through the shining light of publicity were built up into giants of myth and legend.

It was at the very time of the Soweto rising that this formidable attack by the underdogs was launched on the literary front, courageous presses coming into being then to promote the writings of the oppressed, the banned, the exiled, the unpeople. By no means the least among the writers were members of that posthumous army from *Drum*. First were brought out books by those of them who had not published in their lifetime. Ravan Press thus anthologised Nat Nakasa's short stories and articles, following with Casey Motsisi's monthly columns, *Casey & Co.* (Casey's sad death had trailed Can's by a few years only – he died in hospital as predicted, and of the effects of drink on his overburdened frame as predicted, still in his early forties.)

Then the books by *Drum* men that had once been best-sellers abroad but could not legally be read in their own country were rescued from the censor's dungeons by David Philip Publishers. A generation since they were written there appeared for the first time in the bookshops and the libraries of their own land Todd Matshikiza's *Chocolates for My Wife* and Can Themba's *The Will to Die*, together with banned novels from others still alive, Es'kia Mphahlele's *The Wanderers*, my own *Second Class Taxi*, and those by former contributors to and associates of *Drum* such as Peter Abrahams and Harry Bloom, not to mention works by poets, philosophers and ANC statesmen.

Other reprints and re-issues were also to be made of Anthony Sampson's and Bloke Modisane's volumes and of those of that honourary man of *Drum*, Sol Plaatje.

Uniting with this flood was another even more copious one from Bailey's *Drum* Publications, of popular books featuring *Drum*'s men of the 1950s and reprinted material from *Drum*'s archives. In the coffee-table format these steadily publicised our men as heroes through popular and pictorial histories, and through videos and films and television programmes circulating through South Africa and across the world.

The essential value of all this outpouring was to enrich the culture and minds of the people of South Africa, give them champions to admire and great heroes to emulate, while warming their hearts as they prepared to join battle.

Reinforcements arrived from the land of the living too. As the process of unearthing the past continued, Jurgen Schadeberg returned to settle in South Africa and bring more power to the cultural flood, both in collaboration with Bailey and on his own, in reprinting and publishing the writing and photography of his old colleagues. Jurgen came back in spite of arguments by myself and other friends that he would be giving comfort to the government. A restless man, who had consecutively settled – each time 'for good' – in half a dozen different countries where the grass seemed greener, even trying out again the land of his birth, Germany, he found in the end that where he belonged and where he could really make a contribution was South Africa. He searched among the old photographic negatives and contact-pages to work up into elegant form the pictures of the 1950s and have them displayed to the world again.

The living though moribund *Drum* did not itself contribute anything of value to the struggle through this long period and in the end Bailey gave it the *coup de grâce*, selling what was no more than its corpse to its very executioners, the Nationalist press. Another *Drum* murder, but one can't be too critical of its murderer, for Bailey must end with a great balance of credit. If any one man was responsible for the great doings of *Drum* it was Jim Bailey. Those black writers each offered a big contribution, they put their whole lives into it, and Sampson was one of the guiding geniuses and so was Jurgen, but the obstinate man who published it and quarrelled with all of us and contradicted us so pig-headedly – he was the one who kept it alive for so long, who provided and persevered with the true vision.

All credit to him too for continuing into the 1980s and 1990s, when in his old age, to keep the memory of those wonderful writers and photographers alive in his endless publishing and republishing activities.

Contributing to this canonisation of the 1950s people of *Drum* and Sophiatown were all the other entertainment media: stage, cabaret, film, magazines, photographic exhibitions and radio and musical shows, while a course on *Drum* was initiated at Rhodes University. As the movement gathered pace it gathered size, in the style of a snow-ball, Mike Nicol and several other authors subsequently bringing out yet more histories and biographies of the magazine and its men.

This was a giant literary industry – and it was more than that, it grew to be an extra force, a companion army to that of the ANC in the national struggle during the final years, those dead souls of *Drum* its shock troops.

Zeke was another who arrived back in the country in person, a wan-derer no more, in that very significant ycar of 1976. Responding to the stirrings of intuition, he returned to his native land, in his case against the advice and in spite of the strictures of most of his friends and fel-low exiles, concerned that a man of his standing going back voluntar-ily to South Africa would be seen to be 'recognising' the regime.

It was in 1975 that I had caught up with him again while travelling in America, to rendezvous with him and Rebecca at my sister's home in New York State. The two exiles had driven down from Philadelphia where Zeke was a professor of literature.

We talked then about his and Rebecca's feelings on the smothering of their roots and the sad nostalgia that went with it. We talked of the music of Africa and its dance, of its warm, open, noisy peoples, of the grandeur of the country, of the sudden storms and the sodden sun-shine of their native highveld. We talked of the life and song of Zeke's Northern Sesotho language. We talked too of the need to sup-port those who were fighting serfdom, and of what he, Zeke, a writer of his people, could bring towards enriching them in their poverty and strengthening them in their combat.

He did go back, political arguments notwithstanding, his heart and his instincts ruling his decision. He went back to an honoured aca-demic chair at Witwatersrand University and an honoured position in Soweto as sage and prophet to the young. In this environment he was able to work and contribute to Africa and the world. In him you had one of our rare sustained success stories at *Drum*. Zeke was one who survived and thrived, through his perseverance and sense of service and humility.

Had the others lived on, who could tell what destinies they were marked for, whether they possessed the spiritual qualities and could have summoned the strength of purpose to succeed.

Zeke had, of course, matured in fine style since his *Drum* days. Would not the others have grown too – or would they have become middle-aged and fossilised and would their purpose have waned? I have never abandoned the thought that certainly Can could have become that leader of Africa whose future greatness I had perceived in the auspices; and who could doubt that Todd would have contributed to the world's store of music and philosophy?

What of Henry, I wondered, what role would there have been for him, in fact what role could there still be for him and his story? Could not he add his weight in this final battle against the evil forces? After a long interval, I once again looked for Bloke to find out how he was getting on with that long-deferred dramatisation of the Henry mystery. I wanted to say to him, bring Henry and his work back to life, to be enlisted too in the spectral army, to make his contribution in the battle for freedom!

But Bloke was away, for his own life had taken a happier turn. He had married a fair German woman and gone with her to live in Rome where she was working. I knew how difficult it would be for me to cajole him satisfactorily at such a distance away.

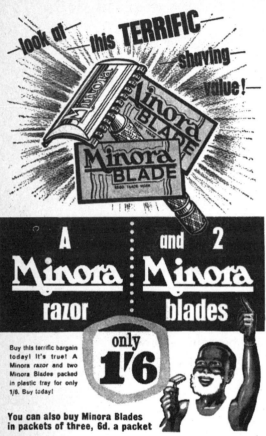

look at' this **TERRIFIC** shaving value!

A Minora razor and 2 Minora blades

only **1/6**

Buy this terrific bargain today! It's true! A Minora razor and two Minora Blades packed in plastic tray for only 1/6. Buy today!

You can also buy Minora Blades in packets of three, 6d. a packet

Samson is strongest lasts longest...

it's today's best value for money

When you buy, look for these points, every Samson Overall has them . . .

★ **BUTTON-UP CUFFS** the sleeves can roll up
★ **MADE FROM FINEST DENIM** strong material for long, long wear!
★ **PLENTY OF ROOM** across the shoulders

SAMSON THERE'S A SAMSON FOR EVERY JOB OF WORK

the name for greater strength

BE THE ENVY OF YOUR FRIENDS AS THE MAN WHO IS ON THE INSIDE OF

ALL THE HOT NEWS

MAKE SURE OF YOUR COPY OF

DRUM SENT DIRECT TO YOUR HOME

Please send me DRUM for 12 / 6 months for which I enclose postal order of 7/6 / 3/9.

Name

Address

Send subscription to: DRUM, P.O. Box 3413, Johannesburg

Headache?
TAKE
Saridone

Toothache?
TAKE
Saridone

Saridone gives quick relief. Saridone is safe. Saridone is the modern analgesic, obtainable only from your chemist.

Saridone

MEN ONLY

● WOMEN LIKE STRONG MEN. If you feel weak and ladies don't like your company then use Powa Pills. After using Powa only a few times you will feel strong. Your blood will pump with wonderful refreshing energy. Your muscles will become hard and strong. You will get more fun out of life and women will love you.

WRITE FOR

Powa Pills

TODAY

Send your postal order for 37/6 (Seven-seven Shillings & Sixpence)

M.M.R. LABORATORIES Dept.

ARE YOU LUCKY?

IF NOT — WHY NOT

29. WHY DO THE NATIONS SO FURIOUSLY RAGE TOGETHER?

That fateful year of 1976 had been responsible for many a side-effect too, influencing lives abroad and setting up consequential developments in our own story within a story.

First it had been Zeke's turn to move away from us and back to Africa and now it was Joe Slovo's, for he needed to edge in closer to the scene of the action; he began to spend his time in those front-line states where the ANC camps were located, and in Maputo, the capital of independent Mozambique.

Others followed back to Africa but, pacific as I was by nature, an unlikely warrior, I was not to travel there, though I did find myself from that same year active on a minor front, my own involvement with South Africa's affairs thus revived. It was in an unusual and in the end not altogether insignificant sphere, that of sport. I had at the age of 50 rediscovered my youthful zip as an athlete, had become a wiry, born-again old sprinter and been invited to participate in international veterans' running championships. There among the over-40 and over-50 members I was confronted with a hardened, ossified, conservative ruling group, who were fraternising with white South Africans, planning to sneak them into the movement despite their being shunned by most international sports associations.

In trying to break up this pro-apartheid conspiracy I sought guidance from Sanroc, the sports boycott organisation run by the exiled Sam Ramsamy, and with help and advice from him waged a 10-year war on those backward old runners from Britain, the US, France and other countries. This campaign moved to and fro across the globe, year after year, to confrontations with pirate South African teams in Toronto, Canada; Malmo, Sweden; then Hanover in Germany; and then Christchurch, New Zealand, where matters took a violent turn, becoming in effect a dress-rehearsal for the big rugby political showdown there a month or two later, in 1981.

This was a lesser element in the immense efforts by Ramsamy and Sanroc to pile pressure on the regime, assailing them from this non-military front as the 1980s rolled on. So from now onwards the main ANC forces inside and outside South Africa, the trade unionists, the writers and theorists inside the country and the promoters of economic sanctions outside, as well as the boycott movement of Ramsamy, were all launching powerful punches from a number of different directions that left BJ Vorster and then F W Botha little time for peace, little tempo for regrouping.

By the middle 1980s it looked as if we might be coming up for a new round of small-arm fire from the literary front too, for at last Bloke seemed ready to tackle an exposé in dramatic form of the case of Henry and his fellow writers. By now he and his German wife had moved from Rome to Dortmund, Germany, on the trail of her livelihood – of both their livelihoods, for his own work was but as a free-lance, with no steady earning power. It chanced that at this time he was making one of his infrequent acting appearances on London TV, and had come over to stay with me for a day or two. 'What's next with me, Syl?' he echoed my question, 'Wait for it, wait for it – it's the Henry story!' He stood there arms raised to acknowledge the applause.

'Oh, ho, it is! At long last! You'll do Henry's story? Marvellous, at last someone will do it!'

'Yup. Screenplay: William Modisane; Starring: Bloke Modisane; Design, camera, sound-track, central casting, key grip, on-location catering, the lot: William Bloke Debonair Modisane.'

'And will you go over there to do it in person, all you Modisanes? Will you actually travel there to interview Florence and the children, will you sniff around among the cops and the *tsotsis* and the Cabinet ministers, and then will you have a few shots of *skokiaan* for me in Fatty's place? Will you? Will you go back?'

'Ja I will, 'strue's God! Ja I will – if they definitely send me,' he put in as a condition, 'Ja, if German TV will send me. Fact is I need the pay bad, Syl.' He went on, become rather piano in mood now and resigned about it: 'Ja, what else can I do? Ja, that's life.' He shrugged, in his very best French: 'Ja, *Sailor V*, Syl.'

The truth of it was, he was not able to rely on his wife any longer for his drinking money, and that drinking of his was now become habitual and necessary. He carted with him around the house while in London one steadily diminishing bottle of whisky after another – and whether it was the whisky that was to blame, who can say, or his advancing age, but the swagger in his gait had become more pronounced than ever, evidence of desperation.

However, this was excellent news, Bloke would at last be turning back the pages of the past to discover something more about Henry's murder, he'd dig out some of the truth, I thought rather smugly. And I hoped it would be more than mere mechanical details about an inebriated reporter wandering around a late-night township, for already through the passage of time the circumstances of Henry's death were becoming elevated from topical whodunit into historical issue. Now there could be a full perspective, a proper focus, and Bloke would be able to look at things with a broader vision, to analyse them more closely.

The very airing of the story would be a hammer force in the continuing battle against apartheid, I encouraged him. 'And you'll be setting down the definitive Life of Henry as well, Mr Boswell,' I teased him.

I had to keep reminding Bloke over the next months. 'Get going. Begin, put something down now ... now, now!' I shouted at him through the telephone to Germany, 'and remember, you need the money. Now! now! now!' But nothing much happened.

Then, at last, action! He rang from Dortmund in great excitement to say he'd had word of a rumour floating around Soweto lately and wafted over to him by friends to the effect that a black prisoner at the Johannesburg Fort, with something secret rotting away on his conscience over all these years, had finally confessed that it was he who had struck down Henry, having been paid a goodly sum to do it by a minor fellow crook, an agent for someone yet further up the line no doubt.

'Yarrah!' I cried, 'we must track him down! Now we'll have something to go on.'

'Ja!' Bloke crowed, 'Ja, and we'll be able to track back from him to that Mr Big – I'll go and beard that fat crooked surgeon with what we know.'

'After all these years the truth at last, it's a damn miracle,' I chortled.

'The truth come home to roost!'

The euphoria of discovery seized us both.   However, a slow counter-current began to build up in my mind, and soon a less positive feeling prevailed. 'Mind, you, ja, Bloke, ja but ... but I don't know, mind you, no, I'm not so sure.' My voice trailed off, a less elated tone in it. 'No, it's too late now, no, no, no ...'

'What *no*?' he shouted angrily into my ear, feeling robbed I suppose at the very moment he had finally caught up with the idea.

'It's all too late.' After that first moment or two of great excitement, I'd realised we had nothing but a stale anti-climax here and I became more and more dismissive of it: 'Bloke, we always knew he was knifed and we always believed some hitman did it, and maybe it was for this motive or that – "girl friend", government panic, *fah-fee* debts, abortion story, you name it – but which particular hitman and what actual Mr Big are mere incidentals now, superficial symptoms of something more basic. What killed so many of them, that's what you have to find out! Mr Big himself isn't big enough, we need to find out what plague it was that history visited on them all.'

It was the wrong thing to say. It must have disappointed him immensely and killed off his enthusiasm and now his conversation tailed away into grumbles of dissent and polite mutterings and snorts.

I rang him again a few days later to have a go at re-enthusing him, but he didn't even return my message. And then still later I wasn't able to reach him on the phone at all, he'd moved, his wife it seemed had pushed him out on his own, not able to tolerate his celebrations of happy hour any longer, and he had no phone of his own. There was one much-delayed letter in reply to several of mine, 'Okay, okay – okay!', then silence again.

I was still hoping to see what first scribbles he might have had ready by now, and still hoping to get him going again and blaming myself for his despondency, so sent another tactful letter but this one was returned unopened, something non-committal in spidery German scrawled across it.

It wasn't long though before I had an explanation. Sadly, drinking as hard and fast as he could, as a way of softening the pain of the old blackskin disease as he would wryly call it, cursing his fate and blaming history for the final time, and never getting far with our big new project or with anything else, he had come to a sudden stop, in a one-way heart attack.

It was a sorrowfully miserable end, for by this time he was living quite on his own in that cold, cold room in that cold German city, with only his bottles of whisky for company.

So now Bloke too had gone – and was I to blame for giving him the last push? That was my first awful rather maudlin thought but then normal human emotions took over and with heartfelt warmth and tears I remembered his life, his jolly buoyancy, his sociability – and his social-climbing – and his charm. Then I recalled his work. His first and only book remained. I re-read it – I had given it a rattling good review in one of the dailies when it was published in London a year or so after his arrival. It had been a surprise to all of us in that long-ago time, *Blame Me on History*, for its perception, its strength, its depth of understanding. It contained far more than the memoirs of Bloke the playboy. There was not only much forceful introspection on the evils of being black, there was accurate political analysis. And finally there was his intense personal recording of the murder of his beloved Sophiatown – an anticipation too perhaps of the murder of Bloke Modisane himself.

It struck me that perhaps Bloke's book could almost have provided the source material for this story of Henry and all the others, as being a study of the mind of a victim of life – Bloke victimised for his colour, Bloke the refugee evicting himself from Sophiatown before it evicted him by exploiting yet another of apartheid's infamous and greedy pieces of legislation, Bloke as the squeezed rag of history. He there set out his own diagnosis of what eventually was to kill him, and in the end killed not only him but all those others too. He had pointed his finger at the causes and pronounced the verdict. He blamed his end as well as his life on history; history, which like nature is red in tooth and claw.

So Bloke died, in a lonely way, following all those others in our little band, and now David Sibeko died too, once our young office messenger who had become by his forties a substantial man, a leader of the PAC ... assassinated at the party's head office in Dar-es-Salaam. And before long there came the death of the affable and resourceful G.R. Naidoo, who'd run the *Drum* office in Durban.

On the day we heard of Bloke's death Arthur Maimane and I gathered for a two-man wake in a London pub on the corner of the television news studio where he worked as an editor. We remembered Bloke and we remembered the others, totalling so many by now, and we recalled the premature epitaph those carefree *Drum* men had adopted for themselves: 'Leave a good-looking corpse'. But it had come about not like that at all, I pointed out to Arthur. On the contrary, whatever their negativist intentions, they'd left behind them more than mere corpses, handsome or not, disfigured by a score of bloody slashes or not: they'd left a significant epitaph, which declared that they had contributed mightily to the fight against the very force that had killed them.

We adjourned to my office, close by, and I was able to prompt Arthur to do the write-up of Bloke's life for *The Times* and incorporate that theme into his obituary notice, which he did. Then my old persisting thought surfaced again, and I asked myself why shouldn't I try to rope Arthur in more closely for him to do the Henry story, persuade him to elaborate on the epitaph-writing? I knew he was another one looking to publish something in book form, so why should he not take on the story, adding Bloke now to its dramatis personae as well as those other dear departed colleagues of ours? I tried him out a few times, said it need not be in dramatic form, a dramatisation in book form would be fine, I cajoled him, I prodded him, I humoured him ... but Arthur was too tied into his professional work to consider it.

'The story of Henry is the story of the whole crowd from *Drum*, Arthur,' I said, having one last go, 'and it's more than that, it's the story of all the people of our country, it's the story of just one of the multitude of crude, cruel struggles of nature, of one powerful ethnic group's domination over another.' But no, it wasn't possible for him ...

So who would take it on?

30. WHO KILLED MR DRUM?
- THE VERDICT OF HISTORY

As I looked for someone who would handle the story, Henry Nxumalo's story – Mr Drum's – and tell the manner of his death, history was continuing to unroll rapidly before me and work up its own considered epitaph for him and the others. This epitaph, what's more, would not be for the *Drum* men alone but, as I'd proposed to Arthur, it would also speak for those other millions of South Africans who like our own men had come to an early end.

History was revealing a great deal in those years. It started, in the late 1980s, to let us know that although the struggle in South Africa was enduring hard still, there were now to be glimpsed a few, first cracks in the surface – cracks that were widening as we watched.

The ANC was armed, both inside the country and in its camps in the frontline states, the world outside had pledged its alliance, the people were become more assertive, not to be put off, and Nelson Mandela sat in his cell, waiting, waiting ...

Within my own humble sector, Masters' Athletics, we had managed to bottle up the South Africans in their own backyard, and that may have assisted in a tiny way with influencing at least one group of sportsmen and their followers into realising that apartheid could and would never prosper. By way of thanks, in exchange for the help I'd had from him, I became a back-room assistant of Ramsamy in his campaign to keep South Africa shut out from world contention in every country and every possible sport. And that campaign was vital, it attacked the white South Africans where it hurt most, at the moral centre of their lives, that is their sport – how it rubbed up the Afrikaners especially! Next to Mandela and his ANC, who was there that would have so much success in forcing the Nationalist government's arm as Sam Ramsamy, with his snatching away from the whites of their international cricket, their beloved rugby, their

Olympics, everything?

Victory for Africa might still be a score or so years away, it was believed at that moment, but battle had finally been joined in force. The Nationalists had real opposition, and knew it and feared it. Though never owning to the fact in public, they now began to treat with the enemy. Stage by stage there were small advances: Mandela was accorded special status, secret negotiations were arranged with him and other ANC people, white liberals and businessmen were called in as go-betweens, and social persecution of the black peoples was in a slight degree eased.

Then, in a rush at the end, coming after all much more rapidly than had seemed possible, De Klerk was put in power instead of Botha, and he from the start understood that he would have to look to more radical measures, he had to forge a completely new policy if civil war was to be averted. A major breakthrough decision had to be taken, and it would be an immense gamble, one his own followers were hardly ready for. Could he convince his party to trust him and follow him?

The gambler's choice was this: either stand firm and risk losing everything to black revolution or give way yard by yard, surrender at first merely the symbols of office, the white electoral monopoly and the language monopoly, but hold on to the real wealth. He had a historical example to follow here, that of Tsar Alexander the Second, who in 1861 emancipated the serfs. 'Better to abolish serfdom from above, than to wait while it begins to abolish itself from below,' the Tsar lectured those aristocrats opposing him – the *verkramptes* (hardliners) of the day.

De Klerk took the gamble, he played that same conjuring trick, he offered emancipation to his serfs; and the gamble worked for him too, for in spite of the formal elements of the offer, which allowed the ANC to emerge as the governing party, it was to leave the Afrikaners in the 1990s hanging on as yet to the fundamental, tangible assets they wanted to keep their hooks on: the land and the wealth it produced (as ever, thanks to the starvation wages paid to the black people). And the English-speaking whites were to hang on to their riches and their privileges too, passive and weak-kneed though they'd

been through the years of struggle, always content to leave the Boers
to fight their battles for them.

That was perhaps the bitter truth the people had to swallow, that
they had won victory but not its rewards – still, it is not to deny completely that some sort of miracle had been played out and that
Mandela was some sort of messiah and that some sort of millennium
is yet to arise ... and long, long before a thousand years have passed,
for freedom, meaningful freedom, is on the way to being achieved
and the spread of wealth to all races will follow from the spread of
formal power to all. Mandela has said himself: 'The truth is we are
not yet free; we have merely achieved the freedom to be free – but the
first step on a longer and more difficult road.'

Certainly the moment of achieving constitutional victory was a
sweet, emotional one for all. All felt proudly that they had done it
alone single-handed – all of us together single-handedly.

How our *Drum* men would have treasured the chance to join the
march-past at Pretoria celebrating the triumph over apartheid. I can
see them, Henry, Can, Todd, Casey, Bob, Nat, Gwigwi, striding out
and Bloke bringing up the rear, shambling in his bandy way off into
the distance, chuckling at those beside him, acknowledging the
crowd's cheers with raised fist.

The change of national mood and the gradual let-up of repression
since Mandela's release and the handing over of parliamentary control has allowed one, even tempted one, to look back into history and
seek explanations for what it was that had been allowed to happen,
and then perhaps to seek excuses for those responsible, those who so
wilfully waged the 100-year apartheid war.

In the scrutiny of our own one small and special area it could now
be clearly seen that it was not drink, drink being but the instrument,
that was the common cause of the death of some 15 and more that
were young and brilliant, of some 15 like Can and Casey, Nat and
Henry, of 15 members of the original wonderful crew of the African
Drum, of 15 who started out with *Drum* in the Earlies but did not live
out their prime. We could in the end satisfy ourselves quite categorically that it was not alcohol but apartheid itself that was the curse,
the plague, the master-killer; alcohol was merely there as its servant,

hitman for Mr Big. There was, after all then, but one single reason, there were not so many different reasons for their deaths, not so many for their turning to drink.

They died long ago and far too early, our men; yet, with a fine kind of irony that would have appealed to them, they are more alive today than those who killed them ... it is they who live on in our histories. Henry and Can and Casey, Bob and Todd and Bloke – who is there in their homeland that can read and breathe who knows them not. They are remembered better than the ruling tyrants of their era and their conniving ministers, or those Special Branch men and those other dirty-tricks traitors.

And when we think of them, those fellow journalists and friends of ours, we have to think too of the many millions of African people of whom they were but a sample batch, of the million others cut down in their prime by the same agency and the same method, by the same single executioner.

And after that has all been said we have to come to look for excuses for those we blame for it all: we have to turn our thoughts to the regime and its followers, we have to try to find explanations for their actions, to justify their responsibility for the extermination of those 15 journalists and those many million others, to look for apologies for them.

We must seek excuses – but shall we find them? It is a terrible task we are taking on, is there really a credible justification for such deeds, committed by a nation who boasted of its civilised Western values, who clung so hard to its dedicated brand of Christianity? Is it open to us to exonerate them, simply on the grounds that, although they were ruthless and uncontrollable in the pursuit of territory and power, they were yet quite correct in their own sanctimonious eyes?

Have we the generosity, have we the *right* to excuse them the horrors they meted out – merely so that they themselves might prosper – in the extinguishing of the lives of a million infants and a score of millions more whom they would not tolerate among their race, the human race?

Is that not all quite as difficult to explain and excuse as the Holocaust itself?

From *MR DRUM GOES TO JAIL,*
by Henry Nxumalo

(*Drum*, March, 1954)

I served five days' imprisonment at the Johannesburg Central Prison from January 20 to January 24, 1954. My crime was being found without a night pass five minutes before midnight, and I was charged under the curfew regulations. I was sentenced to a fine of 10s or five days.

Two constables arrested me at the corner of Rissik and Plein Streets. I was taken to Marshall Square police station, charged, searched, given two blankets and locked up in the cells with 37 others. The night was long. The prison doors kept clanging as more prisoners trickled in during the night. The cell itself was dark. I couldn't tell the day from the night. Only the familiar shout of the young constable carrying a noisy bunch of prison keys told us it was morning.

We had roll-call, breakfast, got back our personal effects and were packed like sardines – over 40 of us – in a truck and delivered to the cells below the court. When we got off the truck into the cells, one elderly-looking prisoner was a little slow to climb off. The prisoners were jostling to get off at once and blocking the way, and when the old man reached the ground he nearly missed the direction the others were taking. He looked about and S saw him. He hit him with his open hand on the temples and told him to wake up.

Before we appeared in court I asked one of the black constables to allow me to phone my employers and my family. He said 'Go to hell, *voetsak*!' Meanwhile, white prisoners in the opposite cells were phoning their families without trouble from a wall telephone near the warder.

After our cases had been heard by the magistrate, we were sent back to the cells. Convicted prisoners who couldn't raise enough to pay their fines employed various methods to get money. They either borrowed from others or bartered their clothes, promising to repay their benefactors as soon as they were out. Discharged prisoners took messages to relatives of convicted prisoners.

This lasted about two hours; we were checked and taken to Johannesburg Central Prison by truck. We arrived at the prison immediately after one o'clock. From the truck we were given orders to 'shayisa' (close up), fall in twos and 'sharp shoot' (run) to the prison reception office. From then on 'Come on, Kaffir' was the operative phrase from both black and white prison officials, and in all languages.

Many of us who were going to prison for the first time didn't know exactly where the reception office was. Although the prison officials were with us, no one was directing us. But if a prisoner hesitated, slackened his half-running pace and looked round, he got a hard boot kick on the buttocks, a slap on his face or a whipping from the warders. Fortunately there were some second offenders with us who knew where to go. We followed them through the prison's many zig-zagging corridors until we reached the reception office.

The office had a terrifyingly brutal atmosphere. It was full of foul language. A number of khaki-uniformed white officials stood behind a long cement bar-like curved counter. They wore the initials PSGD on their shoulders. When they were not joking about prisoners, they were swearing at them and taking down their particulars. Two were taking fingerprints and hitting the prisoners in the face when they made mistakes.

Five long-term prisoners attended to us. One came up to me and said he knew me. I didn't know him. He asked for cigarettes but I didn't have any. Another told us to take off our watches and money and hold them in our hands. These were to be kept separate from our other possessions. Another asked me for 2s 6d but I had 5d only and he wasn't interested. He noticed I had a copy of *Time* magazine in my hand and asked for it. I gave it to him. He hid it under the counter so the warders couldn't see it. Later he asked me what paper it was, how old it was and whether it was interesting. After we had undressed one long-term prisoner demanded my fountain pen.

'That's a fine pen you've got, eh?' he asked. 'How about giving it to me?' I said 'I'm afraid I can't; it's not my pen, it's my boss's' 'Hi, don't tell me lies, you bastard,' he said, 'what the hell are you doing with your boss's pen in prison? Did you steal it?' I said I hadn't stolen it. I was using it and had it in my possession when I was arrested. 'Give it here, I want it for my work here; if you refuse you'll see blood streaming down your dirty mouth soon!' I was nervous, but didn't reply. 'Look you little fool, I'll see that you are well treated in prison if you give me that pen.' The other prisoners looked at me anxiously. I didn't know whether they approved of my giving my pen or not; but their anxious look seemed to suggest that their fate in prison lay in that pen. I gave it away.

We were called up to have our fingerprints taken by a white warder. Before taking the impression the warder made a complaint that the hand glove he uses when taking impressions was missing. He swore at the long-term prisoner who assists him and told him to find it. He was a stout middle-aged man, apparently a senior official. He took my impression, examined it and then complained that my hands were wet. He hit me on the mouth with the back of his gloved hand. I rubbed my right thumb up my hair and he took another impression.

From there I ran down to the end of the wide curved desk to have my height taken, and stood beside the measuring rod, naked. The long-term prisoner taking my height asked for my name and checked it against my ticket. He asked for my address and tribe. He then recited something very long to the white official who was writing in a big book opposite him.

My surname and address were wrong. But I dared not complain at that stage for fear of getting more blows. The only words I recognised throughout the recitation was my first name and 'five foot, *basie*', which is three inches below my actual height. Though I was near the measuring stick, he hadn't measured me; nor did he measure the other prisoners. He merely looked at them and assessed their heights at sight. When finished with a prisoner he would throw his ticket on the floor for the prisoner to pick it up and get on with the next one.

We were then taken to the showers in another room. There was neither soap nor towel. After a few minutes under water we were told to get out and skip to get dry. Then our prison clothes were thrown at us – a red shirt and a torn white pair of short pants. They looked clean; but the side cap and the white jacket which were issued to me later were filthy. The jacket had dry sweat on the neck. From then on we were barefoot and were marched to the hospital for medical examination in double time. Another long-term prisoner lined us up, ordered us to undress and turn our faces to the wall, so that we would not pollute the medical officer with our breath when he came to examine us. While we were being inoculated another prisoner, apparently being hit by someone for some reason, suddenly ran into the others at the end of the queue and there was a general shuffling round of places. We were then told to face front and make urine. Three prisoners were detained and sent to the hospital as VD suspects. Whether the white official in khaki uniform was a doctor or not, I was unable to tell. He didn't examine me. There was a mix-up of prison clothes after that shuffling around and changing of places, so that many prisoners couldn't find their clothes. Everyone picked up the clothes nearest to him. Some said the clothes they were wearing had been worn by the prisoners detained for VD.

After this we were marched down to the main court of the prison in double time. Here we found different white and black warders and long-term prisoners, who took charge of us. Again we undressed and had our second shower in 30 minutes. I was unable to make out my own clothes after the shower and the skipping. The African warder kicked me in the stomach with the toe of his boot. I tried to hold the boot to protect myself and fell on my face. He asked if I had had an operation to my stomach. I said no. He looked at me scornfully. I got up, picked up my clothes in front of me and ran to join the others squatting on the floor.

After another roll-call we were marched to the top of the court to collect our food. The dishes were lined in rows and each prisoner picked up the dish nearest to him. The zinc dishes containing the food were rusty. The top of my dish was broken in three places. The food itself was boiled whole mealies with fat. We were marched to No. 7 cell, given blankets and a sleeping mat and locked in. We ate. The time was about 4.30 p.m. Clean water and toilet buckets were installed. But that water wasn't enough for 60 people. The long-term prisoners warned us not to use the water as if we were at our own homes. An old man went to fetch water with his dish at one stage and the long-term prisoner in charge of the cell swore at him. The old man insisted that he was thirsty and continued scooping the water. The long-term prisoner took the water away from him and threw it all over the old man's face.

There was a stinking smell when prisoners used the toilet bucket at night without toilet paper. At 8 p.m. the bell rang and we were ordered to be quiet and sleep. Some prisoners who had smuggled *dagga* and matches into the cell started conversing in whispers and smoking. The blankets were full of bugs; I turned round and round during the night without being able to sleep, and kept my prison clothes on for protection against bugs.

We were up at about six o'clock the following morning. I tried to get some water to wash my dish and drink. The dish was full of the previous night's fat, and I didn't know how I was going to do it. But the long-term prisoner shouted at me and ordered me to leave the water alone. I obeyed. He swore at me in Afrikaans, and ordered me to wipe the urine that was overflowing from the toilet bucket, with a small sackcloth. I did so. He said I must wipe it dry; but the cloth was so small that the floor remained wet.

He told me to find two other prisoners to help me carry the toilet bucket out, empty it and clean it. It was full of the night's excrement. There were no volunteers, so I slipped to a corner and waited. He saw me and rushed at me. 'What did I tell you, damn it; what did I say?' He slapped me on my left cheek with his right open hand as he spoke. He said he could have me put in solitary confinement if he wished. He could tell the chief warder that I had messed the floor and I would get an additional punishment. I kept quiet. I had done nothing of the sort. Finally he ordered two other prisoners to help me.

We emptied the bucket and washed it as the other prisoners were being lined up in readiness for breakfast. One of my colleagues tried to wash his hands after we had emptied the bucket. The white warder saw him and slashed him with the strap part of his baton. The dish containing my porridge – and many others – still had the previous night's fat. It had been washed in cold water. The breakfast itself was yellow porridge with half-cooked pieces of turnips, potatoes, carrots and other vegetables I could not recognise. No spoons were provided; so I had my breakfast with my stinking soiled hands. I didn't feel like eating, but feared that I would be inviting further trouble.

After breakfast we were divided into many work *spans* (parties). I spent my first day with a span cutting grass, pulling out weeds with my hands and pushing wheelbarrows at the Johannesburg Teachers' Training College in Parktown. We walked for about half a mile to our place of work and I was one of two prisoners carrying a heavy, steel food can, which contained lunch porridge for a party of 16. Two warders escorted us: one white and one black. Once I slackened because we were going down a precipice; my fingers were sore and the burden was heavy.

The old white warder who was carrying a big rifle slashed me on my bare legs with the strap of his baton and said, '*Ek donder jou, kaffir.*' (I will thrash you, kaffir).

We returned to jail at 4 p.m. We were ordered to undress and do the '*tausa*' dance, a common routine of undressing prisoners when they return from work searching their clothes, their mouths, armpits and rectum for hidden articles. I didn't know how it was done. I opened my mouth, turned round and didn't jump and clap my hands. The white warder conducting the search hit me with his fist on my left jaw, threw my clothes at me and went on searching the others. I ran off, and joined the food queue.

One night I didn't have a mat to sleep on. Long-term prisoners in charge of the cells sometimes took a bundle of mats to make themselves comfortable beds, to the discomfort of other prisoners. In practice, a prisoner never knows where he will sleep the next day. It is all determined by your speed in 'tausa,' food and blanket queues. Invariably a prisoner is always using another prisoner's dirty blankets every night.

In the four days I was in prison – I got a remission of one day – I was kicked or thrashed daily. I was never told what was expected of me, but had to guess. Sometimes I guessed wrong and got into trouble.

Long-term and short-term prisoners mixed freely at the prison. For example the famous A- D-, of Alexandra township, who is doing a 10-year sentence for various crimes, was one of the most important persons in prison during my time. He was responsible for the in and out movements of other prisoners and respected by prisoners and warders. Though I was a short-term prisoner, I, too, took orders from A-.

It was a common practice for short-term prisoners to give their small piece of meat to long-term prisoners on meat days for small favours such as tobacco, dagga, shoes (which are supposed to be supplied to Coloured prisoners only), wooden spoons – or to ensure that they were always supplied with sleeping mats.

Many other prisoners shared the same fate. There are no directions or rules read or posted in prison. At least I didn't see any. Thrashing time for warders was roll-call and breakfast time as well as supper time. For long-term prisoners it was inside the cells at all times. Long-term prisoners thrashed more prisoners more severely and much oftener than the prison officials themselves, and often in the presence of white or black warders. All prisoners were called *kaffirs* at all times.

On the day of our discharge we were mustered in a big hall and checked. There was an open lavatory at the corner of the hall. Six men used it, and when the seventh one went, a long-term prisoner swore at him and told him to keep his stomach full until he reached home. He said the man belonged to a tribe that killed his brother. After that none of us could use the latrine.

We were then marched to the reception office for our personal effects and checking out. The long-term prisoners officiating there told us not to think that we were already out of prison. They kicked and slapped prisoners for the slightest mistake, and sometimes for no mistake at all; and promised them additional sentences if they complained. In the office there was a notice warning prisoners to see that their personal belongings were recorded in the prison's books correctly and exactly as they had brought them. But I dared not complain about my pen, which was commandeered on my arrival, lest I be detained. Even the prisoner who took it pretended not to know me.

Before we left prison we were told the superintendent would

address us. We could make complaints to him if we had any. But the fat Zulu warder who paraded us to the yard for the superintendent's inspection said we must tell him everything was all right if we wanted to leave prison. 'This is a court of law,' he said, 'you are about to go home, but before you leave this prison, the big boss of the prison will address you. He will ask if you have any complaints. Now I take it that you will want to go to your homes – to your wives and children – you don't want to stay here. So if the big boss asks you if everything is all right, say "Yes, sir." If he says have you any complaints say "No, sir". You hear?'

In a chorus we said 'Yes.'

Just then one prisoner complained that his Kliptown train ticket was missing from his things. It was a season ticket. The Zulu warder pulled him aside and said, 'You think you're clever, eh? You'll see!' He put him at the tail-end of the parade. The superintendent came and we answered him as instructed. Most of us were seeing him for the first time. The Zulu warder said nothing about the complaint of the man from Kliptown. Later as we were going to collect our monies from the pay office, the man from Kliptown was escorted to the reception office to see the famous fierce discharge officer, C. C said the man's papers showed that he was charged at Forsdburg and not at Kliptown. He was not entitled to any ticket. But the man insisted that he was arrested at Kliptown, charged at Fordsburg and appeared at Johannesburg. The fat Zulu warder said in broken Afrikaans: 'He's mad, sir'. He gave the man a hard slap in the face with his open hand and said; 'You've just wasted the boss's time, eh? On your way ... voetsak!' And the man sneaked out.

One by one we zig-zagged our way out of the prison's many doors and gates and lined up in two's in front of the main and final gate. We were ordered to leave prison quietly and in pairs when the small gate was open. If we blocked the gate we would be thrashed. We were to come out in the order of the line. The man on the left would go out first and the one on the right would follow. The gate was opened. We saw freedom and blocked the gate in our anxiety. If they thrashed us we couldn't feel it ... we didn't look back!

Henry's report was published opposite pictures of the inside of the jail, showing the 'tausa' dance. These, taken through a long-range lens, were a great sensation to readers and served to give the story authenticity. After the article appeared conditions in the prisons improved, though only for a time.